P9-CTB-655

ELIZABETH
·B·I·S·H·O·P·

The Biography of a Poetry

PS
3503
.I785
.Z67

ELIZABETH
·BISHOP·

The Biography of a Poetry

LORRIE
GOLDENSOHN

COLUMBIA UNIVERSITY PRESS
NEW YORK

NOV 3 0 1994

487410

Excerpts from *The Collected Prose* by Elizabeth Bishop: copyright © 1984 by Alice Methfessel. Excerpts from *The Complete Poems, 1927–1979* by Elizabeth Bishop: copyright © 1979, 1983 by Alice Helen Methfessel. Reprinted by permission of Farrar, Straus &Giroux, Inc. Excerpts from the unpublished work and letters of Elizabeth Bishop are used with permission of her Estate: copyright © 1991 by Alice Helen Methfessel.

Permission to quote from the unpublished letters of Marianne Moore is granted by Marianne Craig Moore, Literary Executor for the Estate of Marianne Moore, and by the Rosenbach Museum & Library, Philadelpia. All rights reserved. Permission granted by the Rosenbach Museum & Library for citations from photocopies of Elizabeth Bishop's letters to Marianne Moore deposited in the Vassar College Library.

Excerpts from *Selected Poems* by Robert Lowell: copyright © 1956, 1959, 1962, 1976 by Robert Lowell. "For Elizabeth Bishop 4" from *History* by Robert Lowell: copyright © 1973 by Robert Lowell. Reprinted by permission of Farrar, Straus, & Giroux, Inc. Excerpts from "The Drunken Fisherman" in *Lord Weary's Castle:* copyrighted 1946, and renewed in 1974, by Robert Lowell. Reprinted by permission of Harcourt, Brace & Jovanovich. Excerpts from *Collected Prose* by Robert Lowell: copyright © 1987 by Caroline Lowell, Harriet Lowell, and Sheridan Lowell. Reprinted by permission of Farrar, Straus, & Giroux, Inc. Quotations from the unpublished correspondence and poems of Robert Lowell: printed by permission of his Estate; copyright © 1989 by Caroline Lowell, Harriet Lowell, and Sheridan Lowell.

Columbia University Press
New York Oxford
Copyright © 1992 Columbia University Press
All Rights Reserved

Library of Congress Cataloging-in-Publication Data

Goldensohn, Lorrie.
  Elizabeth Bishop : the bibliography of a poetry / Lorrie Goldensohn.
    p. cm.
  Includes bibliographical references and index.
  ISBN 0–231–07662–2
  1. Bishop, Elizabeth, 1911–1979—Criticism and interpretation.
I. Title.
PS3503.I785Z67   1992
811'.52—dc20   91–21265
                                                                  CIP

Casebound editions of Columbia University Press books are Smyth-sewn
and printed on permament and durable acid-free paper

Book design by Teresa Bonner
Printed in the United States of America
c 10 9 8 7 6 5 4 3 2 1

For Barry, for everything

CONTENTS

Illustrations follow page 138. (Except where noted, all photographs are part of the Vassar College Library collection.)

PREFACE

ELIZABETH BISHOP'S pursuit of truth and accurate description has always existed in fruitful tension with her defense of the unwilled and unconscious life of the mind. For Bishop, dreaming freely in the world of the poem, the body and its burdensomely particular self are released from either encroaching narcissism or despair. Yet the story of other lives, of what she described as the charm of what "really happened," fascinated her. She read widely in biography and memoir, translated a Brazilian child's diary, and in 1971 taught a course at Harvard on letterwriters. But her opinions about the confessional mode were fairly consistent: to her, confessional poets called up a picture of reality in which "we live in a terrifying and horrible world, and the worst moments of horrible and terrifying lives are an allegory of the world."* Her personal code of ethics was one of stoical restraint; she was moved to comment on more than one occasion about certain poets: "The tendency is to overdo the morbidity. You just wish they'd keep some of these things to themselves." † Her early allegories all project selves only indirectly or schematically connected to her own experience.

In spite of this aversion to exposing the self's darker moments, the story of Bishop's poetry still seems to me the story of how from impersonal, spatializing allegories like "The Map" and "The Monu-

---

* "Poetry in an Age of Prose," *Time*, June 2, 1967, p. 68.

† This comment is reported in *Time*, and attributed to her again by Wesley Wehr in "Elizabeth Bishop: Conversations and Class Notes," *Antioch Review* (Summer 1981), 39: 319–28.

ment," she gradually and significantly enlarged her work to include the directly personal. First she uses fantastic speakers who sleep standing up, or crouch on the ceiling, or hang from a ship's mast, and so on. After this phase, she highlights more mundane travelers, and geography becomes a conveyance for history, for the writing of her own history at large in the world. For emotional survival she avoided "morbidity," or openly voicing her fears of abandonment or loss of control, but over the years honesty came to urge that she name and place their looming dimensions. Goaded by her own sense of meaningful event, she bent over the map of her life, gradually signposting more and more of its roads and monuments in her poetry.

A modest person, Bishop nowhere hints that she owes her vision to the elections of poetic temperament. Toward the end of her career, however, she conceded a larger role to poetry, and by various tactical juxtapositions, implied the importance of its mode of truth to her own acts of self-definition. But those acts traced a zigzag path. As events, feelings, and ideas prompted her to drop one line of inquiry, another came to take its place. Once underway, however slowly, subjects generally prospered. Yet Bishop's drafts frequently offer startling insight into her patterns of inclusion and exclusion, of *how* various topoi came to bloom or wither.

In large measure, this book remains a study of texts. I began with the poems and stories, and then the letters and unpublished papers erupted through that opening. Although I've chosen to concentrate on the personal events only where they appear most insistently through the writing, the tangling knots made up of temperament, gender, and sexual proclivity, knots affected by both individual and historical circumstances, nonetheless came more and more to define that writing for me. The questions of Bishop's reticence, the style and substance of her engagement with autobiography, then tied themselves to the development of her narrative and descriptive technique.

Initially, I had a chronological plan in mind, intending a roughly book-by-book study, yet somewhat as Bishop herself almost tripped over a continent on her way around it and then subsequently found herself bound to a seventeen-year residence, I found myself precipitated onto the Brazilian or middle phase of her career. I had made only a last-minute and almost whimsical decision to go to Brazil before writing, but once there, I was fortunate enough to discover a cache of her papers, which included "It is marvellous," a previously unpublished, short, intense love poem, apparently written in Key West, which had been tucked into the backflap of an old notebook and taken along to Brazil. This initial discovery steadily drew me into a rearrangement of my material, as the abrupt force of the poem delivered to me by accident made me question more closely why a later Bishop had treated love and sexuality only glancingly. I wanted to open this book with the years that brought the sharpest delineation of change in her subject matter, and to track what looked like a characteristic advance within a characteristic retreat in her self-presentation.

The first three chapters concentrate on Bishop in Brazil, setting in motion a variety of questions that continue to resonate throughout the book. The first chapter assembles her motives for voluntary exile and briefly describes my finding of "It is marvellous"; the second analyzes this poem, speculating on its relation to the rest of Bishop's poetry. The third asks questions about Bishop's early poems on love and sexuality.

This middle period in Rio de Janeiro and in Petrópolis with her companion, Lota de Macedo Soares, gave Bishop a place to work, a library, a society, and a semblance of family. The early years of her residence crystallize the most hopeful and the gladdest part of Bishop's life. As her orphan's sense of having found a late grounding deepened and stabilized, other concerns opened as the derivatives of place. Paradoxically, Brazil brought her an instinctive identification with exile as a positive movement of place within displacement. The dislocations of exile took her out of the linear, forward march of her life, and back through memory into a simultaneous recognition linking a primitive, childlike Brazil and Bishop herself as a child. Within her view of Brazil, however troubling its appropriations, both her Brazilian present and her Nova Scotian past fused in a triumphantly double narrative.

In Brazil, both Brazil and Nova Scotia came fully alive as subjects. Bishop's poetry shifted from allegory and the representation of objects, as her personae also moved up in the scale of creation from Weed or Man-Moth to Giant Snail or child or Riverman. During these years even her landscapes gained in human rather than animal population, as a description colored more and more by the waking real and less and less by the fantastically dreamed began to take in urban and village life. Folk ballad and dramatic monologue replaced the early surrealist myths. The pairing of north and south begun in her first book settled into an affinity for those divisions in her personal life, so that the myth of the tropical which she seized allowed her to affirm a bipolarity including northern reticence and southern emotional release as the desirable condition of her existence.

But when "It is marvellous . . ." went to Brazil with Bishop, and not to an editor for publication, what had appeared to be a tentative movement "forward" into the new subject territory of erotic intimacy, and a guarded look at the feints and dangerous diplomacies of amorous relation, went underground. Between the publication of *A Cold Spring*, consisting of poems written before her Brazilian sojourn, and *Questions of Travel*, which featured poems written after, Bishop damped her public interest in erotic themes as cleanly as Marianne Moore might have wished.

As she found home both psychologically and geographically in Brazil, Bishop withdrew from the poems of adult relationship that had begun to express both suppressed anger and suppressed tenderness; yet the unpublished "It is marvellous" eludes the social consequence and difficulties inherent in her position both as lesbian and as lover. From within transitional work, as one looks at this protean sample of it, the vivid drops extend from her earliest preoccupying images of prison bars and rainstorm, and forward, faintly outlining future resolutions governing both work and life. In this poem, Bishop puts in place the imprisoned lover who will in future poems break her bonds and assume an openly female body, if only for the most part a child's. As her female identity emerged in print, so did the contours of her identity as poet.

The third chapter looks at Bishop's treatment of erotic themes chronologically, and finds in them the imprint of events from Bishop's early life. The pronoun switches and silences that she drew around erotic subjects began to define themselves even within Bishop's adolescent work. The very first chapter of her 1960 book, *Brazil*, uses an anecdote about a lost and then recovered infant to open a discussion of Brazilian warmth and tolerance. However Bishop may later have repudiated her unsatisfactory collaboration with Time-Life, these choices of subject, drawing together childhood losses with emotional expressivity, seem stamped as her own.

The childhood motif is also introduced as the maternal is eroticized. Bishop's relationship with Lota intersects with the early loss of her mother and her fears of abandonment, so that an embrace of Lota's semitropical Brazil offers a compensatory mythologizing of Bishop's own darker powers and fears. "Faustina, or Rock Roses," as well as a draft of an unfinished piece called "Vaguely Love Poem," appear as paradigmatic poems supplying crucial information on Bishop's responses to race, sex, and gender roles.

·I·

Clearly visible in the middle years, this set of issues radiates thematically outward to both early and late work. At this point, I wanted to pause, and move back yet further, spelling out some broader sense of the traits sustaining Bishop's work. Chapters 4 and 5 look at the continuities between Bishop's juvenilia and her first book, *North & South*. Chapter 6 considers the impact of surrealism and the visual arts, as the visual became a dominant pathway for Bishop's interest in description. Finally, rejecting an orthodox surrealism, she positions herself as a female artist in a nonprophetic, empirical tradition.

Because no description of Bishop's poetic development can afford to ignore them, chapters 7 and 8 weigh the impact of her relations with Marianne Moore and Robert Lowell. Pressed by the need for discretion about her lesbianism, and by her own skepticism and uncertainty about the role of the female, and caught between the inadequacies of Moore's gentilities on the one hand, and Lowell's confessional on the other, Bishop saw both poets as models and counter-models.

In chapter 9, "Brazil, January 1, 1502" and "The Riverman" demonstrate in detail Bishop's particular resolution of the autobiographical problem, as devising her own strategies, she meets Lowell's challenge but differs decisively from his practice. Translation and memoir offer her new ground on which to try out new subjects and new approaches. Not for the first or last time, unpublished work in a fragmentary state offers arresting insight into Bishop's growing awareness of the political and social forces operating within her life in Brazil: once again, however, a geographical relocation, this time with explosively tragic results, forces an emerging subject inward. Lota's suicide in 1967 brought an eventual end to Bishop's Brazilian years. Away from Brazil she drops the more overtly political tenor of her subjects, much as she had earlier dropped the erotic for rather happier reasons. A present-tense involvement with a distinctive community mostly disappears from her work after her return to the United States. "Pink Dog" with its richly Brazilian scene may look like a deviation from this pattern. Yet the first hand-written drafts of it appear in a blue-lined copybook dated 1959, even if the poem was finished and published in 1979.

Several other equally tantalizing counter examples remained immobilized in draft form.

Assessing strengths, the final chapters look closely at *Geography III* and the four poems last published, noting Bishop's growing preoccupation with larger form. Bishop's sense of connectedness through love and friendship with Lota strengthened her work. Yet while the uprooting from Brazil damaged that flow of connection, in the larger trajectory of her life and poetry, whatever additional accomplishment may have aborted along the way, the Boston friendships that succeeded Bishop's Brazilian attachments undoubtedly enabled the brilliant achievement of the late phase.

Back in Boston, Bishop, now a woman in her sixties, was free at last to identify a safely distant autobiographical theme, Lost Love, making her final move within alternate selving as Robinson Crusoe, and as an openly female child. In her middle years, she rechristened her old interest in space and location as "Travel"; then "Travel" turned into a "Geography" situated within a dour but not unilluminating homelessness. In the late narrative poems, as the ampler geography of her last book spreads over its ground, extensivity shades into duration, and space inevitably becomes temporal, and therefore historic, as Bishop's work comes to its impressive close. Stoically, from within art and nature's joint shelter, her speakers count on the precarious acts of memory to call up, house, and transform life.

·II·

Perhaps for no very powerful reason beyond a desire to be faithful to the turns of mind that produce an argument, these chapters cross forward and back, between periods in one country and then another, between relations with a lover, and relations with one's poetic peers, between considerations of the formal manipulations that literary tradition offers, and the original devising of the alphabet of emotions that experience alone hands over to us. Something in the order of this accounting preserves the disruptive force of the actual reading experience on the too-tidy field of analysis—making it easier to pay the open, and I hope, nonpartisan, attention that Bishop's poems really seem to reward. My respect for this poet only grew and grew; in the little moment in the long life of great poems that scholarly pages represent, I wanted to catch and then disperse what fish I could alive.

·III·

There is a rapidly and valuably increasing body of scholarship on Bishop's poetry. David Kalstone's seminal work on the relations between Bishop, Moore, and Lowell is chief among many to which I am indebted, an indebtedness I acknowledge where appropriate. Most of my references, however, are to the poems themselves and to much currently unpublished Bishop material in both letter, draft, and notebook form. To orient my readers, I list here the major collections of letters.

From Elizabeth Bishop:

Ilse and Christopher Barker, Princeton University Library; Anny Baumann, Grace Bulmer Bowers, Dorothee Taylor Bowie, James Merrill, Lloyd Frankenberg and Loren MacIver, Linda Nemer (letters in Portuguese translated by Irene Adler de Aquino Nena), and Joseph and U. T. Summers, Vassar College Library; Carley Dawson, University of Oregon Library; Robert Lowell, Harvard University Library, and the University of Texas at Austin; Marianne Moore, Rosenbach Museum and Library, Philadelphia; Anne Stevenson, Washington University Libraries; Wesley Wehr, University of Washington Library.

To Elizabeth Bishop:

Robert Lowell and Marianne Moore, Vassar College Library.

For these letters, instead of footnoting, reference in the text will be made to the names of Bishop's correspondents and the dates of the letters. Endnotes identify the rare case in which drafts of poems or prose work discussed are housed in other collections besides the Vassar College Library.

My immediate thanks are to the National Endowment for the Humanities, for a grant bestowing both time and travel. The patience, common sense, and loyal opposition that my husband, Barry Goldensohn, furnished at every stage, through hours and years of no doubt interminable discussion, were not less crucial. In the early throes, without the active enthusiasm of Jane Shore, Beth Darlington, and Anita Landa, I could never have gotten the book going. If both

Terence Diggory and Barbara Page at later stages of the manuscript, as well as throughout the process, had not generously supplied their careful reading and probing, meticulous criticism, whatever point the final effort has would be lacking. For continuing support and a vigorous, intellectual stimulus of her own inimitable kind, I owe a great deal to Helen Vendler. Robert Hahn, Frank Bergon, and Paul Nelson helped in the darkest hours, while Reno Odlin provided a stream of notes on style, notes precise, erudite and memorable. For her acuity in formulating the Brazilian questions, though she may not agree with my conclusions, my debt to Regina Pryzybycien is substantial.

I owe many thanks to Alice Methfessel, for her assistance as Bishop's literary executor, to Lisa Browar, formerly Curator of Special Collections at Vassar, and then especially to Nancy MacKechnie, a truly indefatigable and indispensable guide through the Vassar Library, who smoothed a thousand ruts in the road.

I'm deeply grateful for all the help I received at Columbia, for Jennifer Crewe's infectious confidence in the manuscript, for Joan McQuary's sensitive editing, and for Leslie Bialler's resourcefulness in response to my electronic fumbling.

Grateful acknowledgments are made to *The American Poetry Review*, in which chapter 2, "It is marvellous to wake up together," appeared in an earlier version, and to *Pequod*, which published a section of chapter 6, "For a World 'Minute and vast and clear.'"

BIOGRAPHICAL
INFORMATION

Elizabeth Bishop provided the following "Autobiographical Sketch" in 1961.

Born in Worcester, Massachusetts, 1911. Mother Nova Scotian; father half Canadian, half old New England stock. (Paternal grandfather from Prince Edward Island.) Ancestors fought in the Revolution, on both sides. Maternal side left farms in upstate New York to take up land grants in Nova Scotia given to Loyalists by George III.

Only child; orphaned by five. Lived alternately with Nova Scotian and New England sets of grandparents; later with an aunt. Started school in N.S., but was sickly and hadn't much formal education until fifteen. Public and private schools in New England.

Wrote poetry from the age of eight. Literary career started at the age of twelve with a prize, a $5.00 gold piece, awarded by the American Legion for an essay on AMERICANISM. This has vanished, but the first sentence, something about "From the icy regions of the frozen north to the waving palm trees of the burning south ..." seems to have been prophetic, indicating directions taken later by both life and work.

Walnut Hill School, Natick, Massachusetts, 1927–30.
Vassar College, B.A. 1934.
Walking trip in Newfoundland, 1932 or '33.
1935–1939, travelled in Europe, Morocco, Ireland, etc.; lived mostly in Paris.
1939–1948 – lived in Key West, Florida, and New York City

1942 or '43 – Nine months in Mexico. Other trips to Cuba; Haiti; Nova Scotia; Prince Edward Island; Sable Island, etc.

1949–1950 – Consultant in Poetry, Library of Congress, Washington.

Late in 1951 began a South American trip, stopping off in Brazil to visit Brazilian friends. Like the life very much and have lived here ever since, with various trips to New York.

I live outside Petrópolis, in the mountains, most of the time; sometimes in a *pied à terre* on Copacabana Beach, in Rio. I am very interested in architecture, and in Petrópolis I have the good fortune to live in (I think) one of the best examples of contemporary Brazilian work, a house by Sérgio Bernardes. I am also fortunate in numbering among my friends and acquaintances most of the best contemporary Brazilian architects, artists, and some writers.

I've been down the Amazon from Manaus to Belém; made many trips to Minas Gerais, Ouro Preto, Diamantina, etc.; to São Paulo; one to Paraty; frequently spend holidays in Cabo Frio; one trip to Brasília and one to the Xingú River to the Indian Post of Capitão Vasconcelos. I'm about to go to Bahia – I hope.

After giving a brief publishing history, Bishop concludes with the following paragraph:

My mother's family seems to have had a taste for wandering, also for writing and the arts. Two great-uncles were Baptist missionaries in India and one of them wrote the first novel to be written in *Telegu*–besides other works. A third, at the age of fourteen, started painting portraits of sailing ships for the ship-builders then flourishing in Nova Scotia; he grew up to be an academic English painter. Their father, my great-grandfather, was master-owner of a bark in the West Indies trade. He also wrote a small text book on navigation. He was lost at sea, with all hands, off Sable Island in a famous storm in which many ships went down.

Chronology for subsequent years:

1962   Chapelbrook Fellowship.
1963   Two months in New York City.
1964   Spring, in Rio de Janeiro during a revolutionary coup; summer, traveled on an Academy of American Poets Fellowship to Italy and England; visited the Barkers enroute.

1965	Buys Casa Mariana in Ouro Preto, Brazil, historic house dating from 1690s, and begins restoration.
1966	Two terms at the University of Washington in Seattle, first teaching job.
1967	Early spring, Brazil: stern-wheeler trip down the Rio São Francisco. Lota de Macedo Soares hospitalized; in September, dies in New York, apparent suicide.
1968–69	Lives in San Francisco. Merrill Ingram Award. Stays six weeks in Ouro Preto. Awarded Brazilian Order of Rio Branco.
1970	Months of residence in Ouro Preto. Returns late September to Cambridge, Massachusetts, to teach her first term at Harvard, an affiliation lasting through 1977.
1971	Winter through spring, residence in Ouro Preto terminated by severe attacks of fever and dysentery. Fall term at Harvard interrupted by illness, hospitalization for asthma.
1972–73	With Alice Methfessel, trips to Ecuador, Galápagos Islands, as well as later trips to Sweden, Finland, Leningrad, and Norway; from Bergen by mail boat to North Cape and back.
1974	Last trip to Brazil. First of six summers at Sabine Farm, North Haven, Maine. Harriet Monroe Poetry Award. Moves to Lewis Wharf in Boston Harbor.
1976	In April, receives *Books Abroad*/Neustadt Award, first woman, first American recipient. June, attends Poetry International Congress in Rotterdam; June-July in Portugal.
1977	Fall term, teaches at New York University. Severe anemia.
1978	Guggenheim Fellowship.
1979	In May, visits England, Greek Islands, Yugoslavia, with Alice Methfessel. October 6, at home in Boston, dies of a ruptured cerebral aneurysm.

ELIZABETH
·B·I·S·H·O·P·

The Biography of a Poetry

※

In the Footsteps of
Elizabeth Bishop in Brazil

A FOOT-LONG book about as thick as a floor-tile started me off on the Brazilian phase of Elizabeth Bishop's life, and so by attaching me to the geography of her middle years, gave me a quirky, midstream entry into the poetry. *Brazil*[1], a *Time-Life* picture-and-text production found in a secondhand bookshop and passed on to me by a poet-friend, seemed odd company for Bishop, surely a mistress of more than half-tone or quarter-tone illustration. Indeed, hard evidence of her authorship is discreetly withheld from the cover, and the legend "by Elizabeth Bishop and the Editors of Life" appears only on the title-page.

Tropical, subtropical, and multiracial Brazil came in at an angle that I didn't understand: Bishop's relationship to it must have prodded her self-definition as a white northerner, but how that prodding might be bound to her handling of travel themes was no concern of *Brazil*. After the book was published, Bishop was quick to distance herself from it, as she looked over the cut and mangled body of the final text, muttering darkly in a September 1961 letter to Robert Lowell, "No one I know will ever *see* this book if I can help it." Yet there is a peculiar appropriateness to the effort, a fitness that has to do with Bishop's passion for accuracy, and her need, during the onrush of more complex and delicate literary maneuvering, for the blunt stability of the prosaic and literal.

Bishop's poems insist on fact and thingishness, most behaving at first sight as if they were only simple description. Her verbal bearing as a modest, but inquisitive, observer seems a quintessentially feminine strategy: her poised speakers, with their tactical withdrawals of self, a part of an earlier age's good breeding. With few exceptions, she keeps her most pained or bewildered selves undercover in terrestrial or marine disguise as snail, sandpiper, fish, armadillo, man-moth, or moose. In the poems of the late thirties and early forties, she wraps up understanding of self and world within curio: a tiny, cantering horse with a key in its underbelly, or a big bad painting, or a half-man leaning into a mirror to become whole. But throughout both prose and poetry, Bishop refuses to accept the usual species barrier between the fantastic and the real, the poetic or prosaic, the lettered or unlettered, or even the higher and lower cultivations of mind. Or so it might have seemed, as she planned the book on Brazil, helped, perhaps, by substantial cash advance.

I meant to honor Bishop's entanglements in the real by letting myself into the closest approximation of her world that I could find, and to begin with the brightest and strangest piece of it, Brazil. With her good example before me I could move to dismiss the symbol or the letter as insufficient, and try to test letter, story, and poem against the standard of place and fact. A blaze of geography that included several thousand miles of Brazil, four climate belts, and several branches of the Amazon River would spread my stake in the work across genre boundaries, across the gulf between critic and poet, then and now, the real and the imagined, and across all those other binary divisions that exist so implacably in human conversation held in space and time. I was courting a reading of the poetry that would not be too narrow, or too passive. And perhaps my own mind, like hers, refused to accept the nonmateriality of language, its unbearable lightness of being.

· I ·

It was clear from reading her letters and other prose that Elizabeth Bishop had never intended a lengthy residence in Brazil. At the outset, she had taken passage for a long-desired steamer trip around the world. She was forty, and had spent years and months of her life since college in transit through Paris, New York, Key West, and Mexico City. The two years preceding her travel had been particularly unhappy, marked by loneliness, self-doubt, and alcoholism. In Washington, a bad bout of drinking had ended in a five-day hospital stay. In

1947, during treatment for her allergies and her drinking, she wrote to Dr. Anny Baumann, her personal physician for much of her life:

> father had to stop, and his father, and three uncles. It can be done. And I'd like not only to do it but be cheerful about [it] – and shut up about it.

Under the title numbers of her diary for 1950 she had written, "Just about my worst, so far." The problems were never purely alcohol, of course. Months before leaving for Brazil she wrote Dr. Baumann again:

> I was not drunk when I called you, just terribly upset, in fact the last few times this has happened I haven't actually drunk so much – it seems to be more emotional than anything else & I get myself into a fine state of discouragement, panic, sleeplessness, nightmares, etc.

Travel and change proved catalytic. Once having stepped from the decks of the *S.S. Bowplate*, and into the company of Lota de Macedo Soares, the friend she had temporarily stopped to visit in Rio, she was done in by an allergic reaction to the fruit of the cashew: "my head swelled like a pumpkin and I was completely blind. It also affected my hands so I couldn't write," she had written to English friends, Ilse and Kit Barker, in February 1952. Surrounded, and surrendering to the solicitude and kindness of her hosts, for a few days she lay in bed in an apartment in Copacabana, then got up, and stayed on for years, making only temporary removals out of the country. Her residence in Brazil, up to her permanent return to the United States in her late fifties, was to be nearly two decades.

What was it that attracted her for so long? In one description in the Vassar Library, taken from notes for the book on Brazil, Bishop had been living in Rio for some time, and went to see a friend laid up in what was called the "Strangers' Hospital," built for yellow fever victims by the British. Her friend looked out his window and said "This is scenery for an eight-year-old boy." Bishop says of it:

> And it did look like a child's drawing! Four or five unreal peaks; two cable cars dangling on wires; planes landing and taking off; lights coming on all round the bay and a huge signboard giving the hours and the news. . . . Goats lounging on a little footbridge, looking down enthralled by the hour of the "roosh" – all the elements were

there to delight the heart of a child – and yet altogether a delicate and slightly mad beauty.

Then again, writing to the Barkers on July 13, 1953, she invokes a child's perspective, with its magical simplicities, to help her explain the directness and exhilarating power of the impact being made so freshly on her. Here is the description of what she saw:

> Little fire balloons float up across the mountains all evening long and now it is full moon as well, and there are wet patches on top of the mountains – on the sheer rock – that glitter. It is too fantastic – we were driving home the other day more or less southwest and the *lolloping* mts were all pink and the moon came up perfectly white – it was still daylight – like a dinner plate – really like a child's painting.

A few years later, she traveled down the Rio San Francisco on the stern-wheeler, the *Wenceslau Braz*, and in an unpublished essay about the trip describes the progress of this seventy-year-old woodburner in words that are characteristically miniaturized and distanced, but at the arms' length of a child:

> We sported a very tall smoke-stack painted and re-painted with yellow-orange paint. At night this gave off a stream of big sparks; by day it moved along like a yellow wax crayon – as if a big child were tracing the course of the Rio São Francisco for his or her geography lesson.[2]

In the beholding of this metaphor, inevitably suggesting Bishop on board the *Wenceslau Braz* as a big child tracing her geography lesson with adult absorption, the river is tamed, contracted, and locked into a remote viewing. The whole scene has an irrepressible vitality perceived as both primitive and distanced, but the distant primitive is rendered intimate and manageable by the speaker through its transformation into childhood measure. Bishop maintains the miniaturizing wide-angle lens in countless other poems treating landscape from the river Seine to the Florida coast to the northern Brazilian highlands. It is a consistent feature of her approach to the world; but what enters the Brazilian description is Bishop's marriage of the distancing and miniaturizing to the joyfulness of a child's eye, or child's experience, as the traveling wide-angle is wedded to the wide eye, with all of its effervescent possibilities.

In the opening stanzas of "Arrival at Santos," the poem introducing *Questions of Travel*, the new note sounds again. Behind the usual keen observation, something artless, and close to prattle, escapes in the poem's light swiftness across the travel theme, where all of the adjectives registering potentially negative feeling about travel itself are moved off the speaker and safely onto the landscape:

> Here is a coast; here is a harbor;
> here, after a meager diet of horizon, is some scenery:
> impractically shaped and—who knows?—self-pitying mountains,
> sad and harsh beneath their frivolous greenery,
>
> with a little church on top of one. And warehouses,
> some of them painted a feeble pink, or blue,
> and some tall, uncertain palms. Oh, tourist,
> is this how this country is going to answer you
>
> and your immodest demands for a different world,
> and a better life, and complete comprehension
> of both at last, and immediately,
> after eighteen days of suspension?[3]

It is not the speaker, but the mountains who are "self-pitying," or "sad and harsh"; it is only the scenery judged as "frivolous" or "impractical." Generally, the tone is a playful and teasing intimacy, regardless of what is hovering at the edges of the speaker's mood. The poem concludes, "We are driving to the interior," and this is precisely what the first Brazil poems appear to do, as they start from a common geography, exchange the position of tourist for settler, and try out the anchor of family and household more intensively than the poems of either of Bishop's previous books.

In other notes, originally made for the *Time-Life* book, Bishop paints a clear, bright miniature of a coffee plantation:

> the round, almost conical green hills, the Negro women carrying white bundles on their heads, like ants with their eggs, the children playing *futebol*, the dry, broken graveyards – even details like kites, balloons and the way the ever-present umbrella is hanging from the back of the collar. . . .

In the quoted comment, as in the practice of so many other traveling Americans exploring the intoxicating and perhaps disturbing freedom of the unfamiliar tropics, Bishop holds the dark Others, in this case the antlike Negro women with their eggs, at a severe and cautious distance. In similar passages of trans-species communication, footballers in striped jerseys are seen as wasps; on Sundays, Brazilian crowds watch "the bright, drifting, insect-like figures." Distance, and ambivalence, twine as feelings: in the same notes, she writes about the Rio slums how "even the favela architecture is hauntingly beautiful"; showing both "horror and delicacy"; the oriental piling-up in the building of these shacks, in their "wooden lace" something that resembles "swallow or weaver birds on their cliffs."

In these comments the child's perspective gives way to a desire for different emotions and different specificities, but the language is filtered through a long-range, far-sighted aesthetic sensibility responding first to landscape, with an enlarged category of flora and fauna summarily taken as primary focus. In reading all of her poems, essays, notes, or letters, perhaps what we need to bear in mind is what within that view stays large, and what grows small; what is disembodied and hovering, and what is eventually placed. Here, what is newly introduced as subject is not only that large child prowling the outskirts of the vision, but also the uneasy dialogue between the imperial eye that translates the foreign to the animal, and the one capable of establishing the foreign on an equal footing with the observer, or the Other on a par with Self.

Sometimes this capability produces surprising poems like "Going to the Bakery," where rich and poor, North and South American, perceiver and perceived, are all implicated in the poem's view of human distress. Elsewhere, as in "The Armadillo," where acts of the human observer fade, Bishop reverts to earlier discretions, and everybody of symbolic importance turns out to be animal. Sometimes all the projected figures remain reduced in size: in "Brazil, January 2, 1502," it apparently becomes the task of the watchful, off-page observer to see both the Portuguese conquistador *and* the local life as tiny figures in the large-souled weaving of Nature. In "The Burglar of Babylon," Bishop in a letter to her Aunt Grace Bowers in October 1964 pointed out the origin of the poem in personal experience, saying "*I* am one of the 'rich with binoculars!' " or one of the spectators watching from the protected vantage point of tall apartment buildings. But for the poem's duration at least the poet leaves the crowd on the balconies and signs up with the folk in the vivid primary colors of a ballad's cadence and style.

·II·

In a variety of texts, Bishop's travel to South America performed what Lévi-Strauss described as the time-twist inherent in such travel: "The tropics are not so much exotic as out-of-date" he declared in *Tristes Tropiques*, a book Bishop read while in Brazil. For him it was "a way of life which would suggest that you had gone backwards in time rather than forwards across a great part of the earth's surface."[4] While usually avoiding the patronizing judgment about equatorial progress, with its corresponding binary trap defining one country as temperate-advanced and the other as tropical-regressed, Bishop did share the sense of sliding temporality. But feeling floods her style, so that her temporal reversal, or her fascination with the primitive, becomes in part an assumption of a childhood perspective with a liberating and adaptive force.

Backwardness was something not wholly unappealing to Bishop. In her introduction to her 1957 translation of the Brazilian classic, *The Diary of Helena Morley*, Bishop describes the home terrain of the child diarist, a mountain province of mines abandoned or cut back when Kimberley in South Africa eclipsed them, and slavery no longer supplied an exploitable work force:

> [. . .] diamond "mining" [. . .] goes on all around Diamantina constantly, and enough diamonds are found in this way to provide a meager living for some thousands of people. One sees them, sometimes all alone, sometimes in groups of three or four, standing in every stream. Sometimes they are holding a sieve just under the water, looking for diamonds, sometimes they are sloshing their wooden bowls from side to side in the air, looking for gold. The bent heads and concentration of these figures, in that vast, rock-studded, crucifix-stuck space, give a touch of dementia to the landscape.

Lunacy seems so much easier to see when it is foreign; nonetheless, the reiterated chord of this Brazilian lunacy, which could also strike one as human displacement from meaning, or uprootedness, must have touched off a sympathetic vibration in Bishop herself. The favorite landscapes—the rural Nova Scotia of her childhood, depression Florida, and isolated, hilly Ouro Preto—nearly all display loss and abandonment, economic and otherwise: these traits correspond to her orphan's sense of a precarious inner geography, one frequently marginal and shifting. When she gibes at the fragile, or frivolous, or lunatic balance of these places, it is likely that the projected identity with them was strong enough to be seen as a flicker of self-mockery.

To see landscape as the outward semblance of the self, as the mirroring or external correlative of the self's condition, has become nearly automatic to Bishop. The Brazilian poems are the first group resolutely presenting a traveling self, however attenuated in detail, in a landscape deliberately chosen for its contextual value. Another function of her travel follows Johnsonian terms: "the use of travelling is to regulate imagination by reality, and instead of thinking how things may be, to see them as they are." Or perhaps even by determined and relentless travel, to see them as they might be. Landscape may offer its bitter, salutary doses, emphasizing disjunction or savage isolation, but it also offers its powers of enlargement and alteration, as travel through landscape by its very nature means motion and a potentially exhilarating change. In the travelogue, or home movie of the world that her eyes provided, Bishop, born in 1911 and forty when she arrived in Brazil, clearly found hope in her Brazilian transfer, and in it, a means of growth and survival. Certainly that is what this haunted passage, which concludes "To The Botequim & Back," seems to suggest; written after Lota's death when Bishop had serious doubts about staying on in Brazil, about a little walk from Bishop's house in Helena Morley's state of Minas Gerais in the town of Ouro Preto, the passage traverses all the familiar themes. In its ambling, flower-picking, mock-innocent transparence, Bishop tours all the familiar themes — a lunatic disconnection, childhood, and mutability. Here are fragments:

> It is a magnificent sight to the east, seemingly all the way to the coast, miles and miles and miles of blue hills, the nearer ones topped by crazy spars of gray stone, and one tall cross slanting lightly to the north [. . .] The fields are filled with wild flowers [. . .] you realize the ground is carpeted with flowers, short, shorter ones, moss-height ones. I picked dozens of wild flowers, little bright orange-and-yellow ones on a dry fine little bush brilliant like orchids; lovely tall single white yellow ones, each on its own thin green stock; hanging magenta bells. Before you can get these home, they have shut up tight forever. This is the field of the Waterfall of the Little

Swallows, and this is where the stream disappears, like the sacred river Alph in Coleridge's dream. It fans out over the red stone, narrows and rises in cold gray ridges, disappears underground, and then shows up again farther off, dashing downwards now through more beautiful rocks. It then takes off downwards for the Underworld. You can hang over the rocks and see it far below. It keeps descending, disappears into a cavern, and is never seen again. It talks as it goes, but the words are lost.[5]

The little wildflowers are short-lived, and deaf to human desire. Like the cold waters of "At The Fishhouses," the waters, too, are oblivious to human needs, may in fact chastise them; but they also live at the hopeful, underworld brink of knowledge where our human travel takes us, even if we lose the words. Faithful as ever to her empiricist need to test experience by testing space, these words show Bishop at the point where an increasing fidelity to the paths of the surface reveals to her the deeper circuits of myth. These allusions, more specifically to Coleridge, more generally to the Underworld, let us slip from the mileage of home and shop to the minutes and hours of revelation. Here at the lip of the Underworld joining death, imagination, and the unconscious, experience releases us from historical space into the timeless: yet this release from history occurs in Bishop's career when her mapping of the surreal estate of the inward impulse has given way to a greater fascination with a very particular and external geography.

·III·

In the early letters to Dr. Anny Baumann, Bishop writes about her arrival in Rio, and her home in Petrópolis, with infectious exuberance: "I still feel as if I must have died and gone to heaven without deserving to." The comment is repeated, in almost identical wording, to other close friends, the Barkers. In July 1953, giving a full set of reasons for her feelings, she writes to Robert Lowell:

I was always too shy to have much "intercommunication" in New York, anyway, and I was miserably lonely there most of the time– here I am extremely happy, for the first time in my life. I live in a spectacularly beautiful place; we have between us about 3,000 books now; I know, through Lota, most of the Brazilian "intellectuals" already and I find the people frank, – startlingly so, until you get used to Portuguese vocabularies – extremely affectionate – an atmosphere that I just lap up – no I guess I mean loll in [. . .]. I arrived to visit Lota just at the point where she really wanted someone to stay with her in the new house she was building. We'd known each other well in New York but I hadn't seen her for five or six years. She wanted me to stay; she offered to build me a studio – picture enclosed – I certainly didn't want to wander around the world in a drunken daze for the rest of my life – so it's all fine & dandy.

The affection was obviously important. Without feeling encroachment, Bishop's New England or Nova Scotian reserve could accept the greater demonstrativeness of the South American as the manner of the Other, as both deriving from distance and functioning as nearness, surely an irresistible combination for a self-confessed shy person. In July 1952, Bishop explains to Dr. Baumann:

> It is really a wonderful country in some ways – where when you arrive the janitor and the porter and the cook all hug you tenderly and call you "madame my daughter" – and where I looked out the window at seven this morning and saw my hostess in a bathrobe directing the blowing up of a huge boulder with dynamite.

Unleashing great powers, this hostess is also a figure of informal and unstinting affection. Bishop herself working with energy and effectiveness, adds: "the drinking and the working both seem to have improved miraculously. Well no it isn't miraculous really – it is almost entirely due to Lota's good sense and kindness."

The household of Lota de Macedo Soares functioned for her as family—on arrival, Bishop says: "the 'family,' has consisted of another American girl, also a NY friend of mine, 2 Polish counts for a while, the architect over weekends, etc., all a strange tri-or quadri-lingual hodgepodge that I like very much." Even the polyglot nature of that household was comforting; in living where English mattered less, and in living side by side near a language that she acknowledged that she spoke imperfectly, there was free space, an opening for her own work with language to continue, unobserved and unself-conscious. Her sense of groundedness and of authenticity increased as her life drew strength from circumstances rooted somewhere beyond language. Once, in speaking of a scholar friend she describes him in kindly but near-audible contempt as one of those people who does not believe something has happened until it has been written down. One of the seductive compensations of her exile must have been her freedom from this exigency of writing: to practice it without belonging to it, or having her life dissolve through it.

Fresh off the *S.S. Bowplate* and on her way to Rio, Bishop in a journal entry puts heaven in proximity to the question of meta-language: "I don't know why I think it is 'good for one' to get lost in a strange city where one doesn't speak the language etc., but I do. I wonder if they speak Esperanto in Heaven or what." Her comment to Dr. Baumann and the Barkers, "I must have died and gone to heaven without deserving to" becomes interesting for other reasons: heaven appears now in two contexts, where getting to heaven and being in heaven both involve the acquisition of family and a passage across language borders.

In this new household, the cook's child was born as her namesake, and others of Lota's wide and various family from time to time contributed relatives of all ages, ranks, and dispositions. Not even pets, those proto-selves of the child's world, were missing, but here provided on a mythic scale. With unrestrained pleasure Bishop reports to all her friends on the new acquisition of cats and birds. "My lifelong dream . . . A TOUCAN." she announces, dazzled, to the Barkers:

> He eats six bananas a day – I must say they seem to go right through him & come out practically as good as new – meat, grapes – to see him swallowing grapes is rather like playing a pin-ball machine [. . .] and something I'd never known – they sleep with their tails straight up over their heads, and their heads under a wing, so the silhouette is just like an inverted comma. . . as you see I'm still too excited to type properly.

Bishop is rewriting her own childhood, assembling it around her with gifts given her by travel. If we look at the conclusion of "Over 2,000 Illustrations and a Complete Concordance," a poem written and published two years before her arrival in Brazil, the whole fragile enterprise of constructing family takes on deeper and even more urgent dimensions:

> Open the heavy book. Why couldn't we have seen
> this old Nativity while we were at it?
> — the dark ajar, the rocks breaking with light,
> an undisturbed, unbreathing flame,

colorless, sparkless, freely fed on straw,
and, lulled within, a family with pets,
— and looked and looked our infant sight away.

Bishop's own childhood had been split between family affluence
and family warmth. Her maternal grandparents in Nova Scotia, who
took care of the virtually orphaned Elizabeth after her father's death,
and her mother's subsequent institutionalization, seem to have represented the apex of Bishop's shaky experience of intimacy. But in 1917,
when the paternal grandparents swooped down on the six-year-old
Elizabeth, she was torn from that close and familiar village world. As
her words from "The Country Mouse" explain, she was "brought
back unconsulted and against my wishes to the house my father had
been born in, to be saved from a life of poverty and provincialism,
bare feet, suet puddings, unsanitary school slates, perhaps even from
the inverted *r*'s of my mother's family." The household of the paternal
grandparents was to contain the nervous, gloomy world in which she
remarked that she and Beppo, the Boston bull terrier, lived on pretty
much the same footing. After this move, Bishop developed the allergies and asthma attacks that would mark later crises as well. On the
train, going away with these strange and surprising grandparents, she
had referred to the Pullman car's metal sink as a "hopper," and drew
loud and probably quite humiliating laughter from her grandfather for
her farm language. In her early experience then, money and culture
stood in one branch of the family tree, while warmth and acceptance
stood in the other; one branch hung over town space, the other, the
accepting Nova Scotian one, stayed country.

And now we look at her March 1952 description to Lowell of Lota's
Samambaia:

> an ultra-modern house up on the side of a black granite mountain,
> with a waterfall at one end, clouds coming into the living room in
> the middle of the conversation, etc. The house is unfinished and we
> are using oil-lamps, no floors – just cement covered with dogs' foot-
> prints.

No wonder she referred later to her resettlement in this way: "What
I'm really up to is recreating a sort of deluxe Nova Scotia all over
again in Brazil. And now I'm my own grandmother." In her own
person, a grandmother dissolving and resolving the dialectic that each
of her actual grandmothers had played against her. In this home

archaism and modernity, intimacy and sophistication, the manners of both luxury and poverty, the exotic, the familiar, the autonymous and the familial, are all inimical pairs disarmingly blended. In it as well, Bishop finds the indeterminate openness of the evolving creative enterprise. Even in the hopefulness of its unfinished state, Samambaia at that point mimicked Bishop's own paradigm for the creative act drawn from her early poem "The Monument":

> But roughly but adequately it can shelter
> what is within (which after all
> cannot have been intended to be seen).
> It is the beginning of a painting,
> a piece of sculpture, or poem, or monument,
> and all of wood. Watch it closely.

In this household clinging to the side of a mountain, and invaded by the ambiguous boundaries between sky and ground, Bishop's past is being rewritten, its antinomies if not resolved, then at least projected symbolically with increasing clarity and balance.

In 1955, after mentioning the medicines she takes successfully for the allergies that have plagued so much of her life, she describes her working routine to Lowell:

> I get up in the freezing dawns here and begin with all the confidence
> in the world – the mountains look exactly as if floating in *vin rosé*
> then, with a white bowl of milk down below us.

Like a lulled child sustained by a giant breastful of milk, the poet is free to begin her work.

·IV·

This phase of Bishop's life in Brazil lasted for some time—"I had fifteen really happy years," she later writes tersely to Dr. Baumann. In 1960, before the end of those years, before the period when Lota became increasingly tense and strained by the tumbling, climactic politics of her employment as park designer and city planner under the controversial governor of Guanabara, Carlos Lacerda, Bishop took a trip by herself down the Amazon. In 1967 she described a part of this journey in an essay, "A Trip To Vigia," and part in "Santarém," a poem whose writing was not completed and published until long after she'd left Brazil. "I want to go back to the Amazon – " she wrote Lowell, "I dream dreams every night – I don't know quite why I found it so affecting."

For Bishop, poems and experience had their intervals of disjunction as well as fusion. The Amazon for her had bifurcated into the swift, dreamy magic of her poem about the river witch called "The River-man," and into the more prosaic observations contained in a letter to Lota. "Literature," of course, was preternaturally sharp, while "Life," as represented in the letters home to Lota, was full of practical arrangements about cabins and sleeping quarters. "The Riverman" had been written before Bishop ever caught sight of the Amazon, and owed a great deal of its descriptive substrate to Charles Wagley's *Amazon Town*,[6] and to conversations with Brazilian friends. For Bishop there had been prior travelers, prior descriptions, and entangling relations between different temporal and spatial orders of event and image, dream and reality. Lowell was very likely right when he connected "The Riverman" not to Bishop's reading of Brazilian folktales, but to what he called her "fairy tale": to a fantasy that she related to him over a decade earlier in 1948, from Maine, about a mermaid. Before relating the daydream, Bishop writes about "solitude & ennui" and admits to " 'suffering' " from them, placing the topic between inverted commas, and at least in part attempting to brush it away by comic touches:

> That's just the kind of 'suffering' I'm most at home with & helpless about, I'm afraid, but what with 2 days of fog and alarmingly low tides I've really got it bad & think I'll write you a note before I go out & eat some mackerel. The boats bringing the men back from the quarries look like convict ships & I've just been indulging myself in a nightmare of finding a gasping mermaid under one of those exposed docks – you know, trying to tear the mussels off the piles for something to eat, – horrors.

In Bishop's poem about a merman, or river witch, made before she had even tested the Amazon's powers of abundant disposal, the merman has not been abandoned by the sustaining waters, but instead is on the point of entering his proper realm. He is made to speak in a voice full of promises and invitations:

> When the moon burns white
> and the river makes that sound

like a primus pumped up high —
that fast, high whispering
like a hundred people at once —
I'll be there below,
as the turtle rattle hisses
and the coral gives the sign,
travelling fast as a wish,
with my magic cloak of fish
swerving as I swerve,
following the veins,
the river's long, long veins,
to find the pure elixirs . . .
When the moon shines and the river
lies across the earth
and sucks it like a child,
then I will go to work
to get you health and money.

For Bishop, once there in propria persona, the river provided no disappointment; in a letter to Lowell, there is a rather mysterious vignette. She speaks of slides she has taken:

I have some of passengers going ashore in a pouring rain and up a steep ladder, etc. it is like the Israelites. Did I tell you (oh dear I hope not) how we stopped at a place called "Liverpool" late one night – a narrow channel, nothing visible but a few white blurs of houses and candles, and one lantern. The ship waited and waited – then plop-plop – very gently, a canoe came out, a big one. Several men were in it, with two lanterns, one the old-fashioned burglar's kind of dark lantern – they were bringing out a dying man to be taken to the hospital in Belém. It was very hard to raise him up to the ship – in a sheet, I think – an old man with a nightcap on – the lantern light fell on his face, on the red, muddy water – it was quite incredible.

On the mother waters, in a dreamlike darkness evoking the mysterious authority of a biblical image, a near-corpse with lantern and candles is setting forth on the final journey.

Before she ever embarked on the Amazon, its mythology gave Bishop the person and format for a myth of potency in "The River-man"; after inspecting it herself, she returns with images of both death and communal continuities, and writes her later poem, "Santarém," as a narrative of her own experience, and not from behind the masking of dramatic monologue. Like Bishop's other late-published Brazil poem "Pink Dog," originally titled "Goodbye to Rio," or "Rio Blues," "Santarém" is drenched with the sense of leave-taking.

For Santarém, the city on the Amazon that occurs midway as the first real stop between Manaus and Belém, a city of nearly a million souls, a letter of Bishop's said merely "Santarém – I'd like to go there for a rest cure or something – no pavements, just deep orange sand, beautiful houses – and absolute silence – walks along the waterfront and two cafes – just the way a town should be laid out." No lyrical effusion: instead, a longing. Nearly a decade after her arrival in Brazil, Bishop inscribes longing in a strange constellation of images and feelings, pivoting on death, rest, underworld quietude and stasis, and within what looks like the deadly sleepiness of myths of completion and perfectibility.

What had Santarém become for Bishop in the poem finally bearing its name, the poem which, unlike "The Riverman," had actually been based on "experience," that elusive entity? Two-and-a-half pages of raffish gaiety, disarming, wholly appealing:

> That golden evening I really wanted to go no farther;
> more than anything else I wanted to stay awhile
> in that conflux of two great rivers, Tapajós, Amazon,
> grandly, silently flowing, flowing east.
> Suddenly there'd been houses, people, and lots of mongrel
> riverboats skittering back and forth
> under a sky of gorgeous, under-lit clouds,
> with everything gilded, burnished along one side,
> and everything bright, cheerful, casual—or so it looked.
> I liked the place; I liked the idea of the place.

And yet the Edenic freshness of the poem, with its world of innocent animals, zebus "gentle, proud/ and *blue*, with down-curved horns and hanging ears," and tiled housefronts, ends at departure, as Bishop clutches the prize a local pharmacist has given her: "an empty wasps' nest [. . .] small, exquisite, clean matte white/ and hard as stucco." In the very last words of her poem, a fellow passenger, "really a very nice old man," asks, "What's that ugly thing?"

·V·

Why did Elizabeth Bishop choose to live in a strange country whose very strangeness might have made its poverty and pain even more repellant to her? There were practical reasons for staying. She writes Lowell bluntly: "I couldn't live on my money in the 'States' – in fact I find by statistics in *The New Republic* that there I am actually in the 'underprivileged' class." Certainly not her situation in Brazil. It isn't that she romanticizes its perfections. Probing for an explanation of her expatriation, in 1957 she says:

> it's just some lack of vitality in myself that makes me feel so hopeless about my own country . . . and then I feel just as hopeless about Brazil [. . .] But I really can't *bear* much of American life these days – surely no country has ever been so filthy rich and so hideously uncomfortable at the same time.

And by 1960 she can say:

> But I worry a great deal about what to do with all this accumulation of exotic or picturesque or charming detail, and I don't want to become a poet who can only write about South America, etc. – it is one of my greatest worries now – how to use everything and keep on living here, most of the time, probably – and yet be a New Englander-herring-choker-bluenoser at the same time.

There is an increasing anxiety, audible in poems and letters, a need to struggle against preciosity, to open herself to what is troubling and disturbing. She writes to Lowell:

> I'm in fine shape except for these worries about money and whether I'm going to turn into solid cuteness in my poetry if I don't watch out – or if I do watch out –

"Going to the Bakery," published in 1968, points directly at the disturbing qualities of her life in Rio:

> The bakery lights are dim. Beneath
> our rationed electricity,
> the round cakes look about to faint—
> each turns up a glazed white eye.

The gooey tarts are red and sore.
Buy, buy, what shall I buy?

Now flour is adulterated
with cornmeal, the loaves of bread
lie like yellow-fever victims
laid out in a crowded ward.

The baker, sickly too, suggests
the "milk rolls," since they still are warm
and made with milk, he says. They feel
like a baby on the arm.

Under the false-almond tree's
leathery leaves, a childish *puta*
dances, feverish as an atom:
cha-cha, cha-cha, cha-cha . . .

In front of my apartment house
a black man sits in a black shade,
lifting his shirt to show a bandage
on his black, invisible side.

Fumes of *cachaça* knock me over,
like gas fumes from an auto crash.
He speaks in perfect gibberish.
The bandage glares up, white and fresh.

I give him seven cents in *my*
terrific money, say "Good-night"
from force of habit. Oh, mean habit!
Not one word more apt or bright?

Here even language is abashed. But using her habitual understatement, through compression and selective focus, Bishop sketches a domestic scene that is dense with political implication, where neither the foreign American resident nor the home government nor the helpless population is denied corrupt or unpleasant roles. The black man in the purgatorial shade, crashing in the fumes of his native rum, needs to be propitiated by gifts from the traveler so that she, burdened by the terrors and powers of her currency, may pass into her own good night. Wrapped in "my" money, she finds the freshness and whiteness of bread is fever pallor, fever brightness. Bread itself is the helpless flesh of infants, and the baker of it is sick. In this stricken electric light, where the whores are debased children, the almond tree is false, the flour adulterated, and the bandage glares freshly over invisible hurt, even the eyes of the American dim. There seem to be only wounds and fatalities about, and her belief in the restorative powers of that seven cents flickers, its wattage low.

How much more penetrating, unsentimental, and painfully direct the considered language of this poem is than that of this passage, taken from the river trip essay, never finished, that included the crayon image of the smokestack on the stern-wheeler *Wenceslau Braz* previously cited. Here, Bishop takes up the surface, the conventional judgment, in this first-strike sketch of a waif, encountered one evening in Juazeiro:

> . . . A very tiny praça – almost totally dark. One street light. On the corner, a big sheet of sacking or something like that spread out, a few pots and pans, a bundle, odds and ends, all dark and mysterious and travel worn – and in the middle of it all, a tiny, tiny child – sitting up straight absolutely alone. Possibly a year old – possibly more – it's hard to say – a little girl, in rags, her very thin legs folded buddha like – absolutely alone in the praça in the dark, in the river wind. I went over to her. Maybe she couldn't walk yet, maybe she was crippled – the little folded legs were so thin. I tried to talk to her but she looked frightened – at the same time, she automatically held out her hand to beg. Her parents must have gone off to find a place to stay or something to eat – well, who knows. I put a conto – tucked it down inside her filthy little shirt – I was afraid if I left it in her hand someone might steal it. (40 cents now, maybe – but this will still buy quite a bit in those parts.) She didn't speak, couldn't, maybe. 2 or 3 other people had now gathered on the sidewalk in back of me – where the light was – but they expressed sympathy: "Coitadinha – all alone," and so on. – so I left her there, a little silent scrap awaiting God knows what.

This scene isn't Elizabeth Bishop: it's a combination of David Douglas Duncan and Charles Dickens. First the *Life* photographer, the need just to get down the misery that has so moved one; then, the first faint stirrings into literature in the appearance of all those modifiers, and that "dark, in the river-wind." But by the time we have to move to do something, put the coin to the child, literature steps aside for practical action, a crowd gathers, there is public record, public murmur. Unlike her poems, Bishop's last line about this incident moves off, "silent scrap awaiting God knows what" into pathos and an utterly undistinguished and conventional style. In the last handful of Bishop's poems about Brazil, in "Santarém," in "Going to the Bakery," and in the savage "Pink Dog," some of the earlier, bubbly good humor dissipates, and pain and cruelty make more overt and lasting appearances, but the temptation either to "solid cuteness" or journalistic sentimentality is bypassed.

·VI·

On the bus to Ouro Preto, a couple of hours north of Rio, in the state of Minas Gerais, or General Mines, I lean forward in the front seat of a bus climbing heights with an exhilarating recklessness. I have an unimpeded view: the dirt on this ground so iron-rich it is a pure and unctuous red, the blue-violet mountains breaking in waves, while tropical palms and shrubs stick out every which way from the roads and slopes. The vegetation, impossibly shiny, uncountably various in the upward cut and thrust of its leaves, is very beautiful. This is the road that Bishop must have taken every time she left Rio for the house I am going to see.

The house, which the caretaker opens, still has most of Bishop's furniture in it. Things are very simple. Speaking no English, Maria has judged well enough to be able to tell that I *will* be pleased to see the big copper bowl in which Bishop's bread dough rose. Rusted and forlorn, three little loaf pans, American make. Books and magazines in French, Spanish, Portuguese, and English crumble on shelves in the basement. Provocative titles. *Amiel: Une étude sur la timidité. Middlemarch.* Abandoned or forgotten? *El hombre y lo Sagrado. Pão e Vinho.* A littered backyard, a bentwood rocker in the small living room. A painted gourd hangs over the stove, and a Klee faces the dining room over the sideboard; the wooden chairs, table, and blue glass in the cupboard look as if they might have been at home in New England, or in Great Village, in Nova Scotia. Seized with a desire to have *something* from this presence-drenched house, for one disgraceful moment I want a keepsake, a back number of an Italian journal: here is Bishop's poem on Pound, "Visits to Saint Elizabeths" in Italian, and here is an apologetic preface, I can make out this much, for Pound's Fascist politics. It's really a little thing. On the phone, in strained French I try to explain to Linda Nemer, the Brazilian owner of this house, who speaks no English, why the magazine is important, fumbling for reasons to walk away with it. Of course she is cautious, a gentle, reasonable voice on the phone explaining to me that xeroxes are possible in Brazil. Right here in this town of fifty thousand souls who leave screens off the windows and where I can't find electric outlets for my international folding clothes iron, and where the frosted bulb hopelessly awaits adoption, I can find a xerox machine? Apparently I can. I have only to ask Maria to take the magazine for me, she will do it.

When I walked around this house early this morning, trailing it humbly, and suspiciously, it looked derelict. It looked as if it hadn't been inhabited for years. Now that the fog over the valley has burned away I can see where the narrow shoe-box of the back porch leans over the abyss of a hillside, falling steeply down from the house. At least I can tell this much: why Bishop had come to this place, even at a time when her relationship to Brazil was souring, and had fallen in love with this small stucco house dating back to the seventeenth century. It must have been the mountains, and the vertiginous little streets, the fact that one end of a cobbled lane drops so sharply down when you look at it that the arms at your side fly out instinctively—looking for handholds, as the blind toes of your shoes feel for the way over these tilting stones.

And the mountains: views jam on views, perspective on perspective with up and down, big and little, near and far, in a constant dialectic undoubtedly prized by a far-sighted poet from Nova Scotia, whose eyes and pen were trained to release vision at distances. Huge mountains, shrinking the people—it seems the same conversation with space that a shore dweller might have with the sea. I think of Bishop's description of the iceberg as "a breathing plain"; of "Questions of Travel" where the mountains look "like the hulls of capsized ships,/ slime-hung and barnacled." They're all interanimate.

In Ouro Preto collections of soapstone carvings are hawked on the sidewalks and in the shops; churches with high shoulders, frilled doorways and skinny belfries mass along the streets. Gems. On every corner voices soft and insistent or brazen and piercing say, "You buy gems, lady? Gems? Gems?" Besides gems, the big story in Ouro Preto is Aleijadinho, the half-black eighteenth-century sculptor, whose wild and strange statues and carvings can be found in most of the churches. Aleijadinho was said to have modestly worn a sack over his leprosy-eaten face while wielding his chisel, to spare his townsmen and patrons the disquieting spectacle of his features. In her description for Time-Life, Bishop omits the sensational veil and merely talks about the carving:

Aleijadinho's favorite material was the grey-green soapstone of Minas, soft to cut but turning somewhat harder with exposure. It is still much used for pots and pans, and the Mineiros say that nothing is as good as a soapstone pot for cooking the daily rice. Aleijadinho's most famous works are the statues of twelve prophets that stand on the double staircase in front of the church of Bom Jesus de Matosinhas in Congonhas do Campo. Crude, but powerful and dramatic, they gesticulate against the white church with its bright blue doors and against the sweep of bare ore-filled hills.

Characteristic that so much space is given over to a precise account of folk custom and practical detail. Only one sentence at the end paints a tiny, effective scene. Congonhas do Campo was a half-day's trip away, though: so I marched speculatively around and around Ouro Preto's foremost Aleijadinho church, admiring the carved door, closed for restoration and guessing at the splendid altar bolted behind it.

At the tiny inn where I was staying, the English-speaking owner came back and told me a few grumpy facts about his old-time neighbor. Later the hesitant, but friendly voice of Linda Nemer came back on the phone, and we arranged to meet in nearby Belo Horizonte, where she lived. As her French streamed past me, I thought I heard the word "poems" quite clearly; I shrugged, thinking it quite possible that she would have some letters, after all, she and Elizabeth had been friends.

Explaining ourselves over lunch, this large, earnest black-haired woman told me what a pleasure it was to be able to speak about Elizabeth. Elizabeth had been so important to her, allowing Linda to see herself as . . . the concept slipped away from me in the underbrush of her rapid French. Still, this was a very different Elizabeth Bishop from the one that the hotelkeeper in the morning had described. Even through the French, and the mental scramble that it took me to get past the roadblocks of a defective memory of crucial words, our common subject brought us through most of the *churruasco* she had laid on for us, a long proliferation of barbecued meats and waiters rushing to spare us the embarrassment of a nude plate. Why hadn't anyone else come to see this woman? In a deep suspense, I felt myself not to be in my own hands. Negotiating my melon, I did as I saw other travelers do, and awkwardly used my knife to flay the green fruit, slice it with my lefthand knife, scoop it up with my righthand fork. Linda, breaking off in mid-phrase, leaned over the table for a moment, and asked me if it wouldn't be easier this way? Taking the knife from my hand, putting it on the table and placing the spoon, with a lump of melon aboard, into my hand.

She has an *héritage*, she explains to me. Bishop emptied the contents of her desk in Rio, and told Linda that she was likely to outlive her: she must keep these papers. Sell them if she liked, but if so, get a good price for them. What did I think about this? Yes, *of course* I would like to see them.

At her apartment in Belo Horizonte we are still at table. Smiling, Linda brings out a cardboard filebox; another box, wrapped with a stiff tie that looks like the rushes given out on Palm Sunday. These things are old: four black three-hole notebooks, with the metal clasps all rusted, the covers browning and spotting. The blotched blue-lined paper filled with the familiar, pinched handwriting—dreams, handwritten drafts of poems, a travel diary, reading notes, short, explosive little comments—"Marianne's [. . .] democracy [. . .]"; "Muriel Rukeyser – like having a Wurlitzer automatic pipe organ in the home –." There is a first draft of "The Prodigal." An address book, a bunch of folders and letters. Alas, most of the letters in Portuguese, and photographs—is this Robert Lowell? Linda asks. No, it isn't. But then an aerogram from Lowell in England.

Now that the papers are in American hands for the first time, the first American hands since Elizabeth's, Linda is clearly uneasy. Feeling her hesitation I stop and ask in confusion if I may read what is being spread in front of me. She leans forward, and pulling a piece of folded onionskin from one of the notebooks, opens it carefully and hands it to me. Linda reads no English. She has questions about what she is giving me. It is a typescript of a rather remarkable poem, no erasures, a doodle in the corner that looks a bit like a fourposter bed. I've never seen this one before. It's a love poem, beginning "It is marvellous to wake up together. . ." All my signal systems are awash. I can't quite take it all in; I don't even try to figure out when the poem was written. I merely follow the complex, familiar figures and oblique symmetries of the arguments, the tropes. Now a drawing is brought to me, a rather nice black and white drawing of twined lovers with a brief, brilliant *jeu d'esprit* handwritten by Elizabeth in pencil across the bottom. This is a small thing, easy to look at, to grasp.

It is clearly treasured—I ask if I may copy out the poem. Linda eyes me for a moment. No. I may not. Is this a permanent no? While I am reading she leaves the room for what seem to be ages. Does she mean it? Why can't I memorize faster? Is she teasing me, testing me, trying to figure out what I am going to do? Feeling a complete fool nonetheless I copy nothing out. Someone has put me on trust, or is it trussed me with my own word, and like a child or a patient in a harness I am completely incapacitated.

And now Linda's questions begin in earnest, which I cannot begin to answer. What the papers mean to me is not something that I can fix dollars to, others will have to do that. We discuss this subject in the car again. Linda has not allowed me paper and pencil near the notebooks or folders, but she volunteers that she thinks that they should be in American hands. They aren't doing anybody any good in Brazil. We both agree that Vassar, as the site of the major Bishop archive, is a logical owner, although Linda fancies the idea of Harvard. I think of that box in nearby places where I can use its contents, remembering that other life of the library, reading other people's mail, all their little fervent and self-forgetful jottings dissolving their deaths. Nobody seems dead when all this vibrating stuff full of passions still turns in your hands.

The next morning I've thought up a way to take notes and I telephone Linda Nemer. Suppose I read through the papers, spending a little more time with the precious drafts. And then I can't report back to Vassar without notes. I'll write them out, give them over to Linda; she can ask an English-speaking friend to translate what I have written, see if it violates any presiding spirits, any commercial possibilities, for I am by now aware that this is something that Linda will also protect, in addition to Elizabeth's memory. She assents to my proposition, in fact, later waves it all away, and sets me up at a desk in a small room at the back of her apartment, appearing briefly, smiling at the door every now and then to see how the papers and I are faring. Part of what I am reading has to do with Bishop's first trip to Brazil: "It is hell not to be able to speak the language," she writes.

·VII·

When I left Ouro Preto for Rio I had one more mission planned. It seemed silly to want this further thing, but I had determined to find Samambaia, Bishop's retreat outside of Rio, hoping to fetch another signal from the vanished. I decided to take photographs, and wander around the place with the study where she wrote so many poems. Standing there at the gate was the best moment, jumping out to photograph the carved wooden sign announcing Samambaia, Bishop's first mountain retreat from Rio, where clouds held conversations with the ground. But trailing through room after room, and being told that here a wall had been torn down, and a wall put up, and here a frivolous railing in deplorable taste introduced, and there a free wilderness of flowers erased, followed by a trip to a bare and mold-smelling little back cottage, stripped of any clues of furniture or books, I came to the end of the powers of houses and things. This house, this lavish spread of buildings and grounds, was only another rich person's country place. The traces of the occupancy I was interested in had long been eliminated. There was the waterfall, and here was the

> House, open house
> to the white dew
> and the milk-white sunrise
> kind to the eyes,
> to membership
> of silver fish, mouse,
> bookworms,
> big moths; with a wall
> for the mildew's
> ignorant map;
>
> darkened and tarnished
> by the warm touch
> of the warm breath,
> maculate, cherished

The ones who had built and cherished the house were dead. Lota, an apparent suicide in New York; Elizabeth, with less than a decade left of her life after Brazil. As I'd stared around, bewildered, at the small and rather characterless block to which I'd been conducted as the studio Lota built for Elizabeth, bereft of its former occupant's books and clavichord, I found myself thinking, not of studios, but of the boarded-up house in Duxbury, in "The End of March," where "Everything was withdrawn as far as possible,/indrawn" and in that "dubious. . . . .proto-dream-house," the narrator says:

> I'd like to retire there and do *nothing*,
> or nothing much, forever, in two bare rooms . . .

Or of that other house that Bishop described in an early parable, "The Sea & Its Shore," where Edwin Boomer, a stand-in for the poet, lived:

It was of wood, with a pitched roof, about four by four by six feet, set on pegs stuck in the sand. There was no window, no door set in the door frame, and nothing at all inside [. . .]. As a house, it was more like an idea of a house than a real one [. . .] It was a shelter, but not for living in. It was to the ordinary house, what the ceremonial thinking cap is to the ordinary hat.

Then again, how serious was the poker-faced narrator of "In Prison," when he said: "I expect to go to prison in full possession of my 'faculties' — in fact, it is not until I am securely installed there that I expect fully to realize them — ."

In this dank little chamber all the way at the end of my Brazilian travels, a day before going home, it seemed to me I'd found the prolific nothing, the springing bareness at the mind's edges that would be the best guide back through the poems and their unassailable interiority. If I were to learn any more about the inhabitant of twenty years ago, it would not be through the house but through language, through the thicket of letters, diaries, scraps, doodles, and notes I had unearthed elsewhere, and through other sources prosaically found through ordinary outlets, from libraries, from my own books at home. If the browning papers taken from a desk in Rio and put in my hands had given me some sort of thrill, some tremor of impossible expectation about to be fulfilled, my Samambaia of that afternoon had nearly taken that away. It was time to go home, time for the traveler to exit, the scholar to enter.

·T·W·O·

✠

"It is marvellous
to wake up together"

ACROSS FROM me, at the dining room table of her apartment in Belo Horizonte, Linda Nemer held out a sheaf of papers with one hand, and smiling tentatively, pushed over a shoebox full of small notebooks with the other. No other reader had touched these papers, I was sure I heard her say, since Elizabeth Bishop herself. They were an inheritance in English to a woman who spoke no English, who had nonetheless guarded them for nearly a decade.

I unfolded a sheet of brittle onionskin and read through a typed, completed poem I'd never seen before, not in any of the dozens of boxes of Bishop papers currently held for scholarly use. Later, a close draft of the same poem in that small, unmistakable handwriting that looks like frayed smocking turned up in a black looseleaf binder from the shoebox, positioned between other Key West poems. It was a piece probably written in the early forties.

This is how it appeared in typescript, without deletions or additions, or any of those boxed or questioned alternative words or phrases with which the writer usually indicates unfinished work:

> It is marvellous to wake up together
> At the same minute; marvellous to hear
> The rain begin suddenly all over the roof,
> To feel the air clear
> As if electricity had passed through it
> From a black mesh of wires in the sky.

All over the roof the rain hisses,
And below, the light falling of kisses.

An electrical storm is coming or moving away;
It is the prickling air that wakes us up.
If lightning struck the house now, it would run
From the four blue china balls on top
Down the roof and down the rods all around us,
And we imagine dreamily
How the whole house caught in a bird-cage of lightning
Would be quite delightful rather than frightening;

And from the same simplified point of view
Of night and lying flat on one's back
All things might change equally easily,
Since always to warn us there must be these black
Electrical wires dangling. Without surprise
The world might change to something quite different,
As the air changes or the lightning comes without our blinking,
Change as our kisses are changing without our thinking.

It is an intimately first person plural love poem, spoken in that syntactically ambiguous territory of address where one person seems to be speaking to herself or to her companion through the warm cloak of her *we*. In its straightforward but deeply figured way, the poem begins with two people in bed simultaneously awakened by an electrical storm, who then turn to each other, aroused. The poem is at once more joyful, erotic, and tender than anything Bishop allowed herself to publish in her lifetime. The lovers feel the air prickle above, while below there is "the light falling of kisses"; they imagine the house struck, themselves caged by lightning. Fear is deliciously displaced by delight; in this "simplified" world governed by the marvelous "All things might change equally easily." In the last lines, warned by a benevolent and welcome lightning, and "without surprise," the paired speakers, in a language charged with double entendre, bring us not to closure but to a world of potential transformation in which sexual climax will take its orderly place, an unusual theme for Bishop.

Yet this poem, while it differs markedly in subject, still keeps the radiant finish that should attach it unapologetically to the main body of Bishop's poems. Its tone, both subtle and tender, is the familiar, conversational balance of elegance and simplicity; the off-and-on again rhyming playful, authoritative. Here, too, the habit of echoing and reversing phrases becomes another trait tying "It is marvellous" to poems bearing her signature in print.

If we look backward through even the very earliest work, there are other images of wire as release, and birdcage as benign entrapment, and other metaphoric uses of the rainstorm: each of these shaded figures can be seen repeating. And if we trace the meshwork, the overlapping circuits in figure and theme across many poems, then the significance of the newly discovered piece begins to assemble as legible pattern, and its startling subject, love's pleasure, opens new ways in which to read all of Bishop's poems about human connection.

· I ·

There are really only a handful that talk about love. In early work the subject is present through a glaze of abstracting personification: "Love's the obstinate boy. . . . Love's the burning boy." Or from comic distance, as in the second poem from "Songs for a Colored Singer," the only first-person narrator to appear before "In the Waiting Room" as explicitly female:

> The time has come to call a halt.
> I met him walking with Varella
> and hit him twice with my umbrella.
> Perhaps that occasion was my fault,
> but the time has come to call a halt.
> [. . .]
> I'm leaving on the bus tonight.
>   Far down the highway wet and black
>   I'll ride and ride and not come back.
>   I'm going to go and take the bus
>   and find someone monogamous.

Or behind the innocuous cover of loyal friendship, as in "The Shampoo," its domestic intimacies sponged of eroticism, its astronomical metaphor not accenting but attenuating the reach of its tenderness. Or reference is dark and oblique, where those suffering or seeking love exist only in brief cuts. This is the whole of "Insomnia," quoted in full because it is impossible to look at where this short, dense poem is going without considering text and title in their entirety:

The moon in the bureau mirror
looks out a million miles
(and perhaps with pride, at herself,
but she never, never smiles)
far and away beyond sleep, or
perhaps she's a daytime sleeper.

By the universe deserted,
she'd tell it to go to hell,
and she'd find a body of water,
or a mirror, on which to dwell.
So wrap up care in a cobweb
and drop it down the well
into that world inverted
where left is always right,
where the shadows are really the body,
where we stay awake all night,
where the heavens are shallow as the sea
is now deep, and you love me.

In this apparently casual allegory looking with one eye at the moon
and with the other into a bedroom world of daytime sleep and nighttime wakefulness, love jumps into the final line; but only to become,
like the proud, unsmiling and angry moon, a citizen of the mirror
world of contradiction, of reversal, and to borrow Bishop's term, of
inversion. And if the reader blinks twice the subject of this poem goes
right on past.

It is one of the few in which there is a suggestion of same-sex love.
Other readers could complain that inversion is too prejudicial and
negative a word to apply to homosexuality, yet Bishop's application of
that sense of inversion, rather more usual in the early fifties than now,
seems deliberate. In an odd little mid-stanza beat, the center of attention switches from the moon, by way of that reflecting "body of
water," to an indeterminate member of the poem's *we*. And from mid-
stanza mid-poem on out, *we've* wrapped care in a cobweb and dropped
down the well into "that world inverted." For this speaker, love is
only possible in an impossible mirror world of sleepless night, ruled
by a moon in rebellion, in which "left is always right," heaven is low
and accessible, and "shadows are really the body."

We could read "Insomnia" as a simmering, nighttime solitude
defiantly freed from conventional restraints, a condition not linked to

sexual preference at all. But the whole configuration of the angry, deserted female moon, and the drop into a space where lovers live at the bottom of a well in an underground world of erotic connection seems to suggest a more than voluntary withdrawal. There is nothing intrinsically homosexual about the desire to sleep by day and wake by night, or to want to live by shadowy spirit instead of vexatious flesh; yet the emphasis, on dark and subterranean reversals in relation to the conditioning of love, seems loaded with an exceptional anger and anxiety. Our attention flicked by that reading of "inverted," the poem appears to record a constellation of feelings best explained by reference to homosexuality, and its explosive but largely repressed public connection.

"One Art," unlike "Insomnia," is a late poem, but a poem of similarly intense and quite similarly guarded feeling. It shares two characteristics with the majority of Bishop's published love poems: first, to be nongender-specific (a trait shared, too, by "It is marvellous"), and second, to avoid explicit mention of sexuality. "One Art" defines "the art of losing." Dealing with emotional control and the containment of grief as its topic, the poem encloses its story in the formal elaborations of a villanelle. After invoking loss incrementally through keys, then houses, then continents, and then simply, as "you," we arrive at the ultimate disaster with its portrait of the beloved protectively wrapped in parenthesis: "losing you (the joking voice, a gesture I love)." This is the only time that the person who is the subject of grief emerges directly into the text; yet it is the genius of this poem so to manipulate the distancing properties of the villanelle's intricacies as to make ironic capital of them. The repetitions of the key rhyme words, *master* and *disaster*, alternate in the obsessive and tragic dilemma of the grief-stricken speaker, as like a too-tightly wound spring the poem breaks to its conclusion, the painful subversion of language and form by feeling:

> The art of losing isn't hard to master.
>
> I lost two cities, lovely ones. And, vaster,
> some realms I owned, two rivers, a continent.
> I miss them, but it wasn't a disaster.
>
> — Even losing you (the joking voice, a gesture
> I love) I shan't have lied. It's evident
> the art of losing's not too hard to master
> though it may look like (*Write* it!) like disaster.

Once again, the real record of struggle is carried by parenthesis in the final line. Form enters self-reflexively to become ironic commentary on subject, and distance functions brilliantly both as problematic event and as the exploding container of event.

Aside from these rare poems, love, as it touched the more sensitive places in Bishop's life, enters the poems infrequently; yet this is a poetry where the poet usually has no hesitation about identifying its experiences as her own; when love appears as subject, narrative shrinks and abstraction takes over. This stanza from "Argument" opens one of the more direct earlier poems; characteristically, it describes love in a distressed context where distance is the governor:

> Days that cannot bring you near
> or will not,
> Distance trying to appear
> something more than obstinate,
> argue argue argue with me
> endlessly
> neither proving you less wanted nor less dear.

But in succeeding stanzas built with controlled and stylish symmetry, both dispute and disputants remain behind a screen of general and canceling metaphor.

·II·

If "It is marvellous to wake up together" is different in its frank treatment of love, however, it is unmistakably linked to other Bishop poems in its imagery, and in the mechanics and props of its manufacture. Before getting on to the published poem that the newly discovered love poem most resembles, I'd like to look at the initial appearances of wires and birdcage, and at a developing matrix of ideas for the rainstorm.

About those wires: they appear vividly outside poems, too. Teasingly, apparently unconnected to anything but the haphazard chances of a life, this little vignette made its way into a letter of Bishop's to the Barkers late in 1959:

I like oil lamp light – but it was a great relief to stop cleaning all those lamps here when we got electricity up this far – of course nothing works very consistently here – it's part of the charm, as I tell Lota when she nearly goes mad trying to get things working. She's so good a repairman that once a while ago I held the ladder for her along the road while she climbed up the posts and twiddled with the wires – I thought she'd be electrocuted at any minute, of course – and when we got back to the house we did have both lights and the telephone again -

Another set of wires from those meshing in the Key West poem, this set figures forth an experience not easily separable from Bishop's poetry. Both danger and power course along a field of connections that two loving women, one grounded, and one mounting precariously into the air, complete between them; as in a body of poetry, the properly twiddled wires secure both speech and sight. This image, perhaps too exotic and special in reference, was never used in a poem; but both telephone and wires did make their appearance in "Electrical Storm," written at roughly the same time as the Barker letter. In this poem the householders at Samambaia do not resolve their communications dilemma by the poem's ending: "We got up to find the wiring fused,/ no lights, a smell of saltpetre,/and the telephone dead."

Here are wires in a quite early poem from *North & South*, where they are again specifically telephone wires:

> [. . .] we start at
> series of slight disturbances up in the telephone wires
>   on the turnpike.
> Flocks of short, shining wires seem to be flying sidewise.
>   Are they birds?
> They flash again. No. They are vibrations of the tuning-fork
>   you hold and strike
> against the mirror-frames, then draw for miles, your dreams,
>   out countrywards.

But still the wires connect to dreams, to nerve circuits that carry out our dreams of rescue and connection, or that fail to: in "The Farmer's Children," a story written in 1948 shortly before Bishop went to Brazil, the wires also appear, telephone wires humming with sub-animal noise eerily irrelevant to the doomed and helpless children of the story.

Wires with a similarly expanded symbolic mission appear in "Late Air," a poem first published in 1938, where five red lights atop the wires of the Navy Yard aerial distribute "witnesses/ for love on summer nights." And thirty years later, in "Going to the Bakery," not even counting all the wires that fall into poems before or after, Bishop finds uses for "slack trolley wires" for the moon to lean on, where "the wires, at the moon's/ magnetic instances, take off/ to snarl in distant nebulae." In each of these typical cases, wire is anthropomorphized and bears more than its simple chemical trigger, as the wired external landscape takes on the qualities of the body itself. The body is an alert system of circuitry, and in the enlarged World Body these wires are the nerve cells charged with the duty of communicating, of vocalization; they are the news-wire service. This plain and rather prosaic symbol stresses repeatedly for us the poet's view of the world as *natura naturans*, as matter energized, seen as an order of language, and as an immanent speech always accessible to the human forming within that order.

In "Questions of Travel" a similar mesh of meanings is casually present, and here the birdcage appears as part of its embodiment. In the poem, in understated or even blemished form, language, or sound itself, is fixed within a natural design: the clacking of a pair of badly matched wooden clogs makes "a sad, two-noted, wooden tune"; but this dispirited little melody should be pondered in connection with the music of "the fat brown bird / who sings above the broken gasoline pump/in a bamboo church of Jesuit baroque":

> —Yes, a pity not to have pondered,
> blurr'dly and inconclusively,
> on what connection can exist for centuries
> between the crudest wooden footwear
> and, careful and finicky,
> the whittled fantasies of wooden cages.
> —Never to have studied history in
> the weak calligraphy of songbirds' cages.
> —And never to have had to listen to rain
> so much like politicians' speeches:
> two hours of unrelenting oratory
> and then a sudden golden silence
> in which the traveller takes a notebook, writes:

Birdsong, the pour of rain, the weak calligraphy of the birdcage, and the disparate tapping of wooden shoes, and then the flood of golden silence in which the counter-response begins, are all a source of musical speech, a live circuit of telling apparently enclosing us, in which questions of travel implicitly become questions of decoding. Perhaps what is most interesting in this fusion of figures is the extent to which the mute restraint of matter, or its prisoning, limiting self, as cage or wire, or blunt wood, can be brought round into "tune," "fantasies," "history," "calligraphy," and so on. All of the metaphors push us to see essential energy, however intermittently curbed or damaged, as a flow of meaning, a writing. Without invoking tradition through allusion, Bishop's poetry of description swarms with the process of figuration, in which nature acts to become a convergence of truth-tellings, and traveling itself elides into both reading and writing. Here, perhaps, travel as theme, as motion in the world at large, foreshadows its replacement of Bishop's preoccupation with relation to inward, more schematic, and more fantastic worlds.

For early and late Bishop, matter is in motion, both expressive and changing; the boundaries between subject and object blur. A speaking subjectivity invades and animates the body of the world's objects, which somehow inflate, engulfing and transforming the tiny, volatile landscape of the page. Within a structure of consciousness so captivated by flux, it seems only appropriate that water should figure so prominently as metaphor for consciousness of all kinds, as consciousness moves from representation as fluency in language, or the streaming of speech, to representation as water itself.

Its sound circuits and wires notable and conspicuous, the water and storm imagery of "It is marvellous to wake up together" also draws our thinking to parallel tracks in other poems. Three bursting rainstorms and two rainy day landscapes saturate the area of Bishop's published work. Water of all kinds is never foreign to her. Out of the 110 poems published in *The Complete Poems: 1927–1979*, 44, or somewhat less than half, hold water in their mise-en-scène or flush it into their principal activity, while 33 additional poems include a mention of water, often substantial, which makes nearly three-quarters of the poems, minus anything flowing in translation, fairly wet. But all five of the rain poems, plus other specimens of wave and flood in the juvenile work like the love poem "Imber Nocturnus" (Night Storm), demonstrate a satisfying stylistic and thematic confluence with the orphaned and unpublished poem.

In the first of Bishop's adult storm poems, the "Little Exercise" published in a 1946 *New Yorker* originally as "Little Exercise at 4 A.M.," an invisible narrator hovers over the poem, speaking it; the only body located is "someone sleeping in the bottom of a row-boat," an indeterminate "him" seen as "uninjured, barely disturbed." The land-scape seems to be Key West, where Bishop had just begun a nine-year period of off-and-on residence.

But there is some larger, dramatic freight involved in the question of what is illuminated by lightning, and what obscured: the storm reveals and conceals. The whole poem, one of Bishop's most charming and original, is quite impersonal, yet there is something arresting in that oblivious figure a little incongruously asleep in his rowboat, float-ing, and tied up safely like an unborn in the maternal belly waters of the Gulf. The image of the fetal sleeper closes the poem:

> Think of someone sleeping in the bottom of a row-boat
> tied to a mangrove root or the pile of a bridge;
> think of him as uninjured, barely disturbed.

In "Little Exercise," an immanence, a pre-birth tension, safety on the lip of danger; in the unpublished "It is marvellous to wake up to-gether," a dynamic eroticism welcomed within both change and dan-ger. Both stances are open to the future; and, if we take water, con-sciousness, and speech as elements linked symbolically, both of these poems of the nineteen-forties favor the release of speech.

·III·

"Rain Towards Morning," the second in a sequence called "Four Poems" and published in 1951 in *The Partisan Review* is the closest in structure to "It is marvellous to wake up together," and for that reason worth repeating whole:

> The great light cage has broken up in the air,
> freeing, I think, about a million birds
> whose wild ascending shadows will not be back,
> and all the wires come falling down.
> No cage, no frightening birds; the rain
> is brightening now. The face is pale
> that tried the puzzle of their prison
> and solved it with an unexpected kiss,
> whose freckled unsuspected hands alit.

The binary pairs of light/dark and reveal/ conceal join with the bird-cage image of the storm, the ubiquitous birdcage, I should point out, that we found such a suggestive prop in "Questions of Travel," and of course the same feature that more centrally distinguishes the poem I read in Brazil. In "Rain Towards Morning" there are the same dangling wires; a nearly identical, though internal dactylic triple rhyme, here frightening/brightening, rather than lightning/frightening, and the same motif of imprisonment, the same galvanizing kiss, here singular. And yet the major difference between these two rainstorm poems is that "Rain Towards Morning" sketches or barely establishes a context for a moment of love, while "It is marvellous" firmly places that moment within a narrative framework with cumulative dramatic power. It is as if all the properties, thematic and stylistic, are assembling slowly over the years for final use in the manufacture of a single poem dealing for once fairly openly with that climactic event.

If we look at "Rain Towards Morning" carefully, its pale face should probably be claimed for allegory: for the fabulous "face" of heaven, and of the great light cage in which we all pass our days. The face brightens, and somehow those mysterious hands are hardly human, the kiss a grand affair that has more to do with meteorology and clearing skies than with a terrestrial erotic invitation, which would be stimulus of another kind. And yet even in this rainstorm Bishop doesn't entirely rule out erotic stimulus: those freckled hands are obdurately, humanly present, hard to fit into tenor and vehicle; that terminal "alit" sets off another train of response, quite separate from the giant ghostly figures, neither human nor animal that occupy the poem's literal and figurative upper space. In that strange windy arena swept free of any attachment to earth, they are released from prison by an unexpected kiss, a charged brightness. Yet the strategic unfolding of this almost metaphysical conceit suggests that something simpler than heaven and earth is at poem's end being released from its problematic prison.

The moment, that kiss of change and transformation, of release from prison, is featured in both of these rainstorm poems, both of which look written at the same time, because of their extremely close similarities. Dating for both poems is speculative. "Rain Towards Morning" appeared in January 1951, not quite a year before Bishop embarked on the *S.S. Bowplate* for Rio, although its date of publication does not necessarily reflect its date of composition. The untitled sister poem, "It is marvellous to wake up together," comes up in a notebook as a handwritten draft both preceded and followed by other Florida poems, as well as by notes and scraps that echo the images and descriptive language of "The Bight," published in 1948. The notebook, apparently mostly chronological in sequence, seems started in New York and Key West; the last page holds a checked and partly canceled list of items looking like reminders of things to do at banks, consulates, and railway offices before leaving for the 1943 trip to Mexico, and there is a crossed-off reminder to give a "ration book" to a Mrs. R. Then, tucked into the back flap there is a receipt from a post office in Rio dated 2–10–1952, nothing else Brazilian. Of the three notebooks in Linda Nemer's shoebox, only the beige one (not the black notebook containing the handwritten version of "It is marvellous") confines itself to Brazilian notes and events. The "four blue china balls" festooning a ribcage of lightning rods in "It is marvellous" very likely mean a particular house, perhaps the first of Bishop's own houses, the one she bought with Louise Crane in Key West in 1938. But until some memoirist retrieves these in mind or substance from an explicit facade, the ways of attaching the poem more securely to either time or place seem faded.

If we read for autobiography, both poems give us little satisfaction. The interest that they bear goes beyond identifying specific partners in actual moments; in fact, if we think to take on moments rather than partners, another question immediately arises: why did Bishop come back again and again to this moment in a storm, regardless of the people with whom she was experiencing it? It seems to be a figure that corresponds to something equally deep and far-embracing in the structure of her own life and consciousness.

There's something in the flash of its possibilities that she links to enlightenment. In "It is marvellous to wake up together," when the enlightenment theme openly joins a theme of fulfillment or release and resolution through erotic love, then body and world fuse in metaphor: on the magical map of that enlarged body, a figure of extraordinary and exhilarating power, light crackles through the synapses, through both the map of heaven and the map of human skin, and love and knowledge join. Love, passing beyond fear, beyond either the prudent or regressive self that "warns," becomes knowledge, and knowledge power, perhaps most of all, a power for change and transformation. In the best, understated Bishop fashion, the dimensions of the poem enclose something of considerable magnitude, and something clearly charged with relevance beyond the immediately personal and autobiographical.

If we formulate as a serious proposition that all our lives are figures, or symbols, or speech parts for some primary syntax of being, then surely in an openly autobiographical poem a lesson in forms is being served up as well as a lesson in history. And it should be ultimately comforting to think that our dreams and images are connected by navel strings to the literal flesh of our lives. Actually, what the letter should best enable us to do is to rethink the literal: what is most real is not merely what has happened, but what can be dreamed or imagined real; for in so much, without the capacity to choose and invent things into being, much would not come about at all. Or as Blake put it in a "Proverb of Hell" undoubtedly known to that Blake reader, Elizabeth Bishop, "Everything that is possible to be believed is an image of the truth." What we dream, what we imagine, is consistently seeded in both our hypothetical and actual lives; on a dark road holding a ladder for an intrepid friend, or in a moment of reverie over a desk, pushing a pen, we are read and we are reading. Found or invented, remembered or made cognizant, the physical universe in which mind works governs every apparently casual elaboration of our instinctive and habitual use of metaphor. And indeed, little could be more inviting to trace than the little wire mesh, the nerve circuit of our imagining, as it moves into articulation for ourselves or for the writers whose intelligence we hope to follow.

If we look at all of these poems as clusters of an approach to a general state of feeling that Bishop tackled again and again, each poem offers a unique piece of a meta-poem that is very much worth trying to read at each stage of its complex progress. "It is marvellous to wake up together" presents a theme repeated in no other portions of the oeuvre. Other rainstorms, as we have seen, play on security and insecurity, on revelation and concealment; others of the rare love poems like the villanelle "One Art" deal with lost love and grief; yet, unlike the rest, the newly discovered poem puts flash, cage, and erotic fulfillment all on the same axis of personal event.

Bishop did not publish or title "It is marvellous to wake up together" because it seems clear that the meaning of the poem lay too close to the bone for public exposure. This poem has a cargo of openly sexual feelings that the other storm poems, here including 1960's "Electrical Storm," written at Samambaia, do not. With the consistent reticence of a lifetime behind her, Bishop seems to have felt that publishing news about the subjects and objects of her sexual pleasure during her lifetime was neither possible nor desirable. While the figure of the narrator in Bishop's poetry is so often and so readily identifiable as herself, Bishop must have decided nonetheless that some doings were going to be protected from any careless, or potentially hurtful, public viewing.

And yet the poem was made and not destroyed, even as the circumstances of its keeping reflect ambivalence about disclosure. Yet Bishop did not get rid of the poem; she typed it onto that sheet of onionskin as fair copy, and then willed the contents of the notebooks that held the onionskin to a specific keeper, telling her, this Brazilian, non-English-speaking friend, to sell the papers at some appropriate moment after Bishop's death — she must have known that she was placing the poem in some limbo where eventually it would find its way into print.

·IV·

In a few choice places in other water poems running both before and after "It is marvellous to wake up together," there are suggestions of a birth metaphor. It is an intriguing quirk that even 1948's "The Bight," which seems pure description of sea and shore (though nothing is ever quite what it "seems" in this symbol-prone poetry), carries the bracketed subtitle, "on my birthday." Earlier, in the uterine waters of that sleeper safe as a baby in "Little Exercise," we see how he chooses to ride out the storm: there will be no metaphysical, emergent awakening, but there is a suggestion of an embryonic moment nested and waiting. Whatever is going to be delivered or released is still only immanent. But there is no birth or awakening in the 1960 "Electrical Storm," dated at Samambaia. In fact, this poem's hailstorm stays fairly determinedly in the realm of the inanimate and noncommunicative; what the dead telephone has to deliver is not immanent, but stillborn. This time out it is a stripped if not faintly malevolent cosmos:

> Personal and spiteful as a neighbor's child,
> thunder began to bang and bump the roof.
> One pink flash;
> then hail, the biggest size of artificial pearls.
> Dead-white, wax-white, cold—
> diplomats' wives' favors
> from an old moon party—
> they lay in melting windrows
> on the red ground until well after sunrise.

We got up to find the wiring fused,
no lights, a smell of saltpetre,
and the telephone dead.

The cat stayed in the warm sheets.
The Lent trees had shed all their petals:
wet, stuck, purple, among the dead-eye pearls.

The twinings of the warm bodies that heated those sheets are going to stay safely out of sight forever. "Song for the Rainy Season," the other Samambaia piece, also published in 1960, begins "Hidden, oh hidden/ in the high fog/the house we live in," and where the inmates live it is this way:

In a dim age
of water
the brook sings loud
from a rib cage
of giant fern; vapor
climbs up the thick growth
effortlessly, turns back,
holding them both,
house and rock,
in a private cloud.

The "private cloud" or the ribbed cage of this poem encloses, it does not release. The tense future, the mood valedictory, the speaker looks prophetically ahead to a dry "later era," when

Without water
the great rock will stare
unmagnetized, bare
no longer wearing
rainbows or rain,
the forgiving air
and the high fog gone;
the owls will move on
and the several
waterfalls shrivel
in the steady sun.

In "Squatter's Children," published a few years before "Electrical Storm," in 1956, this poem has the same signature elements as Bishop's other rainy weather pieces. A personified landscape, its hillsides are "unbreathing," but "The sun's suspended eye/ blinks casually" — and the children wade "gigantic waves of light and shade." They are very tiny in this huge littoral superimposed by metaphor on a mountain world; rain and lightning, however, command a speech, a language which these children may learn, even if what is there initially is weak and intermitted by a mother's voice "ugly as sin." Still, in the end what they are called to has enabling and therefore consoling power:

> Their laughter spreads
> effulgence in the thunderheads,
>
> weak flashes of inquiry
> direct as is the puppy's bark.
> But to their little, soluble,
> unwarrantable ark,
> apparently the rain's reply
> consists of echolalia,
> and Mother's voice, ugly as sin,
> keeps calling to them to come in.
>
> Children, the threshold of the storm
> has slid beneath your muddy shoes;
> wet and beguiled, you stand among
> the mansions you may choose
> out of a bigger house than yours,
> whose lawfulness endures.
> Its soggy documents retain
> your rights in rooms of falling rain.

Like the sleeper in the bottom of the boat, and like the birthday celebrant sustained by the bight's awful but cheerful ongoing activity, the surface of water provides a protected estate, a womb-room from which "rights" issue. Like the "old correspondences" with which the bight is littered, the soggy documents of this fecund rain constitute the children's empowering, their entitlement. Even though their laughter fusing with the thunderheads may be only "weak flashes," and unstable and unwarrantable at that, these children willfully orphaned from the immediate familial world of the mother's ugly voice, are reparented in the bigger house of nature — much as the orphaned Bishop herself must have wished re-parenting. Here a reader finds the poet intermittently wishing the transmission of personal message that so many of her surface words seem designed to repress.

Placed in the liberating company of these Brazilian children, Bishop permits herself to find a voice free of sin in original nature. For her as for the beguiled children the rain is obligingly echolalic: among these chosen mansions nature will take dictation from the human, and in this poem, and in the later poems of *Geography III* and after, nature ramifies to allow self-mothering and original speech. In "Squatter's Children," in a quite conventional symbolic configuration, water mothers; in the mid-fifties in Brazil, Bishop constructs an amniotic rainstorm that becomes the birthplace of identity. At this point in Bishop's work life, perhaps a dozen years after the writing of "It is marvellous to wake up together," the storm theme detaches itself from the theme of erotic climax to move more firmly alongside the birth or knowledge of identity motif, which replaces it.

Almost a decade earlier, in a collection of poems published before her move to Brazil, Bishop described the mother sea in sterner language. These lines are from "At the Fishhouses":

> I have seen it over and over, the same sea, the same,
> slightly, indifferently swinging above the stones,
> icily free above the stones,
> above the stones and then the world.
> If you should dip your hand in,
> your wrist would ache immediately
> your bones would begin to ache and your hand would burn
> as if the water were a transmutation of fire
> that feeds on stone and burns with a dark gray flame.
> If you tasted it, it would first taste bitter,
> then briny, then surely burn your tongue.
> It is like what we imagine knowledge to be:
> dark, salt, clear, moving, utterly free,
> drawn from the cold hard mouth
> of the world, derived from the rocky breasts
> forever, flowing and drawn, and since
> our knowledge is historical, flowing, and flown.

Down by the fishhouses of Bishop's childhood shore, water, burning like the clouds storing their charges of electricity, does not always help us unequivocally, drawn as it is from "the cold hard mouth/ of

the world," and derived forever from those "rocky breasts." Besides
flux and transformation, a disconcerting indifference also governs the
free character of this northern water. In "The Unbeliever," the Bun-
yanesque sleeper at the top of the mast murmurs in his dream, "The
spangled sea below wants me to fall./ It is as hard as diamonds; it
wants to destroy us all." In these early poems, for each appearance of
the fructifying and enlightening rain and thunder there is a freezing, a
congealing of water into its mortuary opposite, a sea like moving
marble. And if the skies rain down occasional opportune messages,
often as not the passage through the heavens is so difficult that even
the fantastic and brave Man-Moth cannot on a clear night put his
head through the white hole of enlightenment that the moon appears
to be hanging there.

What nature's envelope provides of air, water, fire and ice is full of
constraints, and what it offers to the human, difficult of access. If we
ask further about all this weltering of water we might conclude that
the salty substance Bishop gives us time and again has a more enduring
relation to the welling of tears than to the amniotic, enabling wave.
Certainly this kind of salt water flows freely in many of Bishop's
metaphors—the pond of tears in "Chemin de fer," the crying of the
sea that streaks the boardinghouse of "A Summer's Dream," the
tearstains of the waterfall in "Questions of Travel," the teakettle's
tears that dance on the Little Marvel Stove in "Sestina," even the
bitumen tears that the tycoon weeps in 1972's "Night City"—all of
these tears have their source in a pervasive sadness, struggling to put
its sorrow into acceptable speech.

·V·

Before drowning in the melancholy flood of associations, however,
we might leap to safety within another characteristic figure adum-
brated in "It is marvellous," and return our attention to Bishop's only
apparently unpromising and persistent other prop, the cage.

The cage needs to be thought about in relation to the prison figure,
before we can put an end to an enumeration of what the newly
discovered poem joins in relation to the rest of the poetry, and adds
for us of fresh insight.

Although George Herbert, whom Bishop deeply admired and deeply
studied, wrote an allegorical poem that he called "The Storme,"
Donne's "The Extasie" remains closer to what we might call on for

help in reading "It is marvellous to wake up together" and the brief moment in Bishop's thinking that it represents. While no rain falls on Donne's lovers, his poem does give us an important antecedent for the cage. In Donne's complex argument, he charts the relation between flesh and spirit, body and soul, and finally between eros and agape, asserting the body's proper place and role in the drama of love. His poem counsels:

> As our blood labours to beget
> Spirits, as like soules as it can,
> Because such fingers need to knit
> That subtile knot which makes us man:
> So must pure lovers' soules descend
> T' affections, and to faculties,
> Which sense may reach and apprehend,
> Else a great Prince in prison lies.[7]

In "It is marvellous," the cage of nature is quite delightful. For the poem's willed, imagined enclosure, from a simplified perspective of night and in the extreme vulnerability of "lying flat on one's back," her lovers, in an easy acceptance "without surprise" allow themselves the invasion of the sexual charge. Bishop's "black mesh of wires in the sky" functions something like Donne's "subtile knot": under the stimulus of that clarifying, and "prickling air," the aroused lovers turn to each other in a parallel rain of kisses, tying the change in themselves to the changing air and fire released above them. In the instinctive discretion that Bishop's poetry always practices, the ecstatic moment is off page, in the white full silence that the page's indirection shapes for the mind of the body when it is "without . . . thinking." The poem is poised just at that moment when speech or thinking transform to other articulating forces.

Unlike Donne's lovers, however, Bishop's lovers are not released from prison; that great Prince, spirit or soul, is still encaged in the body. For her, the cage seems stubbornly rooted inside the flesh, as the very ribs. Perhaps an explanation of this point of view originates from within Bishop's thinking about her homosexuality, about the constraints of her separateness, and the conflicts of her identity as both woman and poet. Two features of her writing lead me to this conclusion.

One, the assignment of male protagonists to dominant roles within the poems, particularly when troubling emotions are at issue, or gender is specified at all. It is the "Gentleman" of Shalott who puts in an appearance; the Man-Moth who weeps cool tears; a male Unbeliever who sleeps at the top of the mast; an artist-prince and not an artist-princess sheltered within the Monument and in "Cirque d'Hiver," it is the little circus horse who is favored, and not the shallow dancer: "He is the more intelligent by far." Even through later work, when gender is invoked, the characters and proto-selves, mammalian and non-mammalian, are more frequently male than female: the Riverman, Trollope, Crusoe, the Giant Toad, and the sandpiper, for instance. With the notable exception of the moose in the poem of that name, when the female is delineated it comes out subordinate and pitiable: Faustina, Cootchie, the seamstress in "House Guest," the pink dog, and so on. It isn't until we get to a late poem, "In the Waiting Room," that there is a palpably feminine speaker identified with Elizabeth Bishop herself, and even on that occasion femininity is seen as problematic. In "Gwendolyn," a story written in Brazil, the cloven truths of Bishop's attitude to the feminine surface in a description of her childhood friend, who "stood for everything that the slightly repellent but fascinating words 'little girl' should mean."

Most of the first-person bodies of her poems are nongender-specific, it is true; but the male investitures are not simply a denial of the female, they are a re-cloaking of the imagining self in another body, a male one. A perfectly rational defense could be constructed for this literary ruse, which in Bishop's generation was no doubt frequently, if silently, maybe even on occasion unconsciously, called upon: to be seen as a woman by oneself or others was to be barred from being seen as a poet. Being seen as a woman was to be feared because it inevitably distorted the reception of one's writing. At least some of the negative effects of this internal and external seeing could be warded off by cross-dressing, and by male disguise.

A second suggestive feature of Bishop's writing, both in prose and in poetry, though, is her representation of the delights of prison, in which we might be able to see a backhanded acceptance of the condition of flesh, a subterranean acceptance of gender, as well as a rather self-mocking, morose acceptance of the delights of guilt. Prison is made to look good several times. Once by implication in an early fable, "The Sea & Its Shore," in which the drunken Edwin Boomer, in a kind of lugubrious satisfaction, spends monotonous and constricted days in a cramped shack on the beach. (His name, others have pointed out, is a variant spelling of the common pronunciation of Bulmer, Bishop's mother's maiden name.) Then again, prison is a self-elected pleasure in another early prose piece, "In Prison," which she described to Marianne Moore as "another one of these horrible 'fable' ideas that seem to obsess me."

The protagonist of "In Prison," later clearly identified as male, begins breathlessly: "I can hardly wait for the day of my imprisonment." To amplify his reasons for his perverse choice, he continues:

> As Nathaniel Hawthorne says in *The Intelligence-Office*, 'I want my place, my own place, my true place in the world, my proper sphere, my thing which Nature intended me to perform . . . and which I have vainly sought all my life-time.' [. . .] The reader or my friends, particularly those who happen to be familiar with my way of life, may protest that for me any actual imprisonment is unnecessary, since I already live, in relationship to society, very much as if I were in prison.

Then in the text there is a dreamy little feint, a divagation on the aspiring prisoner's room:

> the room I now occupy is papered with a not unattractive wallpaper, the pattern of which consists of silver stripes about an inch and a half wide running up and down, the same distance from each other. They are placed over, that is, they appear to be inside of, a free design of flowering vines which runs all over the wall against a faded brown background. Now at night, when the lamp is turned on, these silver stripes catch the light and glisten and seem to stand out a little, or rather, in a little, from the vines and flowers, apparently shutting them off from me. I could almost imagine myself, if it would do any good, in a large silver bird cage! But that's a parody, a fantasy on my real hopes and ambitions.

Layer on layer of irony covers, or should one say stripes, the birdcage, and for a moment appears to defy any too-tightly constructed argument: there is something so regular and unconscious about the intrusion of this image into a Bishop text, that the reader should be wary of exhausting the symbol through oversimplification. The image seems so tightly knotted into Bishop's way of looking into the world that we cannot possibly name all the strands of connection. Here the loaded and self-consciously acknowledged parody ambition

of the caged singer ("only a bird in a gilded cage") is introduced, yet
the deep sense of the self as constricted, and not unpleasurably so,
remains. One also cannot help noticing the confusion of foreground
and background in the description of the stripes and vines, the fading
and blending of what is immanent and what is isolated, or the uncertainties raised over the integral connection between self and world.

The next sentences are equally, dreamily extravagant:

> One of the most effective scenes that I have ever seen, for color
> contrast, was a group of these libertine convicts, in their black and
> white stripes, spraying, or otherwise tending to, a large clump of
> tropical shrubbery.[. . .] One bush, I remember, had long knife-like
> leaves, twisting as they grew into loose spirals, the upper surface of
> the leaf magenta, the under an ocher yellow. Another had large, flat,
> glossy leaves, dark green, on which were scrawled magnificent ara-
> besques in lines of chalk-yellow. These designs, contrasting with the
> bold stripes of the prison uniform, made an extraordinary, if some-
> what florid picture.

These leaf designs seem a kind of proto-writing; both the surface of
the prisoners and the surface of the landscape itself are opening into
exuberant text, though a text which the disciplined speaker patronizes
as "florid"; too flowery, too little near the austere realities of the
human in its state as separate from nature. In these examples, and the
following picture of a prisoner, one is not allowed to forget that the
caging is self-chosen, even if doubt is elsewhere cast on the role of
choice in human affairs.

Other prisoner comforts surface much later in "The End of March,"
where after a tramp on the beach the speaker wants to be closed into
"my proto-dream-house," a house she peers at from the outside, and
which suspiciously resembles the cages of her early fabulists:

> I'd like to retire there and do *nothing*,
> or nothing much, forever, in two bare rooms:
> look through binoculars, read boring books,
> old, long, long books, and write down useless notes,
> talk to myself, and, foggy days,
> watch the droplets slipping, heavy with light.

It is much later in Bishop's life, now, however, and unlike the other
prisons she has invoked, this one is boarded up, it locks *her* out: as

maybe she thinks it really should, being only a "proto-dream-house," a "crypto-dream-house," and a "dubious" choice, at that. In the moment of her time that the unpublished poem presents for us, this insight into attractively repellent choices lies in the future. While the lightning is flashing around the lovers securely caged in the house in Key West, acceptance of an outstretched and changing self comes easily, if momentarily, and body, will, mind, and spirit are one in a landscape whose features openly and joyfully echo the interior landscape of love.

If this poem remains a painfully solitary example of this kind of happiness, nonetheless, perhaps what can be said of its brief flare of candor is that that candor may have established a modality in which deeply personal themes could be treated. There are traces of such attempts in the unfinished work, which I'll discuss in a later chapter: a draft of an incompleted poem called "Vaguely Love Poem" gives an intimate, celebratory description of a female lover; another unpublished draft, which ends "hold on, as I love you" is entitled "Goodbye." What Bishop picked up in full from an earlier rainstorm seem to be the rights of the "Squatter's Children": but in the later, public rooms of falling rain their soggy documents dry magnificently into the less cryptically personal and meditative poems of *Geography III* and into the prose of "In the Village," where if not love then childhood can be traced through the early life and landscape of the poet herself.

For this poet, it appears that in the forties the door of the cage closed on the amatory adventures of its occupant, signaled to the tourist, and opened years later on the autobiographical adventures of the child. In her poems, same-sex love and friendship will be curtly named in "Crusoe in England"; the loss of love will make its terse appearance in "One Art"; but published, and spoken in her own person, the poems of Elizabeth Bishop make no further appointments with Eros, or erotic love.

In the brief, lightning-shot moment of "It is marvellous to wake up together," erotic love becomes a path in the mystical tradition, where through the union of self and Other we learn of the parallel junctions between flesh and spirit, heaven and earth, human and divine. "Rain Towards Morning" plays with key elements of this thinking, but only in the most abstract terms; in print, on this subject, Bishop let go the heavy weight of the personal. But perhaps no thinking quite so exhilarating could have lasted long for any of us.

·VI·

Finally, what the rainstorm, or the cage, or the sea has to teach changes to an earlier assignment: to touch in words the birth of another recognition, when we struggle at the edge of self, separating from the troubling other to become a part of the world. The preoccupying wires of the erotized storm of the adult Bishop lead to the cage theme, and then inevitably to the childhood theme. In circling back to the four "Songs for a Colored Singer," published in 1944, I found these lines from the third song stopping me:

> Lullaby.
> Let nations rage,
> let nations fall.
> The shadow of the crib makes an enormous cage
> upon the wall.

The image of the barred crib as cage might not be so striking, if it didn't line up with all those other cages, as well as a draft of a poem called "A Drunkard," circa 1971, which pulls together for us both shadows, fire, and a traumatic moment experienced by a child in a crib:

> When I was three, I watched the Salem fire.
> It burned all night (or then I thought it did)
> And I stood in my crib & watched it burn.
> The sky was bright red; everything was red.
> And my hands holding to its rods
> the [its] brass knobs held [holding] specks of fire

The child is hanging on to the "rods" of its crib, around her the four brass knobs holding fire. Both rods and knobs recall the lightning rods caging the house with the four blue china knobs in the opening language of "It is marvellous to wake up together." (These stubborn knobs in turn call up the white china knob incongruously topping the schoolyard flagpole in "Cape Breton," in the drafts for the poem: a late, unaccountable addition leading us on in the interminably receding vista of similar, autobiographically charged objects rhyming in their intensity.) But in this earlier bedtime scene from "A Drunkard," the memory is not one of casual observation, or of a delight anticipating fulfillment, but one of outright abandonment: "Mama didn't hear/

me calling her." The child stands in her crib and calls and calls, feeling a terrible thirst, which no one comes to satisfy. And since that day, concludes the narrator, she has suffered from "abnormal thirst."

Whether or not or how seriously this account is intended to describe the psychogenesis of Bishop's own problems with alcohol we do not know, but it seems clear that the poem chronicles a moment of betrayal and abandonment burning itself into consciousness with the aid of that fire. If we look at the text of "In the Village," Bishop's prose memoir of her childhood actually written during her years in Brazil, we find a similar moment:

> But one night, in the middle of the night, there is a fire. The church bell wakes me up. It is in the room with me; red flames are burning the wallpaper beside the bed. I suppose I shriek.

This moment is not placed in the child's crib, and grandmother and aunts do rush to comfort her, but the net effect of the evening's events results in the same "abandonment": the fire triggers a reaction in the mentally unstable mother, and after this evening she is returned to the sanatorium, from which she does not emerge again. The front bedroom with its wallpaper of "wide white and dim-gold stripes," where the mother has been staying, is empty.

Many of the elements that we have been tracing, in figure, in language, and in situation, throughout the particular group of poems that can be associated with the unpublished love poem, are present in these extracts. Here they are again: stripe, cage, storm, and a crisis of love. To cling too narrowly to the repetitions and recurrences would rob both poems and prose pieces of their literary qualities, of their larger reference. And yet it would seem a mistake of another kind to ignore these moments and their anchorage in a developing history. After all, the wisdom that they suggest in fairly specific form follows the general outlines of psychological truism: any moment of adult bonding in love returns consciously and unconsciously to the critical moments in our lives as children when our ability to love and trust was first tested.

A firmly contextualized reading of "It is marvellous to wake up together" shows how the props of our lives and memories never really leave us, and demonstrates their conversion through the kindlier offices of the imagination into empowerment. In skirting the sexual in her poetry, Elizabeth Bishop, like Dickinson, Moore, or Stevens, chose not to struggle with the vision of erotic fulfillment leading to that ecstatic transformation of the flesh by the flesh, wherein the mutable is said to be conquered. It was not part of her job description. In this poet elsewhere so much noted for the brilliance and gaiety of her wit, that portion of her adulthood dealing with experiences of love and erotic intimacy, when translated into subject for poetry, seems to have halted, or been blocked, in the rooted sadness of her childhood. Still, a single finished poem, read in the company of many others, testifies at least once to a dreamy openness of mood and image reversing her customary estate.

In her last decade Bishop retrieved her first years for direct treatment in poetry; if life were only more congruent with the patterns our minds show themselves capable of revealing and creating, we no doubt would have had other and equally rich poems from her, from more of the later times and places.

And probably it seems cavalier to ask for them. Yet in that odd way in which an artist's life becomes representative life, a deeper probe into both her life and poetry becomes a deeper probe into ours; the hunger for poems that can be shown to be based on actual experience is after all not a trivial one. Perhaps we wish to be robbed of the belief that invention alone has significance, even, to be relieved from the weight of our fictions.

The Body's Roses

Elizabeth Bishop's reticence about the erotic and romantic did not leave her with a wholly impersonal poetry; but while the speaker of a poem can frequently be matched to the poet herself, self remains a creature only partially and tantalizingly glimpsed in the staging area of the poems. For Mary McCarthy:

> I envy the mind hiding in her words, like an "I" counting up to a hundred waiting to be found.[. . .] I would like to have had her quiddity, her way of seeing that was like a big pocket magnifying glass. *Of course* it would have hurt to have to use it for ordinary looking: that would have been the forfeit.[8]

It is that hiding, in tandem with the sense of pocket magnification, or scale distortion, that stays so provocative, even if we need to take note that McCarthy speaks of the *mind* carrying the magnifying glass, and not the *self* hiding in the words. But the hiding, or the obliqueness of representation in Bishop's transparently deceptive style, makes it often difficult to see how in this most private, apparently least confessional of contemporary poets, her passion for accuracy and exactitude extends to a passion for autobiographical record. Names, places, and dates in Bishop's poetry match up with the known facts of Bishop's life. Outside the ballad stanzas of "Arrival at Santos" there *is* a Miss Breen:

> about seventy,
> a retired ex-police lieutenant, six feet tall,

with beautiful bright blue eyes and a kind expression.
Her home, when she is at home, is in Glens Fall/

s, New York.

This lady was still living in Glens Falls until a few years ago, and eager
to chat with people about her trip to Brazil on the same freighter with
Elizabeth Bishop.

Apart from the obvious use Bishop makes of her residence in Nova
Scotia, Brazil, and elsewhere, she adds to this sense of scrupulous
record with her confirmation of other data. Yes, she *did* have a relative,
George Hutchinson, not exactly an R.A., but someone who showed at
the Royal Academy in London, and who painted a "Large Bad Picture," the subject of discussion in the poem of that title. Yes, she *did*
watch a manhunt for a burglar go on under her windows in Rio, much
as she described it in "The Burglar of Babylon," and yes, the island
scenery of the dramatic monologue "Crusoe in England," at least
once puckishly anachronistic in detail, draws from her knowledge of
many islands visited in her own travels in the Galápagos, Florida, and
Aruba. And of course the "Elizabeth" who shares a February 1911
birthdate with the poet of "In the Waiting Room" and who also lived
in Worcester, Massachusetts, sounds like the poet herself, although
no, the poet's actual aunt was not named Consuelo nor did the 1918
February issue of *The National Geographic* contain what the poet said it
did.[9] Her only partly credulous readers rose to the bait on that hook,
but in the end forebore to swallow.

For Octavio Paz, the lesson of Bishop's poetry contained in her
"enormous power of reticence" comes to lie "not in what words say
but in what is said between them, that which appears fleetingly in
pauses and silences."[10] As Marianne Moore remarked of Bishop's first
book, it is "Spectacular in being unspectacular," and "accurate and
modest."[11] After noting in passing Bishop's early debt to Donne and
Hopkins, Moore reads this indebtedness as partially protective—as
something like the defensive feint of the hermit crab. Or, as Bishop's
mouthpiece from the comparatively late prose poem "Strayed Crab"
cues us, "I believe in the oblique, the indirect approach and I keep my
feelings to myself." Again, in another moral fable, from an equally
insulating layer of self-irony placed between speaker and poet, we hear
her say in the voice of the Giant Snail, "Draw back. Withdrawal is
always best."

Metaphors of shell, skin, screen, or mask seem entirely appropriate. Yet the tough, resilient finish of a Bishop poem, an almost tactile quality that seems to place stress on the status of the poem as an independent object detachable from its creator, also functions as a transparent medium of personality. In one of the paradoxes of her language, its Moebius-like exterior turns to reveal the interior, still keeping its character of protective coating. While her poetic strategy refuses the ego seductions of much overt personal reference in increasing favor of the concrete particulars of the world around the self, the leash of the autobiographical still circles everything both said and not said. In most of this work, a bodiless voice sounds through the poems with Bishop's own unmistakable tone, syntax, diction, and treatment of rhetorical figure. The voice crackles with intelligence, subtlety, and quirky humor as it moves adroitly in and out of its often disconcerting comparisons. In the following poem, typical of her early manner, a simple declarative syntax made up of clearly defined and qualified predicates comfortably unfolds its description of the "Large Bad Picture" painted by her uncle, the reputed Royal Academician:

> On the middle of that quiet floor
> sits a fleet of small black ships,
> square-rigged, sails furled, motionless,
> their spars like burnt match-sticks.
>
> And high above them, over the tall cliffs'
> semi-translucent ranks,
> are scribbled hundreds of fine black birds
> hanging in *n's* in banks.

The diction is balanced between casual and colloquial, poised at a level where it can rise to a more ornate wording like "semi-translucent," but still take on the plainness of sit, hang, and scribble as verbs. The point of view is nicely calibrated as Bishop moves us with typical suppleness in and out of her clashing perspectives. On the one hand, all is shrunken artifice, in the miniature painted world from which, like spectators enlarged to Alice's proportions at her most ungainly, we are first excluded. On the other hand, all is lifelike, and we move with tiny confidence and ease within the scripted world of the "Large Bad Picture," following its contours as Bishop gives them to us in the writing of which those "n's in banks" are the peculiarly fitting sign. Throughout the miniature seascape, the figures of comparison are strangely domestic and familiar, although we never lose our sense of viewing the painting as a painted object from which we are detached. Simultaneously we are within the painting and without it, living suspended on one of those trick two-way perspectives that ask us to be both hare and dog, flat and round, visual and verbal, here and there.

There is rarely insistence or obtrusiveness in the deft manners with which Bishop offers her teasing figures; the tone is always level and unstartled even as a metaphor itself may startle us, as in this example from "A Cold Spring":

> The next day
> was much warmer.
> Greenish-white dogwood infiltrated the wood,
> each petal burned, apparently, by a cigarette butt;

That cigarette burn on the greenish-white flesh of the dogwood has disquieting implications; introduced without warning there is something quite mysterious in the agency producing such a burn, and yet the explanation of the mark on the dogwood petal, for anyone who has ever marveled over them, strikes us as right; there is a fit in the outlandish choice that makes us forever adjust our perception of the dogwood petal. All over this poem there is her control by personification, and yet the figure of the poet making such striking description is nowhere in evidence but in that conversational, equable, agreeable voice. Back of her evolving deployments of memory, there is always the same observer and respecter of contexts who sees human and animal as equal occupants in a landscape, and who fuses inanimate objects and animate persons in consciousness within the concentrated field of the poem. These implicit, perhaps occasionally terrifying, assumptions finally expand the notion of the autobiographical self to an unsettling inclusiveness, as within the poetry all voices and objects represent aspects of the consciousness both feeding and hearing it. At its best, consciousness playing in this work feels like a sympathy without skin extending deeply and unnervingly everywhere.

In "Cirque d'Hiver," a poem in the early manner dealing more concentratedly with objects and with interiors of all kinds, it is difficult not to read one of the events in the poem as the only partly whimsical identification of the speaker with the horse's mute, animal intelligence. The speaker hovers over the small theater of the poem, invisible until the last line of the penultimate stanza. First there is detached description of the major characters:

Across the floor flits the mechanical toy,
fit for a king of several centuries back.
A little circus horse with real white hair.
His eyes are glossy black.
He bears a little dancer on his back.

She stands upon her toes and turns and turns.
A slanting spray of artificial roses
is stitched across her skirt and tinsel bodice.
Above her head she poses
another spray of artificial roses.

And yet those reiterated artificial roses stitched across a surface of tinsel do in the possibility of taking this evocation of the feminine artist seriously. No, it is the courtly horse holding up the silly dancer that catches the speaker's sympathies:

His mane and tail are straight from Chirico.
He has a formal, melancholy soul.
He feels her pink toes dangle toward his back
along the little pole
that pierces both her body and her soul

and goes through his, and reappears below,
under his belly, as a big tin key.
He canters three steps, then makes a bow,
canters again, bows on one knee,
canters, then clicks and stops, and looks at me.

But tied as he is to her—and our attention to the piercing tie is made to loop syntactically across their separate stanzas—it is not the self-absorbed dancer who can engage the poet in dialogue, but the key-keeping horse:

The dancer, by this time, has turned her back.
He is the more intelligent by far.
Facing each other rather desperately—
his eye is like a star—
we stare and say, "Well, we have come this far."

It may be that a Maker has linked him to the dancer's distressing female materiality, whose anatomy appears alarmingly close to shaping her destiny. Another function of that big tin key, hung below the circus horse's belly, its slightly ambiguous position displacing phallus with omphalos, may be to blur or decentralize questions of gender, as the starry vision of the little performing horse moves beyond the frame of the poem and looks squarely back at its author. The best they can do for each other is a rather desperate and monosyllabic exchange of teeth-gritting survivalism. In this early phase, Bishop may be playing out at the literal edges of perception both acceptance and rejection of the masculine as the appropriate costume of her poetic identity.

· I ·

Bishop's understated and oblique method of self-reference remained directly counter to everything that most of her other contemporaries were interested in doing. Yet Robert Lowell, Bishop's poet friend with considerably more confessional manners, is the colleague for whom she herself felt most affinity. She wrote to Anne Stevenson in March 1963: "Cal [Lowell] and I in very different ways are both descendants from the Transcendentalists." This seems surprising. Much that Bishop relies on for original energy in poetry does not appear to come from the traditional quest for the transfigured moment that so much of her understated poetry looks bent on deflating, her coolness and habitual self-possession a compress descending casually but unerringly over any inflammation of the word or deed. In her poetry, Blake is a skittering, confused sandpiper; Baudelaire spends his time on the frivolously exotic, turning the natural fumes of the harbor to marimba music; Trollope is a queasy traveler; Wordsworth is forgettable; her late metaphor for art is an outdated dollar bill, and so on. Art, in her late and last celebration of its goals, is only cramped, memorious, "The little that we have for free, the little of our earthly trust."

Yet in a 1951 letter to Lowell, she deprecatingly refers to herself as a "minor female Wordsworth." At this stage in her career we are far from the quietly soaring, serenely pastoral transformations of her late poems. Her estimate of her own work is always without vanity, and full of what must have been an occasionally painful self-insight. Writing to Anne Stevenson in 1964 she says:

Because of my era, sex, situation, education, I have written, so far, what I feel is a rather "precious" kind of poem, although I am very

opposed to the precious. One wishes things were different, that one
could begin all over again.

At our peril we ignore her cautionary estimate; we need to ask if
"rather precious" in her work becomes strategic understatement, ironic
reversal or, on occasion, failure of nerve, or a misplaced devotion to
modesty. Perhaps the prisoner Bishop, within the privacy of her cell,
too much and too frequently beat up on herself, confining her feelings
too harshly to darkened quarters.

In most of her poems Elizabeth Bishop the person occurs off-page
as a body clad in a voice that hovers over the small field of the poem,
or as a child. In all of her published work, the more volcanic emotions
required containment within the vessel of form; overtly autobiographical feeling is poured into sestinas or villanelles, cooled into rhyme,
wired into rhetorical figure or only allowed *sotto voce* transmission. Her
stoical pride, especially to the gossip-loving among us, or to those who
hunger to touch the naked flesh of the eminent, may be considered in
some cases extreme: about confessional poets she once said, "You just
wish they'd kept some of these things to themselves." To Wesley
Wehr, she is reputed to have said (we wonder how jokingly), "You can
never have enough defenses."

In an era when literary conventions favor revelation, and in a
society the private tenor of which the sociologists never tire of describing to us as isolated, fragmentary, and unstable, we require the extended personal credential, even in poems. Feeling, we have long been
taught by post-Romantic canon fire, is the lyric's subject, and in a
natural adaptation we run to the making self as the *fons et origo* of
feeling. To switch even from Bishop's later and more personal work
in *Geography III* to Lowell's *Day By Day*, or to Berryman's *Dream Songs*
—and these are two of her contemporaries that Bishop admired—we
get the full difference between her reticence, her subtle, ironical, and
implicative style, and Berryman's and Lowell's no less subtle or ironical but certainly louder and more calisthenic myths of self-making. At
times these poets might seem airless and narcissistic in reference; yet
there is a hold-your-breath power and dash in the headlong enterprise
of Berryman's and Lowell's walking naked that arrests our interest and
affection. Unlike Bishop, they found in their work rich uses for pity,
as well as irony. In "Dream Song 53" Berryman quotes Gottfried
Benn on the often desperate strategem of those who free-lance out

along the razor's edge: "We are using our own skins for wallpaper and we cannot win." Then there is the political dimension, especially to Lowell's work, which at least initially, until the later Brazilian poems, remains understated in Bishop, almost willfully, or is it embarrassedly, oblique. Her subject area, though not her style, technique, or perception, stays small. Beside the expansiveness of Lowell's themes, what Bishop herself fondly quoted as his "black-tongued piratical vigor," Bishop's range can look contracted.

Her poems, wary of post-romantic subjectivity, insist on the distance and relative impersonality of the tie between reader and writer, between poem and audience, and between poem and experience all the while that the poetry itself speaks in one of the most idiosyncratic of voices yet to be invented in American poetry.

It is not coincidental that Emily Dickinson's writing shares this property of originality, or that both of these poets were women. Bishop struggled with her assessment of Dickinson in both poetry and prose. A poem planning to yoke Dickinson and Hopkins, unabashedly an early favorite of hers, never got beyond notes, in which both Hopkins and Dickinson appear as internal exiles: "They chose, themselves, their cages." The poem was to turn, apparently, on the hidden strength of feathers: "Feathers are really horn, horny outgrowths"; seen as poets of paradoxical strength within fragility, Hopkins and Dickinson are "divided like (St. Elmo's?) fire" and "The same god in both sustained their songs with iron." In addition to sharing a voluntary obscurity, both poets agonize over their relation to divine love; yet Hopkins' management of his ardent feelings seems to trouble Bishop less than Dickinson's concentration on this love.

In an unpublished review of Emily Dickinson's letters in which Bishop notes with exasperation Dickinson's "constant insistence on the strength of her affections," Bishop's remarks reveal her own need for a compensatory modernity that will distance her from anything even remotely resembling the nineteenth century's stereotypical female sentimentality about love. She writes:

> In a sense, all of Emily Dickinson's letters are "love letters." To her, little besides love, human and divine, was worth writing about and often the two seem fused. That abundance of detail — descriptions of daily life, clothes, food, travels, etc. — that is found in what are usually considered "good letters" plays very little part in hers. Instead there is a constant insistence on the strength of her affec-

tions, an almost childish daringness and repetitiveness about them, that must sometimes have been very hard to take. Is it a tribute to her choice of friends, and to the friends themselves, that they *could* take it and frequently appreciate her as a poet as well? Or is it occasionally only a tribute to the bad taste and extreme sentimentality of the times?

In Bishop's own poems and letters, of course, we will find just those descriptions of daily life, etc. Her reading tastes, too, ran to such letters; in the 3,000 volumes of her library, biography, memoirs, travel and collections of letters are copiously represented, with very little room given to critical exegesis of poetry or literary theory. She continues to muse on the "embarrassing" nature of Dickinson's expression:

> At any rate, a letter containing such, to us at present, embarrassing remarks as "I'd love to be a bird or a bee, that whether hum or sing, still might be near you," is rescued in the nick of time by other sentences such as, "if it wasn't for broad daylight, and cooking stoves, and roosters, I'm afraid you would have occasion to smile at my letters often, but so sure as 'this mortal' essays immortality, a crow from a neighboring farmyard dissipates the illusion, and I am here again."

The admired sentence, predictably the one with roosters and cook-stoves, contains Bishop's own subjects for poetry. And Bishop's embarrassment modulates into qualified, then finally unqualified approval. First she notes that "if we are sometimes embarrassed by E.D.'s letters we are always spared the contemporary letter-writer's frequent cynicism and endless 'humor.' " If not the cynicism, that very "humor" often masks Bishop's own letters, a practice which here she is indirectly acknowledging. But she concludes with a positive comparison, likening Dickinson to George Herbert, and then says:

> it is nice for a change to know a poet who never felt the need for apologies [. . .] or even for long sentences. Yet these letters have structure and strength. It is the sketchiness of the water-spider tenaciously holding to its upstream position by means of the faintest ripples, while making one aware of the current of death and the depths and darknesses below.

In this closing, Bishop pays tribute to her predecessor in a figure of speech that returns Dickinson to the solid dignity of natural phenomena, a characteristic feint that Bishop seems to have reserved for her own deepest feelings. It seems a mild irony, though, that in these passages a guarded Bishop, by contrast, seems to make a poet of candor and frankness out of the recluse of Amherst. It is not by much that women have advanced their freedom in poetry.

Through the gradual invention of a personal style that kept her person peculiarly at bay within the poem, Elizabeth Bishop managed to elude the dominant focus of her era on a narrowing concern with the emotional business of the first person singular, and to develop a lyric poetry that remained faithful to the phenomenal world and to her broad interest in it. To be personal meant to be misread, to be trapped within the conventional feminine. Evading this experience, wherever possible, and with as much ingenuity as she could muster, Bishop stabilized her work in a nongender-specific environment, leaving for later readers the problem of uncovering the hidden allegory at a level of interpretation beyond her firm literality. The story of her development as a poet, however, is the story of how, like a weed in the cracks of a sidewalk, or like William Carlos Williams' "greeny asphodel," the personal intruded itself between the tight planes of her interests, gradually breaking the poems open to the more troubling issues of her life in ever more far-reaching symbolic equivalents. In reaction against Wordsworth's Egotistical Sublime for the whole of her career, Bishop nonetheless came eventually to terms with his inheritance. Neither of her chosen female progenitors, Dickinson or Moore, gave her the right purchase on these materials; yet by swerving toward Lowell and the confessional, Bishop finally managed to make sense of the impact of her sex and gender on her life and work, and in characteristic fashion, to make reticence itself bear on her formal and substantive solutions.

·II·

Some of Bishop's resistance to self-display must derive from her position as woman and lesbian, or according to some reports, as bisexual. Very gradually, in her last years, it became permissible to speak publicly of herself as a feminist; and in a late interview with George Starbuck[12] she displays this candid bleakness about the influence of gender on her life: "I wish I had written a great deal more. Sometimes I think if I had been born a man I probably would have written more. Dared more, or been able to spend more time at it. I've wasted a great deal of time." The whole thrust of her early public experience seems to have been to avoid being ghettoized as a woman; she resisted that tenaciously. I think we should not misunderstand or overlook the very quiet bitterness emanating from sentences like these, sifted as they are through Bishop's fairminded lucidity:

> Most of my life I've been lucky about reviews. But at the very end they often say "The best poetry by a woman in this decade, or year, or month." Well, what's that worth? You know? But you get used to it, even expect it, and are amused by it.

It's hard not to believe that her "amusement" wasn't a little qualified, especially when the gender confinement that she notes came from close and admired friends like Lowell. She appreciated his review of *North & South*; in fact, fresh on in their friendship, on August 14, 1947, she is "overwhelmed" by it:

> It is the first review I've had that attempted to find any general drift or consistency in the individual poems and I was beginning to feel there probably wasn't any at all. It is the only review that goes at things in what I think is the right way.

Yet in the review in question, Lowell, that inveterate and tireless ranker of poetic reputations in speaking about "Roosters" and "The Fish" places them as "the best poems that I know of written *by a woman* [italics mine] in this century." [13] And there he was, not even halfway through the century.

If only subliminally, this must have stung even as it complimented. Lowell's review appeared in 1947; it isn't until 1977 that Bishop is heard in a journal interview talking to George Starbuck, a younger poet, about how laurels for women poets are garnered, or rather sequestrated. If, then, Bishop felt that her status as poet would have been unfairly colored by her identity as a woman, what must she have felt about her sexual identity, clouded in contour for us even after her death, as more and more discussion enters public notice about her life. During her lifetime her homosexuality surfaced nowhere in print; yet her sexual preference seems an inseparable if mostly puzzling part of the other factors she herself named as determinant: her "era," her "sex," her "situation," and "education."

Bishop's public self kept a remote and self-possessed dignity; for Howard Moss, she was "an original"; with "the air of having been born civilized, and as at home at a Parisian dinner table as she was traveling into the Brazilian interior."[14] She never entirely excluded sexual phenomena, at least not in the animal kingdom: there is that lizard in "Brazil, January 1, 1502":

> The lizards scarcely breathe; all eyes
> are on the smaller, female one, back-to,
> her wicked tail straight up and over,
> red as a red-hot wire.

And yet it is interesting to see that folded into a back cover of one of the Brazil notebooks is a torn slip of paper with some faint pencilings, dealing more explicitly with that lizard in saurian heat. These observations, a little abortive proto-poem, step in and out of rhyme:

> The male lizard chases the female lizard around the tree
> Blows out his beautiful rose balloon . . . to see – a line of
> little ants intercepts, the female hides . . . all her tail, all
> her tiny horny sides.

Even a lizard's sexual life requires muffling in her published poetry; precise naturalist that she was, Bishop in print still upholds a certain propriety for her animals. The scrap of lizard courtship designed for print makes us pause, but the moment for sexual contact remains in the fold of a notebook.

There is a cheerful and casual allusion to a weekend tryst during college at a hotel on the Cape with someone she called "my then-boyfriend," an incident revealed as Elizabeth Bishop, Vassar '34, chats in an interview comfortably with Elizabeth Spires, Vassar '74.[15] Her sophistication is flawlessly discreet. In a memoir essay called "The Country Mouse," which was published posthumously, Bishop includes a description of her childhood attraction to "a beautiful boy named Royal Something." She says "once when he helped me buckle my arctics, as I looked at his long shiny hair, neat starched collar, and red necktie, I felt a wonderful, powerful thrill go through my stomach." The eroticism Bishop calls on is clearly heterosexual in reference. Even here in late work she is instinctively building a one-sided picture, omitting the homosexual erotic feelings that would expose her to the hazards of conventional misjudgment.

In her poems the only references to homosexuality, whether hers or anyone else's, are quite oblique or allegorical in nature. As Lee Edelman has persuasively traced these erotic feelings, the child protagonist of "In the Waiting Room" maintains a fascinated interest in female parts, as well as a terror of being imprisoned within the unempowered female body appearing within the poem: she is mesmerized by "those awful hanging breasts" as she stares at a native woman whose naked portrait appears in the copy of *The National Geographic* which the seven-year-old Elizabeth holds in her hands and is "too shy" to stop reading.

Yet the fascination with the female seems as closely linked to the theme of the abandoning mother, as it does to the seductive, eroticized female body, whether powerless or not. We could as easily associate the fear of breasts with a suppressed longing for them, and for the monstrous and disturbing power they still retain to evoke longing; negatively colored feeling could be said to stem from early deprivation. David Kalstone supports this reading in his comment on "At The Fishhouses," and the poem's final lines:

> It is like what we imagine knowledge to be:
> dark, salt, clear, moving, utterly free,
> drawn from the cold hard mouth
> of the world, derived from the rocky breasts
> forever, flowing and drawn, and since
> our knowledge is historical, flowing, and flown.

Here, according to Kalstone, is "the flicker of human drama, of a vestigial implacable female presence behind the scene." [16] This is not an unempowered presence. The lines also indicate once again how erotic subjects concerning the female never move very far in Bishop's work from issues of parental abandonment and the subsequent development of an uneasy and orphaned selfhood.

But until *Geography III* there is little material arising openly about either the making of female identity or of erotic attraction and repulsion. Given Bishop's habitual discretion about the topics of gendering and sexuality, her early prose piece, "The Thumb," published in *The Blue Pencil*, the Walnut Hill School's literary magazine, is certainly worth noticing. In this story, as in her other *Blue Pencil* pieces, the protagonist is male; at tea with Sabrina, a woman he has been taken to see, he muses on Sabrina's smallness, lightness, and the underwater glimmer of her dress, qualities that show the nineteen-year-old writer determinedly evoking the nymph Sabrina. Bishop's narrator is intrigued by her, and says: "though fortunately unliterary herself she really had quite a little influence — friends among all sorts of artists and writers." Speaking in character, Bishop's stolid male protagonist expresses disdain for bluestockings.

Yet this experimentation with role-playing in a bohemian world culminates in a discovery. The narrator has been admiring Sabrina's left hand, "small and fine," and now turns to her right hand:

> Why did I keep on looking? There was something queer about that hand—I couldn't tell right away what it was. There was no mark, no deformity. Good God!—the woman had a man's thumb! No, not a man's,—a brute's—a heavy, coarse thumb with a rough nail, square at the end, crooked and broken. The knuckle was large. It was a horrible thumb, a prize fighter's thumb, the thumb of some beast, some obscene creature knowing only filth and brutality . . .
>
> [. . .] I was horrified. In the midst of that charming, sunny room, that friendly atmosphere, I was frightened. Something mysterious and loathsome had crept out of the night and seized me as I sat there drinking tea.

After further sprinkling the thumb with "a growth of coarse, black hairs," the adolescent Bishop enlarges our understanding of her symbol by poking us with Baudelaire: "What was that phrase? 'Flowers of Evil'—Yes."

Yet there is more than a programmatic and naive flirtation with the postures of Romantic satanism in this exercise. The revulsion that the protagonist feels is directed at more than the thundering menace of a decadent art world; identity is still a fresh, more slippery matter than it will be later, and so the piece opens readily inward to a window of commentary on the writer's own feelings about selfhood.

The protagonist determines to continue seeing Sabrina. "But it wouldn't work. Every time I saw her I felt more and more a peculiar shivering fascination that made me look down at her hand, to those lovely fragile fingers and that horrible misshapen thing that was one of them. Yet I couldn't blame her. She was the most natural thing in the world—the trouble must be with myself." Within the self-conscious transposition of the female writer's imagination into the male there is both the horror and fear of the male bursting out, as well as the strong sense of self-transgression in continuing that transposition, with its denial of the female. Yet the parallel horror also seems to be layered into a recognition and fear of the speaker's own developing homosexuality and denial of the male. Sabrina, with a "Madonna" face, both sexes somehow grafted onto her, is "the most natural thing in the world." The choking rage and madness that the ultimately contravened narrator feels is directed at the courtship pattern toward which Sabrina invites him:

> I put out my hand slowly and laid my fingers across the back of her hand. It was cool and soft—and then I felt that rough, swollen knuckle, those stiff, coarse hairs against my palm. I looked at Sabrina quickly and I found that she was looking at me with a peculiar tender look in her eyes and what I could only describe as a simper across her mouth. I have never felt the disgust, the profound fear and rage of that moment. She thought—well—she thought I was going to tell her I loved her.

It is hard to avoid thinking that the underpinning to this encounter is Bishop's own previous experience of a male erotic invitation: the fictive layering allows her sexually transposed Sabrina to meet a sexually transposed narrator, and to play out the symmetries of several crucial dilemmas.

Ultimately, however, the narrator's loathing closes with his rejection of all the confusions of Sabrina's sex and gendering, leaving Bishop the writer with the inadequacies of her available models for either loving or imagining; the theater of her story, a kind of salon world in which she tries out the writer's life, ends in untenable relation. Like the adolescent Mary Shelley, whose symbolic fantasies of transposed gender in Frankenstein gave her a brief, free space in which to trace female fears and angers through the opacities of cross-dressing, Bishop did not produce anything for public consumption this concentrated or explicit in her adult life. The very rawness and ardent overstatement of the feeling was never duplicated again.

For all the happiness of the years in Brazil with Lota, when same-sex love surfaces pointedly within "Crusoe in England" there is a heart-numbing discouragement, a depleted energy governing its effects. Friday turns up for Crusoe at the end of a vortex of fear and despair; Crusoe names his nightmares of meaningless labor conducted within unending solitude:

> nightmares of other islands
> stretching away from mine, infinities
> of islands, islands spawning islands,
> like frog's eggs turning into polliwogs

of islands, knowing that I had to live
on each and every one, eventually,
for ages, registering their flora,
their fauna, their geography.

And at that point, when the voice behind the voice of Crusoe most resembles the tireless describer, the elective sandpiper, who is Bishop herself, Friday enters:

Just when I thought I couldn't stand it
another minute longer, Friday came.
(Accounts of that have everything all wrong.)
Friday was nice.
Friday was nice, and we were friends.
If only he had been a woman!
I wanted to propagate my kind,
and so did he, I think, poor boy.
He'd pet the baby goats sometimes,
and race with them, or carry one around.
— Pretty to watch; he had a pretty body.
And then one day they came and took us off.

Friday isn't heard from again in the poem until the closing lines, similarly dashed as in the observation that ends this verse stanza, similarly echoic in structure:

— And Friday, my dear Friday, died of measles
seventeen years ago come March.

Friday was nice . . . Friday was nice . . . pretty . . . pretty; Friday, my dear Friday. The muted, deadened and repetitive baby speech here signs a helpless burden of unacknowledgeable feeling that swells somewhere blackly behind the voice, choking it.

If in reading this poem we repeat too cautiously to ourselves that we musn't confuse the actor with the role, the poet with the poem, we will not hear a numbed Elizabeth Bishop after her return to her homeland, reacting to the traumatic death of Lota de Macedo Soares. To fail to hear the pressure of particular experience behind and within the poem (a poem possibly begun in Brazil and finished climactically in North America), is to deny it its fullest vocal range. There is also a curious moment when a longing for children of one's own also rises from within the fictive character, Crusoe. At this moment an attentive reader of Bishop's letters remembers her lighthearted brag to Joseph Summers, that after ten weeks with Lota's grandchildren, they were such experienced hands at childcare that they could "give three baths and three shampoos in half an hour flat." The poet is the same Elizabeth Bishop who in 1961 eagerly passed on the latest book on painless childbirth to a pregnant relative, saying that the book "is a wonderful thing – just about as important, it seems to me, as splitting the atom." [17] It is the same Bishop who gave an Easter egg dyeing party in San Francisco for a mob of children, because she loved dyeing eggs, and the same Elizabeth Bishop who one afternoon picked a waif off the streets of Ouro Preto to bathe and care for: all episodes from a life in which the issue of sexual preference may well have made "propagation" a desire to be repressed. To some degree, the desire to have children always clashes with other basic human needs, for women or men, but in a lesbian life the problems are only intensified. To fail to hear that apparently dry "I wanted to propagate my kind" as a subterranean desire of the "real" shadow speaker performing the poem would be error.

Yet it seems most likely that an exact recovery of the subject of her own feelings about love, let alone the breeding of children, was never Bishop's intention. Her disapproval of Dickinson's narrowing of poetic subject to "love, human and divine," leads one to think that Bishop may have considered a part of her own twentieth-century emancipation from stereotypic womanhood to have been release from that entrapping woman's subject, love.

Her impatience may have been assisted by the same secularization that made older poets like Pound, Eliot, and other High Modernists favor scientific pragmatism over what Pound called in one context the "slither" of Romantic sentimentality, and what T. E. Hulme in another called "spilt religion." Temperamentally, Bishop seems to have joined Eliot in favoring the "depersonalization" of art. But turning one's back on unacceptable emotionalism, its messiness and supposed lack of precision, in both generations of poets, meant a common rejection of what was perceived as an unwanted feminizing of the arts, growing out of what poet-critics could see as the social place for poetry as increasingly marginal and trivial. In certain of Bishop's poems, first in unpublished and fragmentary work, then more guardedly in the late published work, the poems turn to renegotiate that rejection as she slips loose from her ideas of love and the feminine as tethering subjects.

It is certainly our loss as much as hers that for women of her generation a self-description and an inclination toward an analytic and logical mode of discourse, or a bent for the scientific, could push one to feel that love was a paltry female obsession, from which all intellectual ambition and daring were absent. An artist, a poet, was already dangerously close to that slithering in fogs of emotion by the very nature of her trade; perhaps Elizabeth Bishop found a well-bred repression of the psycho-sexual, and distaste for the traditional female sentimental, to be too close in kind to resist evading the too-large presence of either in her work. Moves stressing balance would push her style toward a cool, perhaps on occasion restrictively cool, elegance understating the too-volcanic, the too-volatile world of feeling.

Adrienne Rich suggests that we examine how she placed herself within existing limits as a commentator on the unempowered and silenced, and that we look at the social, psychological, and political implications of Bishop's indirections on love and sexuality, which in spite of her reservations do make their fleeting or subterranean appearances. As a model for such a reading of Bishop's work, Rich offers us "Sonnet" as a cryptic parable of lesbian identity.[18] Two fragmented sets of notes for poems, both of which appear to have been written in the early forties, around the time of "It is marvellous," offer additional insights.

Notations for a poem in the Nemer journals read:

> I had a bad dream
> towards morning, about you.
> You lay unconscious
> It was to be
> for "24 hrs."
> Wrapped in a long blanket
> I felt I must hold you
> even though a "load of guests"
> might come in from the garden
> [at] a minute
> & see us lying
> with my arms around you
> & my cheek on yours
> but I had to
> prevent you
> from slipping away

There are other brief lines of description, and then the draft closes:

in the deep of the morning
    the day coming
that loneliness like feeling on
the sidewalk in a crowd
that fills with slow, elaborate show
the sidewalk rises, rises
like absolute despair

Another fragmented phrase repeats, "fear and embarrassment." In the seclusion of a notebook Bishop did head toward direct, candid and painful autobiographical material, in which potential embarrassment itself surfaces as an issue.

A draft of another poem appears in a pile of unfinished poem fragments. The reference to rose rocks may place it with other Key West material of the early forties, when Bishop wrote the poem entitled "Faustina, or Rock Roses." The question about an Army or a Navy house bolsters this suggested dating. The draft is headed "Vague Poem (Vaguely Love Poem)," and establishes a setting on a trip west: "I think I *dreamed* that trip." An unidentified woman appears at a ramshackle house. The tone of the poem is hesitant, self-questioning. The speaker is looking for rock roses from a woman:

An Army house? — No, a Navy house.
      Yes,
        that far inland
there was nothing by the back door but dirt,
or that same dry monochrome, sepia straw I'd seen every where.
Oh, she said, the dog has carried them off.
(A big black dog, female, was dancing around us.)

Later, as we drank tea from mugs, she found one,
"a sort of one." "This one is just beginning. See —
you can see here, it's beginning to look like a rose.
It's — well a crystal, crystals form —
I don't know any geology myself . . ."
(Neither did I.)
Faintly, I could make out — perhaps in the dull,
rose-red lump of soil (apparently?)
a rose-like shape; faint glitters. . .
      Yes, perhaps
there was a secret powerful crystal inside.

I *almost* saw it: turning into a rose
without any of the intervening

roots, stem, buds, and so on; just
earth to rose and back again.
Crystallography and its laws:
Something I once wanted badly to study,
until I learned that it would
    involve a lot of arithmetic, that is, mathematics.

Just now, when I saw you naked again,
I thought the same words: rose-rock, rock-rose . . .
Rose, trying, working, to show itself, forming, folding over
unimaginable connections, unseen, shining edges
Rose-rock, unformed, flesh beginning, crystal by crystal
clear pink breasts and darker crystalline nipples,
Rose-rock, rose quartz, roses, roses, roses
exacting roses from the body
and the even darker, accurate rose of sex —

Almost like a dream chant, the poem that is groping into being ends as a powerful affirmation of the whole of a woman's body, from center to circumference, without fear, without false shame, and with a full appreciation of beauty and secrecy fused in a primary symbol for women.

Unfinished and sketchy as the poem is, it also lifts a curtain on possibility: *if* Elizabeth Bishop had been born thirty years later into another public decorum, and *if* her keen, Moore-trained observer's eye had been released from the Moore prohibitions, the same poet who can see the sexual body as one more interesting object in the world's cupboard might have given us brilliant description, wholly original and incisive in its daring. This tantalizing little proto-poem is in its quiet ambition, and in its penetrating vision of the private body, far more revealing than much writing that later passed for "confessional" by both men and women.

The draft also moves to appropriate, or reconstitute an earlier image, placing it in a less frightening light. We can see clearly David Kalstone's "vestigial implacable female presence" existing behind the scenes in "At The Fishhouses"; it is there in "the cold hard mouth" and "the rocky breasts" of the poem's maternal sea world. In "Vague Poem (Vaguely Love Poem)" those rocky breasts become a warm, almost-breathing crystal; while the image is still stiffly mineral, the negative context of the earlier image has been subverted, and turned inside out to represent love, and intimacy; the "implacable" female is in retreat.

Yet where would Bishop have wanted to publish such a poem? It isn't really finished; but she is in total control by that ending: its very hesitance, its tentative groping toward subject have become the drama of the poem's revelation. It seems such an enormous loss that there was no place, either in those years of her life or in any other of them, for such loving, or for such a mixture of pride and tenderness to become vocal. One can only wonder, too, at the cost of such a choking off of speech. Still, a partial, or at least livable speech forms within the splendid secrecy of that rock crystal at the center, an invisible beauty solidly connected to the visible world, broken out and displayed in its own good time.

It is a suggestive and enigma-producing linguistic parallel that the public rock roses named in the title of "Faustina, Or Rock Roses" should be so stubborn and obtrusive an emblem of the female sinister, or of the female unempowered. In the opening of this poem,

> Tended by Faustina
> yes in a crazy house
> upon a crazy bed,
> frail, of chipped enamel,
> blooming above her head
> into four vaguely roselike
>   flower-formations,
>
> the white woman whispers to
> herself.

The sick white woman the protagonist has come to visit lies in "her white disordered sheets/ like wilted roses." Above her head, blooming from the bedstead at a level paralleling that of the face of her black attendant, Faustina, Bishop hangs the "four vaguely roselike flower-formations." The poem concludes with a look at Faustina:

> Her sinister kind face
> presents a cruel black
> coincident conundrum.
>   Oh, is it
>
> freedom at last, a lifelong
> dream of time and silence,
> dream of protection and rest?
> Or is it the very worst,
> the unimaginable nightmare

that never before dared last
    more than a second?

The acuteness of the question
forks instantly and starts
a snake-tongue flickering;
blurs further, blunts, softens,
separates, falls, our problems
becoming helplessly
    proliferative.

There is no way of telling.
The eyes say only either.
At last the visitor rises,
awkwardly proffers her bunch
of rust-perforated roses
and wonders oh, whence come
    all the petals.

We are back to the female implacable here, made to notice the sinister potential of our bonds to the maternal or surrogate maternal presence; we are not celebrating the crystalline flower core. Faustina was somebody Bishop actually knew in Key West; she is a local character who sells lottery tickets, and whose one preserved letter to Bishop is quite inoccuous. But the face in "Faustina, or Rock Roses" is terrifyingly unreadable, moving in and out of protectiveness and malevolence in the flick of a watching eye. The roses framing the poem partake of the "cruel coincident conundrum" and, for our eyes, say only that the nature of the female is a splitting "either." In this setting, the unpetaling roses that the visitor proffers so awkwardly in the disarray of the poem's ending, are actually, metaphorically, and syntactically, as disintegrative as the prostrate, invalid female.

There are further pairings of interest in "Faustina." Not so faintly, a mother-child is subsumed in the master-servant relationship. Bishop suggests the double character of the classic master-servant dilemma by the races of her protagonists, in their mutual interdependencies. What happens when one crosses the boundary separating north and south, and separating racial boundaries? What happens when searching for that "lifelong/ dream of time and silence[. . .] of protection and rest," white child and white mistress put themselves at the mercy of the acknowledged black Other? Each member of the pair is made to vibrate within the questions raised by union. Although a race-blind child may still, perhaps, rest in helpless innocence on the bosom of her need for a race-blind mother, as soon as we set a needy white in the care of a powerful black servant, age and weakness cannot modify the historically corrupted terms of such an exchange. Bishop is treading here within a dreadful assent, no less potent because implied, to the very old projection throwing white fear onto the figure of the black servant, whose exploited weakness and subjugation is made to grow into a back-lashing vision of frightening power.

In several poems, Bishop projects the problems of trust within love and intimacy onto the more remote arena of the world of servants, where power or control might then have seemed deceptively simpler issues. In the formal distances of that relationship her own doubts about intimacy can be safely tried, their terrors probed. A letter presents a nearer and more complex picture of mistress and servant in this description of Lota and her maid Joanna, which Bishop sent to the Barkers in the winter of 1965:

> Lota lay on her bed, in *negligee* [. . .] – barefoot, looking very *dark*, and Joanna squatted on the floor beside her – the two watching a samba school on a portable tv set [. . .] – everything so absolutely relaxed, tropical, and lush, – exactly like the old prints of Rio interiors, the mistress and the slave.

This view, as well as the Barker letter in 1959, with its glimpse of Lota up on the ladder twiddling the electrical wires, shows Lota's power. Within the mythos of this relationship, from inside the perspective of "old prints," Bishop moves into a species of pastness to befriend her own dark side, taming and domesticating her vision of the malevolent female. In that "*dark*," "absolutely relaxed, tropical, and lush" space, light-bearing Lota, in Bishop's life a mothering and loving friend, reverses the trend of Bishop's perceptions of Faustina, the earlier Key West servant whose face presented only a "cruel black/coincident conundrum."

Through Lota, the vertical relations of mistress and servant, black and white, loved and feared, implacable mother and vulnerable daughter are, if not canceled, at least qualified. In the tumbling arena of revolutionary Brazilian politics, other polar distinctions like left-wing or right-wing, upper-class or lower-class, radical or conservative, as Bishop observed and wrote to others about them, appeared to clash. It is not the complex relation with Lota alone that accounts for the total impact of Bishop's exposure to Brazilian life. Over and over, in letters far more than in poems, Brazil confronts Bishop with unworkable binaries and provocative social and psychological paradigms in which her own relationships are confusingly set in broader contexts, in which personal urgencies undoubtedly distort her exile's reading of Brazilian realities. For illumination of these complex and culturally crossed issues Brazilian writers are greatly needed.

But the complexities and confusions of these race-haunted relations in Bishop's life are indelibly positioned for any reader. I am reminded of this in the swift sketch of Lota that Bishop presents to her Aunt Grace Bulmer Bowers in a letter of 1957. Lota is wakened by Betty, the cook's child:

> when she was jumping up & down on Lota in her bed the other morning Lota said "my mother certainly would have been surprised to see me with a little nigger on top of me like this!"

As patron, Lota gave gifts in an environment less bound by racially restricted behavior than her mother's. Attempting to mitigate the poverty and narrowness of her servants' lives, she remained the privileged white benefactress, even as in her final years she labored at enormous physical and mental cost to transform an urban landfill in Rio into a public park. For Bishop, on the mythic map of her southern descent, her Latin American lover, however aristocratic, or however correctly *engagée* in upbringing, could represent in the chain of color an embrace of a darker, more primitive self and a less conflicted definition of the feminine. While the 1965 letter, written at a time when relations between the two women were beginning to fray, emphasizes Lota's tropical darkness and otherness, in August 1953 Bishop reported on Lota's aristocratic and leftist background with gleeful pride to Ilse Barker:

> Until Vargas, her father was always in politics – he was exiled several times; they have the straw hat with a bullet hole through the brim he was wearing one day when shot at; Lota says at the convent for a few years the girls whose fathers were in prison – hers was – didn't speak to the socially inferior girls whose fathers were out, etc. . .all in the best South American tradition.

Both women seem to have taken free relations with Black people as a necessary consequence of their own political, social and psychosexual liberation. Writing on March 13th, 1965 to Grace Bulmer Bowers, her favorite aunt, Bishop scolds her "severely" for following southern opinion about Martin Luther King's leadership, and points with satisfaction to having recorded for a Brazilian newspaper her own approval of King's being awarded the Nobel Peace Prize. She says to Aunt Grace: "You have no idea how the rest of the world feels about how the U S treats its colored people—and particularly here, where there is no problem at all. It is one reason I like living here, after ten years or so in the 'south.' " And then she tells a story:

> Don't forget I did live in the south. – My dear old laundress's (black) son was murdered by the Key West police because one of them wanted his wife.- Everyone knew this and nothing was done about it. The laundress was given her son's body in a coffin, straight from jail- She said "I looked at his arm – Miss Elizabeth, – it wasn't an *arm* any more . . . " etc etc

More on the subject crops up again on May 18:

> After living in the south off and on for more than ten years – you have no idea what a relief it is to live here and see people of all colors happy and natural together. (All miserably poor together, too – but even so, it is more civilized than what we have in the U S A, I'm afraid.) At the grand opening of Lota's "park," a few weeks ago, there was a new outdoor dance-floor – and it was so nice to see all the different colors dancing together – one young couple dancing *with* their baby, about 10 months old – a tall black man, a beautiful dancer. Our mulatto maid went, all dressed to kill, and all Lota's architects – young white men – danced away with her and she had the time of her life. Now that is what I call being civilized! It is something I feel very deeply about.

Once again, Brazil represents her world of harmonized opposites, of the place in which the "broken-down luxury" of Lota's living quarters in Rio, as she once referred to it in correspondence with the Barkers, afforded her a vital and earthy shabbiness within privileged comfort, of a place where one can have the service of maids and still have them watch television with the mistress and dance away with their betters on "civilized" public occasions. (It is worth noting that while Bishop was perennially eager to see the dissolution of racial barriers, her interest in dissolving class barriers was rather less keen.)

Bishop, dependent on Lota for her well-being in Brazil, saw her in their happiest years as the longed-for generously nurturant presence. (Lota's mothering is something both women accepted as defining their relation, but Lota was actually no more than a year older than Bishop.) As their relation grew more strained, a vision obtrudes in which Lota as the dark "mistress" emerges, perhaps guaranteeing her freedom in an upside-down world of exile ruled by the Southern Cross, in a reverse heaven like that of "Insomnia." Nine months before Lota's apparent suicide in September, Bishop writes to the Barkers in 1967 of one upheaval. Lota, near mental collapse, is

> unconscious most of the time, kept at home. Since I am closest to her of course I am the one she turned against – or feels a certain ambivalence for – there have been six months now of this up-and-down, but the last few weeks were by far the worst and it was decided (and I'd already decided myself) that the only thing for me to do was to get out, which I did, in about half an hour, while they took her to the dr.[. . .] So here I am after fifteen years with a few dirty clothes in a busted suitcase, no home any more, no claims (legally) to anything here, etc.

The women were eventually reconciled. Bishop, writing in the days immediately after Lota's death, to both the Barkers and the Summers, tried to make sense of her friend's last days, repeating to each correspondent in turn that her hours in New York with Lota had been free of agitation. To Anny Baumann she reports the events, finding Lota's body with the empty pill bottle in her hand, and having to be the official witness. To the Summers she says: "I was with her for only a few hours, actually, and there was no quarrel or discussion of any sort." To the Barkers, she writes:

> I'll never really know whether it was deliberate or a mistake or what – she brought her good clothes, for parties, many presents, pounds & pounds of coffee, etc. – so it doesn't look as though she had meant this consciously – but I know she was desperately unhappy. Our few hours were peaceful and affectionate, thank god – but oh oh – if I hadn't gone to sleep – if I had just managed to say the *right* thing, some how –
>
> I now know, from Rio, that all her friends and *three* doctors tried to keep her from coming – but I could not seem to resist those pathetic cables – and at least, she did want to be with me – that's my only comfort so far.

And to the Summers again, "I just feel worse & worse all the time – but I suppose this will wear away – but don't think for a moment that love does, because it doesn't."

For years afterward Bishop tried to make a go of returning to Brazil. Yet the arc of this experience with one woman and one country represented much material accessible in poetry for Bishop in only carefully controlled bits. There is only limited evidence in both letters and poems for trying to determine what blackness meant by way of symbolic counter to Bishop. Yet neither Bishop, with the instincts of her liberal background, nor Lota, seem free of an appropriation in which the wholeness of the black Other disappears or is obliterated within the narcissistic back-projections of white fear and white self-congratulation. It seems clear that Bishop's fascination with blackness, in poetry and in her personal life, becomes part of the mechanism by which race comes to stand in for our fears and desires for intimacy: in casting one's lover for a role in the drama of approaching the Stranger or black Other, fears of intimacy and of being overwhelmed by intimacy are given their ritual place, and a kind of valor attaches to overcoming those fears. And yet through whatever clouded personal perceptions, both women, often with courage, generosity, and style, rushed to free themselves from malignant practice and from the recursive dilemmas of race and gender within which we, even in our reflective hindsight, seem still entangled.

·F·O·U·R·

"Time's Andromedas"

BRAZIL ADDED to Elizabeth Bishop's growing repertoire of land-scapes and larger views, and sharply changed her list of dramatis personae: after the nineteen-forties, the count on objects and fantastic fabrication went down, and the count on animals, servants, and super-numerary actors rose. Before going on to speak about Bishop's re-sponse to Moore's reticences and Lowell's confessionalism in her evolving interest in biographical inclusion, and before tracing the newer themes based on her Nova Scotian childhood, as well as the attitudes about art emerging in late poems and translation about artists and art objects, I would like to pause, look backward, and steady the frame on the picture at the outset of her career.

An extended analysis of any one of Bishop's major poems will reveal formidable consistencies of language, focus, format, and imagery, and show us a poetic intelligence that forgot nothing. Whatever made its way into language for Bishop stayed there in the mental workshop as tool and supply awaiting further use. Because Bishop's work, from the earliest, has had such cool elegance and finish it has seemed skewed to speak of maturity; from the time that she was a baby poet her pieces were cleanly wrought and intelligently whole. Many features, stylistic habits, and images besides the caged, wired and watered ones already noted in chapter 2 remained eerily recurrent. "Behind Stowe" was written when Bishop was sixteen:

> I heard an elf go whistling by,
> A whistle sleek as moonlit grass

That drew me like a silver string
To where the dusty, pale moths fly,
And make a magic as they pass;
And there I heard a cricket sing.

His singing echoed through and through
The dark under a windy tree
Where glinted little insects' wings.
His singing split the sky in two.
The halves fell either side of me,
And I stood straight, bright with moon-rings.

In its adolescent design, there is still to be seen the characteristic binary form, the familiar intricacies of rhyme (less freely ordered here than later), the persistent preoccupation with animals in a largely untenanted nature, the same fascination with animal iridescence, and the same aerial wire, here called string, with an unorthodox mission. The poem by itself, authorship unknown, would hardly be worth looking at. Its second stanza line, "His singing split the sky in two," is perhaps an unconscious borrowing from another Vassar poet, Edna St. Vincent Millay, from her own famous adolescent production "Renascence." Millay's couplet isn't much different, or much better: "The soul can split the sky in two,/And let the face of God shine through." Bishop's cricket, however, unlike Millay's soul, does not direct us upward to the divine, but downward instead to the transfigured human, in a sophisticated but characteristic reversal of Millay's more conventional piety. The accumulation of parts foreshadowing the mature poet within the twice six lines of "Behind Stowe" is impressive.

At sixteen, Bishop is alive to the glint of insect's wings; at twenty-nine, she sees engine oil that spreads a metallic rainbow on the water from which "The Fish" is drawn, and at thirty, it's roosters that have "all that vulgar beauty of iridescence." At forty, she looks through the eyes of the Prodigal Son and sees a sunrise that "glazed the barnyard mud with red;/ the burning puddles seemed to reassure." And a scant two decades later, while "Going to the Bakery," oil flashes in a ditch and calls up for her the blue iridescence of the Morpho butterfly. In "Sonnet," published in the year of her death, the "rainbow-bird," her ambiguous final emblem of freedom, flames from "the narrow bevel/ of the empty mirror." For the whole of her life, it was worth observing how the world's light fractured into color over oil and water.

It isn't merely the frequent scheduling that matters most about iridescence. Bonnie Costello,[19] in her discussion of Marianne Moore's "luminosity, phosphorescence, iridescence and metamorphosis," provides several reasons for Bishop's preoccupation with these qualities of light, via Moore. The volatile properties named "flashes of appearance and disappearance, luminosities" suggest for Costello "the invisible power of the visible." In this formulation, "Luminosity is a metaphor of immanence in modern literature, of truth shining through its representations. And 'truth' is connected with the thing itself." In her reading of Moore's "Poetry and Criticism" Costello then concludes:

> We are left with an awakened sense of something "beyond" the representation, but with no direction by which to account for that experience. Moore's poetry holds out the possibility that this magical presence is really the presence of the text itself, as a construct of the imagination.

In this view, words, or ideas, seem firmly a reality prior to matter; Costello points out, however, that at this interesting juncture Moore "equivocates": it is not clear whether the "invisible world" is for her "anything more than creativity itself." Costello quotes Moore through a dense thicket of interrelations including the voices first of Joseph Conrad and then of Howard Nemerov, as Moore emerges from this philosophical underbrush first quoting Nemerov as to the union of language and vision, and then declaring her own sense of the proximate fusion of that invisible world and its orders with "soul" and "creativity":

> "Seeing, and saying;—language is a special extension of the power of seeing, inasmuch as it can make visible not only the already visible world; but through it the invisible world of relations and affinities." The world of the soul? Difficult as it is to define the soul, "creativeness" is perhaps as near a definition as we can get.[20]

Moore is far more stubbornly secular and unhierarchized than Coleridge's account of the origin of the poetic impulse, with its "repetition in the finite mind of the eternal act of creation in the infinite I AM."

Bishop sustains Moore's secular bent, but turns Moore's reading of the relation between visible and invisible orders, between the material and the immaterial, into a different description of reality's quarrel with the imagination. In her fidelity to things, Bishop also came to include more of the thingness of her own life, recognizing ever more intently as her territory what the irreducibly particular I of the eye will grasp.

Like Moore in chasing the flickers of iridescence, Bishop as an adolescent instinctively acknowledges a form of "the invisible world of relations and affinities." Yet Bishop seems even more hesitant than Moore about yoking the flux of creativity with a purposive order, although for both poets language wrests no easy triumphs from a nature neither readily knowable nor compliant. Here Bishop's ideas seem close to Williams' often paradoxical nominalism, a label which she accepted for herself later, writing to the literary critic Joseph Summers in June 1965, "I just looked up 'nominalist' in the dictionary and discover it is what I've been all my life." While nature *is* persistently seen in her poetry as a language, there are "No ideas but in things"; Bishop's own form of assent to the doctrine of "res non verba" keeps a fierce faith in the ultimate thingness of truthful words, which like the other things of man in nature have their incurable habits of evanescence and dissolution.

In "Over 2,000 Illustrations and a Complete Concordance," first published when Bishop was in her late thirties, a key descriptive passage closely echoes the language and perceptions of a prose epiphany taken down by her as a college student, a passage appearing in 1933 in *The Vassar Review of Undergraduate Studies* as "Time's Andromedas." In the Hopkins sonnet, "Andromeda," to which Bishop's title alludes, "Time's Andromeda" hangs on rude rock, "doomed dragon food," waiting for deliverance by Perseus.[21] The reference to this waiting suspension merely hangs in abeyance, however, above the essay; the events Bishop notes are entirely unmythological, and beyond the title she makes no direct use of Hopkins' complicated symbolism of Perseus as Christ the redeemer of universal human time. In 1933 Bishop simply appears to be watching birds flying south:

> They were fairly high up, a fairly large sort of bird . . . almost speck-like . . . They spread across a wide swath of sky, each rather alone, and at first their wings seemed all to be beating perfectly together. But by watching one bird, then another, I saw that some flew a little slower than others, some were trying to get ahead and some flew at an individual rubato; each seemed a variation, and yet altogether my eyes were deceived into thinking them perfectly precise and regular. I watched closely the spaces between the birds. It was as if there

were an invisible thread joining all the outside birds and within this fragile net-work they possessed the sky; it was down among them, of a paler color, moving with them. The interstices moved in pulsation too, catching up and continuing the motion of the wings in wakes, carrying it on, as the rest in music does — not a blankness but a space as musical as all the sound.

In a characteristic impulse, Bishop switches foreground and background, and reads the conventionally negative space of interstitial sky as positive — not a blankness — and active. Order among the birds materializes almost as volition, as threads pulling the birds into connection. These extremely precise notations, in a Darwinian intensity of observation, continue over the course of another day, as the unnamed birds constellate in an image of deep order, of one of the prior orders of the world, yet one that may be approached in descriptive language. She concludes that this motion of bird migration results

> in a thing so inevitable, so absolute, as to mean nothing connected with the passage of time at all — a static fact of the world, the birds here or there, always; a fact that may hurry the seasons along for us, but as far as bird migration goes, stands still and infinite.

A natural constancy, an observed pattern transcends time almost through a platonic ideal form, which in characteristically Bishop terms also transforms the language of time into the language of space. But in contrast with the ardor of Hopkins' longing Andromeda, fitting the Christian scheme of a time supervened through divine ordinance, Bishop offers something more neutral. Her seasons may "hurry" for us, may fragment into a "here or there"; but from the timeless, comprehensive perspective of the natural order, they stand "still and infinite." The conclusion must have been important for her; she puts the idea away. The language of the discovery, however, resists sidelining. Its contours are burnt too stubbornly into an awareness, and sure enough, the words rise again in much the same conformation, but in another context.

In "Over 2,000 Illustrations and A Complete Concordance," published fifteen years after her college notations of birds in flight, she juxtaposes an early image of order and meaning, the illustrated concordance of her childhood, uneasily against the troubling weight of experience, against an image from her trip to the Holy Land. Never content to leave to merely metrical feet her hold on a subject, Bishop's reflections on the metaphysical, unlike Moore's or Dickinson's or Hopkins', wait for literal grounding. Yet the final verse paragraph records a dizzying and frightening continuance of disorder: "Everything only connected by 'and' and 'and.' " Further, "what frightened me most of all," is the holy grave of the poor prophet paynim, completely empty, and lacking any trace of even the dust of its former occupant. Remembering those undergraduate days spent before a window, Bishop takes the language of her earlier posting and puts it here into this brief description of a picture from the illustrated concordance:

> Always the silence, the gesture, the specks of birds
> suspended on invisible threads above the Site,
> or the smoke rising solemnly, pulled by threads.

Although the poem cannot at this moment reassure its speaker that order does not disappear from the universe with the dust of the prophets, the routing of the language, drawn from Bishop's early preoccupations at the window, retrieves that conclusion for some later time, within the expanded sites of voluntary exile. When strings and threads are drawn into pattern again in future poems and prose as undulant stripes, ribs, cage-bars and wires of rain, the picture of order, even if order within ominous limits, will have been restored and internalized.

The comfort of a reinforced sense of enduring order, or at least of an enduring religious order, is missing in "Over 2,000 Illustrations And A Complete Concordance." The faith of Hopkins isn't invoked even skeletally: but the mind, drawing from that astonishing cupboard of past musings, pulls out the same 1933 language and the same physical conformation of the birds, perhaps to counter the disappointments of the observations of mid-life, or perhaps once again to reveal the inadequacies of religion. In place of the order of religion, Bishop calls on the balance of natural science, always more attractive to her as a born literalist of the imagination. In another early musing, Bishop invokes Huxley on the governing size of things as naturally as Hardy for an explanation of the proper dimensions for a novel; even as a student she found no conscious bar of unlike enterprise between the formal explanations of artist and scientist. Direct conceptualizing is always less welcome to her than the laying up of treasures of observation; it is through the pragmatic accumulation of layers of narrative description that immanent form reveals itself.

The threads of the network of birds in flight recall Bishop's other persistent metaphors. In their shifting visibility the threads of 1948 sketch a hesitation about the order of foreground and background, even as they pose counterforms of Bishop's enduring questions about the relationship between chaos and order, and fixity and flux, in nature. As threads, they are first positive and then negative views of the existence of order; as we have seen in the previous chapter, cage and stripe and other vertical danglings are Bishop's emblem of the body's limits or of the body's internal wiring for change.

If we look at the configuration of bird and network once again, where the interstices of sky space feature as prominently as the birds cutting across it, we see how Bishop's contextuality emerges. Contextuality, or the expanded view of placement, becomes a habit of mind: while the published, older Bishop questions increasingly the lost or wavering mesh of circumstances that escape her control of context, she never relinquishes that scrupulous notice of the fluctuating ground between observer and observed, between foreground and background, and between stationary and moving objects, appearing and disappearing as they do in their flight from the bereaved eye.

In that early record-keeping by the window, we cannot fail to notice that unlike prior treatments of the bird symbol, in which the soaring skylark or nightingale becomes an emphatic emblem of a transcendent human aspiration in solo flight, Bishop ties her observations firmly to bird communities, and to the actual medium which they inhabit and which supports them. The symbol itself is woven of materials fixing it to her overall habits of design; they are the materials of a thoughtful student nearly as much drawn to music and science as poetry. Birds stay birds, and they flock; they do not move too quickly to become stand-ins for something else, such as light-winged Dryads of the trees, blithe spirits, or scorners of the ground. In this prose passage, much closer to Bishop's later style than some of her earliest poems, personification and hypostasis as technique take a back seat to a more literal machinery of observation and likeness-taking. If there is aesthetic reference it is to the production or sober craft of musical manufacture, with very little attempt at changing or exalting the language of process and description, a language for which Bishop kept an increasingly augmented fidelity.

· I ·

Just as the body of Bishop's poetry offers no internal inconsistency or jarring evidence of change, her own insertion into a traditional lyric poetry seems equally smooth. Although the work is markedly original, Bishop's formal choices, her rhymed stanzas, and her easy, predominantly iambic lines look nonexperimental. It would nonetheless be mistaken to simplify her complex modernity. Her forms, necessarily governed by experience, and necessarily shaped by context, undergo the same wrenching relations of time and space that earlier poets like Pound, Eliot, and Williams acknowledged in the dislocations of their line breaks, and in the discontinuous rhythms of their discourse. Bishop's consciousness of modern propositions about space and time in relation to knowledge never issued forth in the revolutionary poetic form so visible in the productions of these or other twentieth century writers, but she remained, in her own way, and in her own preoccupation with mutability and the regulatory impact of vantage point, faithful to their perceptions.

In an undergraduate essay she titled "Dimensions for a Novel," Bishops quotes T. S. Eliot from "Tradition and the Individual Talent" on the artist's duty to the past:

> The existing monuments form an ideal order among themselves, which is modified by the introduction of the new (the really new) work of art among them. The existing order is complete before the new work arrives; for order to persist after the supervention of novelty, the *whole* existing order must be, if ever so slightly, altered; and so the relations, proportions, values of each work of art toward the whole are readjusted; and this is conformity between the old and the new.

In treating the famous statement, Bishop immediately places the idea of a changing order within the text itself, aligning her own thinking with a whole present and future host of writers struggling with the concept of open, and indeterminate form within what is the apparent fixity of the literary text. After examining the representation of changing sensibility in Joyce's *Portrait of the Artist as a Young Man*, she notes a defect, or a swerve from truth:

> Joyce's "moocow" is blurred, but blurred at the age at which he beheld it; when the reader reaches the end of the book he is still in possession of, as a hard fact, Stephen's earliest days.

She sees this representation of "hard fact" contradicting its earlier nature, represented as essentially blurred:

> Some attempt has been made to get around this problem by the kind of novel (Proust, for example) that picks one moment of observation and shows the whole past in the terminology of that particular moment. This method achieves, perhaps, the "conformity between the old and the new," at least one instance of it, but since the conformity itself must be ever-changing, the truth of it, the thing I should like to get at, is the ever-changing expression for it.

Reverting to personal experience for her illustration of "the ever-changing truth," she says:

> In conversation we notice how, often, the other person will repeat some word or phrase of ours, perhaps with quite a different meaning, and we in turn will pick up some adjective or adverb of theirs, or even some pun on their words – all unconsciously. This trick of echoes and re-echoes, references and cross-references produces again a kind of "conformity between the old and the new."

Her striking account of this experience, putting Eliot in her own words, and appropriating his idea for personal rather than literary event foreshadows her later inclusions of the autobiographical in her poetry; we might notice that even at twenty no fence of genre intrudes between art and life. Bishop's description is also congruent with our current theories of reconstitutive memory:

> A symbol might remain the same for a lifetime, but surely its implications shift from one thing to another, come and go, always within relation to that particular tone of the present which called it forth. We live in great whispering galleries, constantly vibrating and humming, or we walk through salons lined with mirrors where the reflections between the narrow walls are limitless, and each present moment reaches immediately and directly the past moments, changing them both.

Bishop defines these moments and Eliot's "monuments" of literature, and the order in our literary and actual lives in which they occur, as functionally the same. Bishop says: "At five years one looks around the dinner table at the cumulative family with as great a sense of recognition and understanding as ever comes later on." Firmly, she joins both life and art, saying "I can think of these existing moments which make up their 'ideal order' as existing first of all as these moments of recognition." Moments of recognition, a reader might add, greatly resembling Virginia Woolf's "moments of being," and also moments owing quite a lot to Proust's moment of the madeleine dipped in tea, his fork rapping the glass at a dinner party, and so on. There is also a striking resemblance in Proust's preoccupation with a moving perceiver, studying the objects of his perception as they are influenced by that movement: as the boy Marcel rides the box seat of Dr. Percepied's carriage on the way home to Combray, Proust remembers his intense exhilaration while he watched the steeples of Martinville and Vieuxvicq group and regroup in intoxicating pattern before and behind the path of the moving carriage.[22] An intoxication, we should note, that reached its apex only as the experience moved from memory into language.

What is notable in Bishop's discussion is her junction of Eliot's monuments with these moments, as like Proust, she gives herself the ground of memory as the essential force constituting her own work. These definitions of the work of memory also indicate clearly the ways in which readers must not be misled by the emphasis on geography in her work (what Herbert Leibowitz once referred to as her reading of life as "more an affair of places than people")[23] into misreading how space, or geography, progressively intersects with her grasp of temporality. Temporality in the course of her work defines itself more and more as the cumulative action of memory becoming the history of persons. The young Bishop summarizes her argument:

> the moments I have spoken of occur so sharply, so minutely that one cannot say whether the recognition comes from the outside or the inside, whether the event or the thought strikes, and spreads its net over past and sometimes future events or thoughts. Over all the novels I can think of the author has waved a little wand of attention, he holds it in one position, whereas the shifting produced by the present over the past is this other shifting, rhythmical perhaps, of the moments themselves.

What will persist, too, in our experience of all of Bishop's work is just this signal fusion of inner and outer space, and conflation of past and future temporality.

While Bishop's analytic intelligence was at all phases of her career quite keen, and at its student outset easily and naturally extended to prose speculation, another one of the ways in which she chose not to model herself on Moore was to decline Moore's life as a reviewer and essayist. Her adult rejection of the role of critic and theorist was nearly total; it is interesting to see, then, in this college work not only an authoritative handling of such speculation, but also a relevant and consistent thought sustaining her later poetic development. Hard, too, for a reader not to regret that this particular vein of thought-mining can rarely be heard in Bishop beyond her twenties. In an early college essay on Gerard Manley Hopkins' poetry, she continues to explore metaphors of time, space, and literary production. Later she wrote about the Hopkins essay to Marianne Moore, raising the possibility of revising and publishing it, an idea she dropped rather quickly.

In the essay on Hopkins, subtitled "Notes on Timing in His Poetry," she writes:

> A poem is begun with a certain volume of emotion, intellectualized or not according to the poet, and as it is written out of this emotion, subtracted from it, the volume is reduced—as water drawn off from the bottom of a measure reduces the level of the water at the top. Now, I think, comes a strange and yet natural filling up of the original volume with the emotion aroused by the lines or stanzas just completed. The whole process is a continual flowing fullness kept moving by its own weight, the combination of original emotion with the created, crystallized emotion, – described by Mr. T. S. Eliot as "that intense and transitory relief which comes at the moment of completion and is the chief reward of creative work." Because of this constant fullness each part serves as a check, a guide, and in a way a model, for each following part and the whole is weighed together.

The passage, like passages in "Dimensions for a Novel," is concerned with the relations between work and artist and in the waterworks of its expressive functions Bishop shows yet again the consistency of her evolving formal perceptions. The earnest hydraulics, the mechanizing and quantifying of issues in this section also parallel Eliot's use of chemical metaphor as an explanation of the relation between personality and poetry in "Tradition and the Individual Talent." Yet in both cases, the investigative mode with its empirical language surely reflects each writer's sense of the urgency of the topic. For Eliot and Bishop, emotional distance, functioning as reserve in the one case and reticence in the other, were to pose problems for the style of the self's involvement in poetry. Here, Bishop sees emotion free of idiosyncrasy as a necessity of form; she also finds it operating within a metaphor of balance, system and regularity.

Bishop notes how Hopkins' system of sprung rhythm, with its rove-over, enjambing feet, and outriding syllables plunging in at the heads of lines, creates momentum and immediacy. She gives an example of what she names *quasiacope* and the contribution of its "excited" effects to the general effect of "intense, unpremeditated unrevised emotion," presenting us with an early theoretical justification for her own habitual use of an unrehearsed, spontaneous-sounding diction.

Yet her most interesting justification of spontaneity comes as she works out her approval of this poetry in which "the boundaries are set free, and the whole thing is loosened up" and its "fluid, detailed surface, made hesitant, lightened, slurred, weighed or feathered as Hopkins chooses." This looseness, or fluidity, Bishop further develops through the metaphor of the shooting gallery, a metaphor of course familiar to later readers of her poetry in the 1936 poem, "The Colder the Air," in which she says of "the huntress of the winter air":

> air's gallery marks identically
> the narrow gallery of her glance.
> The target-center in her eye
> is equally her aim and will.

In the poem, when vision and will, or self and seeing, are too narrowly concentrated in the shooting gallery of the glance, the seer is a sterile and wintry prophetess. And yet in this general discussion of poetry, self and seeing are both inevitably held within a constant and interactive flux, in which the poet's stance and timing are critical;

> A man stands in a shooting gallery with a gun at his shoulder aiming at a clay pigeon. Between his point of aim and the pigeon he must allow the necessary small fraction of space which the pigeon will cross in exactly the same amount of time as it will take the bullet to travel the length of the shooting gallery. If he does this accurately the clay pigeon falls, and his *timing* has been correct. In the same way the poet is set on bringing down onto the pages his poem, which occurs to him not as a sudden fixed apparition of a poem, but

as a moving, changing idea or series of ideas. The poet must decide
at what point in its movement he can best stop it, possibly at what
point he can manage to stop it; i.e., it is another matter of timing.

The issue of timing is set up within a metaphor that simultaneously
includes positioning, or stationing in space. Even the network of bird
flight representing time in the previous meditation, "Time's Andromedas," could not be read without its being spatialized. From the first,
temporality for Bishop is instinctively represented by clear spatial
reference. Later, this space comes to exist more and more within
time's ruinously insolvent estate, where the debit of the past never
equals the credit of present and future. By spatializing time, though,
Bishop posits a control over the safe passage of her life and work:
time's dismaying dissolutions can be stopped first by being fixed in
language; second, by positioning, or deployment in space; third by
allowing the body to mimic that flux through motion, through a kind
of sympathetic magic, as her hurrying, soon-to-be compulsively travelling body mimed and neutralized the endless motion of the clock by
literally running it down.

But the fixed distance between the striking hunter and the stricken
target of the poem in this early discussion has to be mediated; the
relation of poet and poem still looks like a simple binary, and yet the
poem cannot be described as the objective prey of the subjective
thinker; somehow, in a leap of appropriation the poet wrests from out
of the world a piece of reality which he paradoxically lays claim to as a
piece of his inwardness. Bishop continues her shooting gallery metaphor:

> Perhaps, however, the image of the man in the shooting gallery is
> incorrect, since the mind of the poet does not stand still and aim at
> his shifting idea. The cleavage implied in the comparison is quite
> true, I think – anyone who has tried to write a single poem because
> he felt he had one somewhere in his mind will recognize its truth.
> The poem, unique and perfect, seems to be separate from the
> conscious mind, deliberately avoiding it, while the conscious mind
> takes difficult steps toward it. The process resembles somewhat the
> more familiar one of puzzling over a momentarily forgotten name
> or word which seems to be taking on an elusive brain-life of its own
> as we try to grasp it. Granted that the poet is capable of grasping his
> idea, the shooting image must be more complicated; the target is a
> moving target and the marksman is also moving.

As in Ezra Pound's words from *Gaudier-Brzeska*, Bishop appears to be moving toward an image of the birth moment of a poem as that moment when "one is trying to record the precise instant when a thing outward and objective transforms itself, or darts into a thing inward and subjective."[24] As she returns to Hopkins, she points out that this marksman aims his poems to begin "at the point in their development where they are still incomplete, still close to the first kernel of truth or apprehension which gave rise to them." In this description spontaneity is not a trivial quality of the poet, but an intrinsic quality giving life.

This vitality in Hopkins Bishop names as a consequence of the baroque, and traces his practice to M. W. Croll's discussion in "The Baroque Style in Prose." In the extract she saved for her journal, Croll says of the baroque writers of prose:

> Their purpose was to portray, not a thought, but a mind thinking. . . . They knew that an idea separated from the act of experiencing it is not the same idea that we experienced. The ardor of its conception in the mind is a necessary part of its truth; and unless it can be conveyed to another mind in something of the form of its occurrence, either it has changed into some other idea or it has ceased to be an idea, to have any existence whatever except a verbal one.[. . .] They [. . .] deliberately chose as the moment of expression that in which the idea first clearly objectifies itself in the mind, in which, therefore, each of its parts still preserves its own peculiar emphasis and an independent vigor of its own—in brief, the moment in which truth is still *imagined.*[25]

The moment in which, we might add, both subjective and objective truths are joined, and again the dynamic moment in which both inner and outer worlds fuse, and the question of word as thing or idea, as made of or as making reality, is begged. Applying these characteristics to Hopkins, to declare his baroque nature, Bishop says further:

> At times the obscurity of his thought, the bulk of his poetic idea seems too heavy to be lifted and dispersed into flying members by his words; the words and the sense quarrel with each other and the stanzas seem to push against the reader, like coiled springs in the hand.

She never doubts the validity of this enterprise, however, and all of her metaphors press us to admire the general force and exaltation of Hopkins' poetry. Bishop's own sentence here roughly paraphrases a

further piece of Croll's description of the baroque: "There is a progress of imaginative apprehension, a revolving and upward motion of
the mind as it rises in energy, and views the same point from new
levels; and this spiral movement is characteristic of baroque prose."
Yet what might interest a later reader about her own rewording of this
thought about thought in flight is how she catches Hopkins in the act
of having his flight checked and literally weighed down in a moment
of poetic strain, and poetic inadequacy. This sense of poetry as a
weight-lifting assignment, defining language as a weight to be sent
upwards in transport, away from the strain of its tie to the material,
stays an important physical image for Bishop. There is something
about art's powers, viewed as heroically transformative, or as ecstati-
cally transcendental, that she instinctively mistrusted.

Weight, the recurrent sub-theme, severely qualifies the flight-wor-
thiness of language in the closing poem of the last book published in
Bishop's lifetime, *Geography III*; in "Five Flights Up," we find this
strained, checked moment in the closing lines:

> —Yesterday brought to today so lightly!
> (A yesterday I find almost impossible to lift.)

Even in a poem she chose to translate, Octavio Paz's tribute to Joseph
Cornell, "Objects & Apparitions," in which the bodiless faculty of
vision tilts stubbornly against the weight of the tactile, Bishop affirmed
again the magnetism of her early perspective. Through the medium of
several makers and at least two art forms she refracted the problematic
thrust of the material world, as the artist struggles to hoist experience
into art, and keep it there, lighting the blindness of touch through
vision, for whatever length of term she or he can negotiate. Bishop has
Paz saying:

> The apparitions are manifest,
> their bodies weigh less than light,
> lasting as long as this phrase lasts.
>
> Joseph Cornell: inside your boxes
> my words became visible for a moment.

But quite apart from this late translation, the early descriptive terms
of what her own project in poetry should be are taken from her early
reading, framed in an image of her own making, and then so deeply
internalized that in the last years of her writing she reaches in and

brings out the diction again for that penetrating moment at the window in *Geography III*, in which an understated, somber conclusion about the limits of both art and artist finds characteristic form in an image straying very little from an obdurately physical reality.

She plays with the properties of the sublime, of the transcendent, in literature through a literal-minded testing of images of poems in flight, clearly attaching the fantasy of the flying weight to more poets than Hopkins. Approximately at the time that she is working over the Hopkins essay, she saves this whimsical scrap in one of the Nemer journals:

> It is hard to get heavy objects up into the air; a strong desire to do so is necessary, and a strong driving force to keep them aloft.
>
> Some poets sit in air-planes on the ground, waving their arms, sure that they're flying.
>
> Some ascend for a period of time, then come down again; we have a good many stranded planes.

Then there follows a cryptic note about a fire balloon, linking this theme subliminally for us, perhaps, to the much-later "Armadillo," where "frail, illegal fire balloons" appear to haunt the animals of the Brazilian nightscape, as the fire balloons climb the heights in their "Too pretty, dreamlike mimicry!" and mock those who only tread the earth.

·II·

Other constants in Bishop's early work appear, but the timing and genre chosen for development are suggestively different. While her early student prose may furnish us with an easy and natural conflation of the personal and literary in metaphor, narrative, and theoretical proposition, the poems will not move so unguardedly. In early poetry, Bishop opts for place and position over character, and keeps that choice allegorized, fantasized, and impersonal.

It seems fair to say about the relation between Bishop's poetry and prose, that in a conventional process of development, Bishop's prose allowed her theoretical possibilities which the poetry would act on later; prose could point the way, or provide a rationale for what the poetry could subsequently be asked to perform. The early prose, following Hopkins and Eliot, speculates freely about spatio-temporal relations in poetic thinking, and in unforced metaphor justifies auto-biographical inclusions, for instance, in theory: yet in her own working life, her poetry took decades to catch up to what her theory cut out for it. The fruitful link between prose and poetry remains an interesting one for the figure of Bishop's whole career: in Chapter Nine I make some brief demonstration of how a deep immersion in prose narrative while in Brazil was another such necessary developmental step for her poetry.

Most male poets of an older generation, like Yeats, or Stevens, or Eliot, or Pound, or Jarrell and Berryman among Bishop's own contemporaries, wrote both poetry and prose with equal fluency and point, assuming the traditional role of man of letters with ease and confidence. But the gender that bonds all of these literary acts under the rubric "letters" can hardly be seen as accidental or unimportant. Most women poets do not so readily pull under this harness: Moore, Bogan, and Rich have been significant American exceptions.

Ultimately, both male and female poets who, in growing numbers, decline all prose outside the relatively passive form of the interview, must question the usefulness of refusing alternate ways of spelling out a life in letters, of formalizing, abstracting, and generalizing on one's relations to a profession and a vocation. One might say that for Bishop in particular, concentrating on poetry allowed her to duck the rigidi-fying public mask, to have assured her public right, also, perhaps, to a kind of indeterminacy and playfulness. Assuming the role of man of letters is still an uneasy act for most women, who feel, or are made to feel, acutely marginal to the social manifestations of writing as a profession. But Bishop's most important reason for preserving her status as an itinerant poet may have been to protect her life from behind what James Merrill called "her own instinctive, modest, life-long impersonations of an ordinary woman,"[26] in a space where poet and person could function unself-consciously. In a letter to Marianne Moore she once described her reaction to public notice in a crowd in quite forthright terms. Bishop had come late to a lecture, and as she moved to her seat, Marianne Moore called out a greeting from the podium. Bishop writes: "I enjoyed every moment except the one in which my own name struck me like a bullet, and I felt myself swelling like a balloon to fill the auditorium."

A shy person, she evidently wanted to remain in movement without the burden of a possibly type-casting public life. Yet hidden within the burdens of a public life are undoubtedly some acts and functions giving a poet's intelligence alternate routes of discovery through a greater variety of formal languages. Yet the ease and dash, the pungency cultivated in Bishop's private papers, make them wonderfully free reading. Throughout her large correspondence, I am struck by the precision with which, like any great letter-writer, she adjusted tone and stance, and varied and inflected the information she delivered to scores of correspondents, all standing in different relation to her. When her letters are eventually collected and edited they will be seen as a significant addition to the published work and as a casually brilliant portrait of a life, exactly that sort of portrait, in fact, which she herself enjoyed reading. As a teacher at Harvard, she recognized this taste more formally by offering a course on letter-writers of all kinds.

It would be easy to see the decision to forgo prose about literature as merely a matter of temperament: Bishop herself provides us with incidental language for that. With comic humility she explains to Marianne Moore her hesitations about doing a review of Auden:

> I shall send the story today and possibly enclose a review I've been trying to do – my first – of Auden's "Look, Stranger!" – the reviews I have seen I thought were so poor. When I remember your review of Wallace Stevens in POETRY, however, my very pen shakes. Once more I am overcome by my own amazing sloth and unmannerliness – can you please forgive me and believe that it is really because I want to do something well that I don't do it at all?

Like Bartleby, she'd rather not. Something of Bartleby's reliance on a provocative brevity seems instinctively hers, along with impatience about explanation. In a rather grumpy little statement in response to a questionnaire, she once said:

> The analysis of poetry is growing more and more pretentious and deadly. After a session with a few of the highbrow magazines one doesn't want to look at a poem for weeks, much less start writing one. The situation is reminiscent of those places along the coast where warnings are posted telling one not to walk too near the edge of the cliffs because they have been undermined by the sea and may collapse at any minute.
>
> This does not mean that I am opposed to all close analysis and

The Mappings of
North & South

While Elizabeth Bishop's respect for the stubbornly material is one of the deepest and most enduring characteristics of her work, in *North & South*, Bishop's first collection of poems, curiously enough, the first appearance of place as subject is analytic in style, an odd, pervasive blending of the fantastic and the schematic from which any figure of the poet as person is also absent. During the book's progress, houses, objects, and mythic figures who stand in for persons and dreams, are put in place through an elegance of manner both comic and remote; later books will naturalise their settings. But here already, in a mapping of space that reproduces the main points of Bishop's life, there are geographic opposites, northern and southern hemispheres, New and Old Worlds, and country and cityscapes. Even in this first book a poem like "Jeronimo's House," which bears traces of a Key West milieu, also suggests touches brought in from Bishop's early travel in Cuba, and thereby opens up the Latin American settings that later blossom into the heavy interest in Brazil of *Questions of Travel*.

"Jerónimo's House" directly foreshadows the later Brazilian poems; it is also the first of Bishop's house poems, with its provisional homesteading, its fragile dwelling both beloved and suspect. The poem opens:

> My house, my fairy
> palace, is
> of perishable

                    clapboards with
                  three rooms in all,
                      my gray wasps' nest
                  of chewed-up paper
                      glued with spit.

The description of an interior from this 1941 poem is in harmony
with other early poems, and yet here is the discordant wasps' nest
already, a prop with unavoidable symbolic cargo that turns up a continent and three-and-a-half decades later in the final lines of "Santarém," when Mr. Swan inquires "What's that ugly thing?" Even if
named in a voice in which, in Thomas Travisano's language, "bitterness almost chokes affection,"[29] the "fairy palace" isn't so far away in
substance from the magical burrow which the Brazilian river witch
enters as home in "The Riverman." The naive Jerónimo, a Cuban
patriot in exile, resembles the naive Manuelzinho, the servant of Bishop's poem of that name.

   In structure, "Jerónimo's House" is also a prototype for Bishop's
later dramatic monologues. Unlike other early poems, which when
they feature first-person narratives do so only in fantastic or mythic
form, this is the first of Bishop's poems to adopt a first-person speaker
apparently drawn from a man she knew. But the prosaic is mixed
evenly with something a little spooky and marvelous to both house
and owner, romantic mystery suffusing the penetration of its interior.
The poem closes:

                  At night you'd think
                      my house abandoned.
                  Come closer. You
                      can see and hear
                  the writing-paper
                      lines of light
                  and the voices of
                      my radio

                  singing flamencos
                      in between
                  the lottery numbers.
                      When I move
                  I take these things,
                      not much more, from
                  my shelter from
                      the hurricane.

A waif with "a love nest," Jerónimo is the first of Bishop's folk protagonists, both valiant and shabby, to inhabit a precarious household if not beyond the reach of mutability then at least tucked in against the storming, hurtful dark. Perhaps the poem owes the slightness and emotional thinness of its charm to its concentration on static description, or to a refusal to open out perspective. For the time being, in this mode, Bishop relies fairly little on dramatic narrative, or on subjectivising character, features that make the later poems with southern settings more compelling. Nor is the theme of the magic burrow, or the fertile, marsupial pocket, very much more than lightly etched. *North & South*, abounding in dream and fantasy landscape, alone among Bishop's books slights the description of places through full, loving, naturalistic detail. Yet long before Lowell's confessional poetry thrust the challenge of the historical and autobiographical as subject before Bishop, she moved toward that choice in three steps: first, toward the general structures inhabiting the world of her mind through poems that primarily take on the inner and allegorical world of the sleeper, of dream and fantasy; second, by moving toward description of the objects and places comprising her external world; and third, by electing the world of memory. The poems of *North & South* accept the first assignment in stationing, in which geography will be largely abstract and apparently impersonal, and move tentatively towards the second.

The very first poem in the book is "The Map," as if from the beginning Bishop has known that her interest in space and in geography is integral to her positioning herself in poetry and in the world. The first of several poems marking the New Year that Bishop would write or translate, the poem "was inspired when I was sitting on the floor, one New Year's Eve in Greenwich Village, after I graduated from college. I was staring at a map. The poem wrote itself." [30] It is not merely the exact delineation of physical property that will concern her in her explorations of global surface and the objects in motion upon it, but all the vibrating questions of depth and connection that lie behind a traveling or extending surface. In this first book of poems Bishop tests spatial metaphor as a means of recognizing both inner and outer dimensions, as through them she finds her way to both poetic and personal identity.

Travel is only partly the key to place in these poems: something more primitive and troubling is initially at the base of movement here, and the element of will and control between person and place that the word "travel" suggests skirts something vital in Bishop's movements, and in the engagement of her narrative with language in motion over space. While it is a commonplace to observe that travel is a Bishop theme, there is in reality only a limited correspondence between places traveled and places written up: a good deal of restless wandering never made it into either verse or prose. With few exceptions, the places she wrote about were not the places she was passing through, touring, but the places in which eventually she became a settler, or had been a settler, like Key West or Boston or New York or Nova Scotia or Brazil. While she named a whole collection *Questions of Travel* after a poem meditating on these concerns, travel in her poems largely remains the idea of travel. While titles and dedications have intense significance as Bishop's own framing device for the poems, the word "travel" has a faint whiff of the ironized, its motion partly concealing the more radical and unhappy meaning of motion contained within "homelessness," pointing as such a word quite painfully does towards the onset of her life as a virtual orphan.

If we look at her book titles, they dissolve in a series of acts of orientation, each more comprehensive than the last: first a pair of compass points, *North & South;* then *A Cold Spring,* including a temporal observation to suit an almanac; then the general rubric, *Questions of Travel;* then the last and third, yet more general and diffusing, *Geography III.* Each specific "travel" poem is always inscribed within a larger narrative, which is that of the anticipated, deferred or displaced home-coming; this is true even of the Brazilian series that might be said to begin with "Arrival at Santos" and conclude with "Santarém," a poem which finally gives up on Brazilian repatriation. Even in the early "Large Bad Picture" it is sunset and the ships have reached their harbor, and in the conclusion of the "Cape Breton" of 1949, "a man carrying a baby" is last seen heading for his "invisible house," while on down to 1975's "The End of March," during a beach walk, Bishop moves the protagonist both toward and away from a fancied home. With richness and complexity the poems take in the many points of the settlement of the spirit in its material housing. But grandly or simply, traverse is always the often magical, frequently troubled moment in which identity comes home, and in which domesticity has its hidden function. Perhaps for an alienated person making her condition her occasion, the domesticating impulse obscured within the word "travel" stands for our will to take on or absorb the strange, either as Other, or as Helen Vendler put it in her discussion of "The Moose," as the "Otherworldly."[31]

Possessed of a small amount of independent income, from her

graduation from Vassar in 1934 until taking up residence in Brazil in 1951, Bishop rarely lighted in one place for more than seasons at a time. Even including the years from 1938, when she bought the house in Key West with Louise Crane, she was still shuttling more or less between New York, Key West, and elsewhere. In 1934–35, she was intermittently in New York; in 1935, summering in Brittany, wintering in Paris. 1936 brought a visit to London, travel in North Africa and Spain; part of the winter of 1936–37 she spent on the west coast of Florida, then went fishing in Key West; then a tour in Ireland with friends, back to Paris for six months of 1937, and on to Provence and Italy. The fractions of years and seasons are dizzying: even after Bishop bought the house in Key West there were more trips, to North Carolina, to Nova Scotia, and to Mexico, more intermittent asthma and intensifying problems with alcohol.

Part of travel must have been stimulating, even exhilarating: yet in the early letters to Marianne Moore which represent her movements at their most bravura and engrossing, there are small admissions of discontent. She wasn't looking for local color in any ordinary sense; writing to Moore in 1935 from Douarnenez in Brittany she says:

> Douarnenez is too PICTURESQUE for much longer than a month — maybe even for that. The picturesqueness is just like the water in Salt Lake, you simply can't sink in it, it is so strong. I am afraid I am boring you with a long letter — but perhaps you would like to hear that the fishnets (it's a center of sardine fishing) are an acquamarine blue, so the fish can't see them when they sink in deep water.

The small and graspable detail of the colored net fades into the larger stimulus of Douarnenez. Some combination of the foreign and estranging if not the picturesque seems her necessity, an active marker roping off herself from her surround. But she writes in 1942 from a stay in Mexico:

> I am not so transfigured & upraised [by travel] that I didn't almost weep when your letter was handed to me. We had just been through a rather bad stretch, and any modern big city is depressing just at first.

And after thanking Moore for writing she describes what she must be in pursuit of as "that uneasy heightening of sensation that I think is really essential to travel!"

Travel was her *work* in the world; her tether to experience; its rigors could only prove the reality of her attachment to it. During these years before a manuscript is accepted for publication, and before any human connection within either work or love seems to yield either satisfaction or stability, she unburdens herself to Moore several times. In 1940, during the course of confessing a very great unease about her writing she says:

> I scarcely know why I persist at all – it is really fantastic to place so much on the fact that I have written a half-dozen *phrases* that I can still bear to re-read without too much embarassment. But I have that continuous uncomfortable feeling of "things" in the head like icebergs or rocks or awkwardly-shaped pieces of furniture – it's as if all the nouns were there but the verbs were lacking – if you know what I mean. And I can't help having the theory that if they are joggled around hard enough and long enough some bit of electricity will occur, just by friction, that will arrange everything – but you remember how Mallarme said that poetry was made of words, not ideas – and sometimes I'm terribly afraid I am approaching, or trying to approach it all from the wrong track.

Large, hard, integral and static, the inward iceberg, rock or furniture of words will not dislodge; but through a frantic and constant joggling there may be a chance that a galvanizing connection can be made. Motion or travel fixes images, sets them within the flux in which a view of space glides imperceptibly from extensivity on to duration and into the temporal, in a continuum toward history and away from geography. The urge to move and see around a thing in context, to place and measure through multiplying perspectives, seems a function of travel approximating time and yet denying its linearity: a warding off the wearying and dizzying moment of the homeless in which the world slides away, leaving one solitary, orphaned.

From within this state of siege Bishop wrote the poems of *North & South*. One of her very earliest poems to be published, "The Map" initially appeared in *Trial Balances*, the anthology in which Marianne Moore introduced the twenty-four-year-old poet. Placed on the opening page of *North & South*, the poem emphasizes that all representations of space are hopelessly allegorized. Perhaps the poem can be said to represent her answer to Mallarmé: that poems are made of words which are ideas-as-things. In that curious way that Bishop poems seem to possess, and through the force of that as yet unslaked desire to be stationed, to find the point at which the world stabilizes in welcome, the object of an abstracting representation itself turns steadily material.

Like the "Large Bad Picture," published over a decade after, the contracted bodies on the map are super-animate, brilliantly lit, and conspicuously touchable:

> Land lies in water; it is shadowed green.
> Shadows, or are they shallows, at its edges
> showing the line of long sea-weeded ledges
> where weeds hang to the simple blue from green.
> Or does the land lean down to lift the sea from under,
> drawing it unperturbed around itself?
> Along the fine tan sandy shelf
> is the land tugging at the sea from under?

As in other spatial descriptions, there is confusion about the relation of foreground and background, about top and bottom, depth and solidity. From the beginning, Bishop treats space in this poem as if it were both space and ideation about space. Almost as if seen from satellite distance, the countries are both actual map and actual country. If we squint at the edges of those earth bodies, do we see shadows, or a film of water? How is the land "in" water anyway: does it sag passively into its support, or is it subversively "tugging" at the sea, looking for a deeper bath? What should be said to be acting upon what?

All the questions are contained in neat boxes of doubled quatrains. In the second stanza, perturbation enters the form itself:

> The shadow of Newfoundland lies flat and still.
> Labrador's yellow, where the moony Eskimo
> has oiled it. We can stroke these lovely bays,
> under a glass as if they were expected to blossom,
> or as if to provide a clean cage for invisible fish.
> The names of seashore towns run out to sea,
> the names of cities cross the neighboring mountains
> —the printer here experiencing the same excitement
> as when emotion too far exceeds its cause.
> These peninsulas take the water between thumb and finger
> like women feeling for the smoothness of yard-goods.

And the quatrains with their tidy, infolded *abba* rhymes give way, not to resume until the third and final stanza. Giants erupt here, the "moony Eskimo" oiling the whole of Labrador, and "we," equally enlarged, stroking the toy bays. Next, in one of those deft and understated transformations, the sheen of the map surface hesitates between glaze and glass. Then, like a theatrical scrim, the slightly translucent page dissolves, blossoming to reveal the depth concealed behind the inanimate map, where in their clean cage vital and invisible fish are prowling. Excitement builds. The next lines are crucial:

> The names of seashore towns run out to sea,
> the names of cities cross the neighboring mountains
> — the printer here experiencing the same excitement
> as when emotion too far exceeds its cause.

Whose excitement is exceeding what cause? The lines are wonderfully suggestive, as Bishop exploits the distortion of scale, the slippage between mediums of representation. In picturing, or the mimesis of paint, "reality," or what's in front of us, is merely flattened and shrunk to fit on the recording canvas; in print, life contracts to abstract, non-mimetic symbol, but here in the funny world of map, mimesis sways between picture and sign, between flatness and depth, between what is out there, and what is in our minds about what is out there. Here in the poem, the print system doesn't fit: names run over the hidden towns out to sea and straggle over the neighboring mountains, failing to observe actual, drawn-to-scale boundaries. Our feelings about this spillover must parallel what we know of reading, naming and describing in other enterprises; there is a discrepancy between naming and picturing, between the object and its representation, a distance often governed by unruly desire. Shorn of rhyme and meter, and pumped up an extra three lines beyond its exclamatory dash, the middle stanza of this poem allows us to experience the discord between naming and having or being; we vibrate, in fact, not only between conventions of print and conventions of picture, but over the fact of border or boundary itself. Is it only the "printer" who feels the discord? Surely not. The stanza closes on an extravagant image of touch, as the shopper/peninsulas palp the waters between thumb and finger — testing the map's truths for strength, durability, and colorfastness. (Bishop's emphasis on the tactile seems only another way of closing the gap between boundaries, the hand closing on otherness, converting the strange into the familiar.)

The final stanza is almost sedate. The quatrains with the *abba* rhyme form return:

Mapped waters are more quiet than the land is,
lending the land their waves' own conformation:
and Norway's hare runs south in agitation,
profiles investigate the sea, where land is.
Are they assigned, or can the countries pick their colors?
—What suits the character or the native waters best.
Topography displays no favorites; North's as near as West.
More delicate than the historians' are the map-makers' colors.

In that apparently artless question beginning the second quatrain, Bishop explores the tentative nature of the connection between sign and experience, which our mind's recognitions alone force into being. In a chapter on maps from *Eccentric Spaces*, Robert Harbison points out:

> Maps say that each trip between the same two points is the same and suggest that if you have been to a place that is the end of it, something is achieved, so going back has no map meaning.

In short, "North's as near as West." Through these identities, Harbison says, we attain a certain liberty:

> A map reader's exhilaration comes from the sensation of not being tied to Place, of having broken the bonds of the local, and [. . .] what a sense of freedom it gives.

Further:

> places [. . .] must be pieced together at home, an effort which forces on the learner the truth that everyone's home is his own mind and looking at a map a way of pulling in the boundaries and gathering things up into himself. The perusal can be consuming indoor work that leaves him feeling like one of Beethoven's prisoners, startled by the daylight outside.[32]

And here we come upon that freedom to be wholly mental that winds up looking like bondage. In the world of the imprisoned narcissist, the imagined or thought-up space of the map is liable to induce what Bishop has described in another early poem as the Unbeliever's motion-sickness and paralysis, as he rides his mast high above a threatening sea. The mapmaker's colors are not only more delicate, they may be more fugitive than the historian's. While "The Map" provides an unforgettable parable on the relations between knowledge and travel, and between writing and being, this poem, and its neighbor travel allegory, "The Imaginary Iceberg" provide the impetus, the programmatic, or conceptual impulse, for the following books to be released from the world of abstraction and fantasy to enter a more external, particularized, and populous terrain. At some point the icebergs, rocks, and furniture of the 1940 letter to Moore set sail from their anchorage in the head. Beyond the two-point perspective of *North & South*, the poetry will curtail the hovering inwardness of the allegorical and fantastic, and begin the more outwardly naturalistic and detailed narratives. Within this first book Bishop is readying the perceptions, occasionally in only skeletal form, that will provide the underpinning for nearly all of her later work.

We might look at "The Imaginary Iceberg" as an ironic counterbalance to Kafka's image of the frozen sea, and our need to plumb our emotional depths:

> If the book we're reading doesn't wake us up with a blow on the head, what are we reading it for? [. . .] we need the books that affect us like a disaster, that grieve us deeply, like the death of someone we loved more than ourselves, like being banished into forests far from everyone, like a suicide. A book must be the axe for the frozen sea inside us.[33]

But in Bishop's view of the iceberg:

> This is a scene a sailor'd give his eyes for.
> The ship's ignored. The iceberg rises
> and sinks again; its glassy pinnacles
> correct elliptics in the sky.
> This is a scene where he who treads the boards
> is artlessly rhetorical. The curtain
> is light enough to rise on finest ropes
> that airy twists of snow provide.
> The wits of these white peaks
> spar with the sun. Its weight the iceberg dares
> upon a shifting stage and stands and stares.

Both transparent and impenetrable, an obstacle from within the sea that obstructs us from without, the splendid iceberg provides a parable for the untouchable and dangerous wealth of the mind's interior. Yet the poem, with its echo of Moore's 1924 piece, in which the mirroring and rapacious sea is also "A Grave," ends enigmatically:

> Like jewelry from a grave
> it saves itself perpetually and adorns
> only itself[. . .]

Good-bye, we say, good-bye, the ship steers off
where waves give in to one another's waves
and clouds run in a warmer sky.
Icebergs behoove the soul
(both being self-made from elements least visible)
to see them so: fleshed, fair, erected indivisible.

"We'd rather have the iceberg than the ship" may not be an especially smart choice; warmth is not something to be safely renounced, even for fair and indivisible erections, so it's a careful, non-axe-wielding good-by to them.

If in the theater of the imagination the self-made, solitary iceberg can beckon attractively, there is little doubt about the morality of opposing the Unbeliever's stance in Bishop's poem of the same name, another poem that continues her inquisitive probe into tilting perspective, binaries of depth and surface, of near and far points of view, of background and foreground, and of the external and internal territory of authority. A doubting immobility invades Bunyan's Unbeliever, who "sleeps on top of a mast"; his mind wandering in company with a cloud, "Secure in introspection," peering narcissistically at his watery reflection below. The message about the Unbeliever's distance is clear; while there is no language from Bishop to support an overt message about religious faith beyond the poem's brief reference to Bunyan, the Unbeliever's distant, frozen relation to sea and surface is dangerous, and unlikely to end well:

he sleeps on the top of his mast
with his eyes closed tight.
The gull inquired into his dream,
which was, "I must not fall.
The spangled sea below wants me to fall.
It is as hard as diamonds; it wants to destroy us all."

Ultimately, surface invites penetration, and the consciousness lying at depth, however dangerous, demands a waking acknowledgment.

Evaded consciousness, or dangerous feelings held at bay, seem the submerged subjects of the group of poems with a Paris setting. While Florida in the poem of that name is present in *North & South* as the place most rooted in the actual, and rooted in "Seascape, and "Little Exercise" as well, Paris is invoked merely by name and by interior. In a grouping of four poems, "Paris, 7 A.M.," "Quai d'Orléans," and the paired poems "Sleeping on the Ceiling" and "Sleeping Standing Up," the inward and subjective feel to the space is accompanied by no real interest in external description, and a very guarded interest in internal states. The precise spatial and temporal locations are odd indications of a displaced specificity, because the last thing that seems to interest Bishop in these poems is a description of the complex emotions and events assailing her during the months of residence that these poems represent. In the space of the Paris poems, the poet's state of mind can be approached only by a concentration on structure; on position, balance, antithesis and parallelism; all placement gives way to this focus.

As David Kalstone points out,[34] the writing of these poems occurred shortly after a terrifying car accident in France, in which Bishop and her friends Louise Crane and Margaret Miller, traveling to Paris from Burgundy, were forced off the road by a truck. The car in which they were riding overturned, and Margaret Miller's right arm was injured and subsequently amputated near the elbow. Margaret Miller was a painter. "It is heart-breaking," Bishop wrote to Moore, describing Miller's immediate efforts to learn to draw with her left hand. During the first months of Miller's convalescence the friends stayed in an apartment on the Quai d'Orléans, later joined by Miller's mother, to Bishop's discomfiture: "Mother-love," she wrote to Frani Blough, "isn't it awful. I long for an arctic climate where no emotions of any sort can possibly grow, always excepting disinterested 'friendship,' of course." Bishop herself, emotionally strained, was hospitalized for asthma for ten days.

Much as she treated a period of severe emotional crisis later in Washington by concentrating on precise notations of the geometry of the Capitol Dome in word and sketch, Bishop in Paris stayed with the noncommittal surface of buildings, bridges, and water-traffic. "Paris, 7 A.M.," stalls almost frighteningly in its inward-turning manipulation of geometrical figures, of star, rectangle, circle, and square, and in the tangles of its play with metaphors of infinite regress. Bitterly, it muses: "Winter lives under a pigeon's wing, a dead wing with damp feathers." Thought jams, unable or unwilling to tell forward from backward, as the speaker looks down into a courtyard, like the sea of the iceberg preserving externally a deadening interiority:

> Look down into the courtyard. All the houses
> are built that way, with ornamental urns
> set on the mansard roof-tops where the pigeons
> take their walks. It is like introspection

to stare inside, or retrospection,
a star inside a rectangle, a recollection:
this hollow square could easily have been there.
— The childish snow-forts, built in flashier winters,
could have reached these proportions and been houses;
the mighty snow-forts, four, five, stories high,
withstanding spring as sand-forts do the tide,
their walls, their shape, could not dissolve and die,
only be overlapping in a strong chain, turned to stone,
and grayed and yellowed now like these.

Snow-forts collapse into sand-forts, either giant children or pygmy adults live in these vertiginous structures graying and yellowing like teeth or bone, and looking more like mausoleum than house or monument, Bishop's other favored habitats.

Both of the paired poems "Sleeping on the Ceiling" and "Sleeping Standing Up," not very far into their lines, retreat to the indefinite landscape of dream. If we scrutinise the lines of "Sleeping Standing Up," a continuity of imagery still rises against the thematic discontinuity. Look at the final lines:

How stupidly we steered
until the night was past
and never found out where the cottage was.

The lines echo a trip in "The End of March" from *Geography III*, where a house is similarly inaccessible:

And that day the wind was much too cold
even to get that far,
and of course the house was boarded up.

Both of the Paris poems subvert the space in their titles; both substitute dream landscapes for the sleeper's bedroom, and thus discard and ignore the problematic interior space in which they open. The different treatment accorded the Florida poems demonstrates, perhaps, Bishop's own impatience with what she may have felt as the congealing abstraction of this early style: very shortly it will occur to her to move outdoors and welcome her natural territory.

The general preoccupations of *North & South* with positioning and dissolving internal and external perspectives, with reversing foreground and background, with fluid heights and depths, govern the monument in the poem of that title. "The Monument" seems born in some measure out of early dialogue with Eliot's "monuments" in "Tradition and the Individual Talent," yet Barbara Page finds another linkage more persuasive. Looking into two of the notebooks kept in Brazil by Linda Nemer, and referring to them as "The Key West Notebooks" because of their probable dates of composition, she outlines the poem's connection with Wallace Stevens' *Owl's Clover:*

> Midway in the notebook that opens with commentary on Stevens' Owl's Clover, (published in 1936), she produced a pen and ink sketch of the figure she would describe in her poem "The Monument," in its setting at the shore, preceded by a lined-off text reading, "Take a *frottage* [rubbing] of this sea." [. . .] In form and tone, Bishop's "Monument" answers Stevens' "Old Woman and the Statue" and "Mr. Burnshaw and the Statue," in *Owl's Clover* poems almost crushed by the burden of the past, in which mannered minds fend off the death of things in the impending night of cultural collapse. By contrast, Bishop's seaside monument visually and verbally builds a figure of undetermined possibilities by insisting not on the pre-established meaning of the thing but on the activity of making it, like a child at the shore unconcerned with the source of the flotsam incorporated in her sand castle.[35]

As in the Paris poems, the monument, "a figure of undetermined possibilities," remains ambiguous about where its inner space stops and where it starts. While in Page's sense the symbol may not be culturally or aesthetically overdetermined, Bishop's monument is difficult of access, and even more tellingly, the lines cannot locate for us whether the bones of the "artist-prince" being commemorated may reside "inside/or far away." A childlike sand architect released from portentous prophecy may be freer than Stevens' figure, yet the ramshackle puzzle of the monument's connection to its maker and making may be less playful than Page's metaphor suggests. The poem also contains the first occurrence of the motif of the empty grave so prominent in "2,000 Illustrations and a Complete Concordance," the poem of a later decade, in which the grave passes from its symbolic status as the terror of the shut self, and moves to a more ontological fear. Yet the drying monument is in a clearly transitional stage of significant promise "much better than real sea or sand or cloud":

> It chose that way to grow and not to move.
> The monument's an object, yet those decorations,
> carelessly nailed, looking like nothing at all,
> give it away as having life, and wishing;
> wanting to be a monument, to cherish something.
> [. . .]

It may be solid, may be hollow.
The bones of the artist-prince may be inside
or far away on even drier soil.
But roughly but adequately it can shelter
what is within (which after all
cannot have been intended to be seen).
It is the beginning of a painting,
a piece of sculpture, or poem, or monument,
and all of wood. Watch it closely.

1939's "The Monument" is not ready for the "abidance" of art in 1972's "Poem," but its rough adequacies, "splintery sunlight," and "long-fibred clouds" do house that future possibility.

Bishop's originality is not premised on the absence of repetition or interlocking in her themes and figures; the signs of her unique preoccupations hang over each line of her poems, and yet have their own system of interrelations. Bird in relation to flight, prophet in relation to believer, flesh in relation to spirit, poet in relation to poem — the potential readings in the poems are many and various, but very early all are pegged on questions of space and position.

When we look at the title of "Quai d'Orléans," published in 1938, we might think it a possible exception to the non-naturalistic treatment of place because the title sounds so specific. Concentrating on a single facet of description, the poem opens with an extended figure:

Each barge on the river easily tows
    a mighty wake,
a giant oak-leaf of gray lights
    on duller gray;
and behind it real leaves are floating by,
    down to the sea.
Mercury-veins on the giant leaves,
    the ripples, make
for the sides of the quai, to extinguish themselves
    against the walls
as softly as falling-stars come to their ends
    at a point in the sky.

But even in this poem, the emphasis turns inward dizzyingly, to a dreamy subjectivizing, as the protagonist stands stone-still to watch "light and nervous water hold/ their interview." Twice, the poet tells us that the leaves, the small leaves, that she watches drift away are "real" — but when the nonreal leaves of the waves "extinguish" themselves against the walls of the quai, the speaker sees this process like "falling-stars come to their ends/ at a point in the sky." "Real" leaves, and the backwash of a river barge making waves like leaves, leaves which in turn are disconcertingly like stars, all disappear "modestly, down the sea's dissolving halls." In this passage, the glance downward into a river becomes a glance upward into the sky; space stands on its head, and identity and scale are subverted as leaf movement turns both solid and fluid, both small as oak leaves and large as a barge's wash downriver. The speaker turns to assure her companion of the longevity of these "leaves"; but change and mutability sternly refuse to permit the subject to fix a landscape of objects in which we are enough at home to name them familiarly, locally. Kalstone's summary of this poem feels right: "It is colored," he remarks, "by all the losses the accident entailed and recalled, though none of them is specifically its subject: her friend's mutilation; her own childhood losses; the loss of self-control and surge of vulnerability she experienced when Miller's mother appeared."[36]

While the poems in *North & South* may shy away from personal exposure, the poems maintain a dense network of interconnection; "From the Country to the City" has Bishop's recognizable interest in close observation, as the poem brings a visual effect into philosophical contact with time and motion. The poem asks, what really happens in our visual field to the line down the center of the road when we are driving? What do we really see when the telephone wires streak past us: "Flocks of short, shining wires seem to be flying sidewise./ Are they birds?" It's almost as if Bishop wants to test out the High Romantic themes of vision and imagination pragmatically. Keeping the traditional focus on the relations of self and matter, of ordinary earth in relation to extraordinary heaven, the prosaic in relation to the sublime, she exercises her thematic legs while testing her own perceptions rigorously.

Blake described the absorbed attentiveness of the poet as a matter of being secretary to the Imagination, but for Elizabeth Bishop, in twentieth-century reaction to nineteenth-century excesses of poetic ardor, something less passive and farther from the postures of submission or adoration is needed. "Queen Elizabeth, in the newsreels," she wrote to her friends the Barkers, in one of those throwaway moments of observation when she was obviously just tuning up her prose, "waves like someone unscrewing an electric light bulb." This is not a passage which will or should appear later in a poem. It is simply here in a letter because the poet reflexively observes and translates the relations between things and people.

But some of these early poems, in part perhaps because of their too-rigorous repressions of the personal, stay too close to exercise. It is only in the richer, less worked, less clever poems, that Bishop's almost obsessive interest in mechanical positioning subsides sufficiently to gain her other resonances. Although smoothness of style and clean articulation of parts characterise Bishop's poetry from start to finish, and the overall level of the published work is unusually high, no poet seems entirely free from an apprenticeship to the muse. In this first, conspicuously brilliant book, a younger artist is still trying out her equipment with a disciplined, if perhaps overly methodical, intelligence.

"Florida," the first of the poems in *North & South* to break away from fantasy and allegory as the dominant mode, and to emphasize the naturalistic details of description, is still a poem which could be read as *paysage moralisé*, something in the style of Marianne Moore's "Virginia Britannica." But the details climax in a drama all of Bishop's own.

Her poem begins by announcing a quality it will certainly subvert through irony:

> The state with the prettiest name,
> the state that floats in brackish water,
> held together by mangrove roots
> that bear while living oysters in clusters,
> and when dead strew white swamps with skeletons,
> dotted as if bombarded, with green hummocks
> like ancient cannon-balls sprouting grass.

The contrast between the first and second lines is extreme. From the second line on, Bishop stakes out Florida's territory as dead, dying, and imprisoned, and does so largely through adjectives. The harsh and somber adjectives do not diminish the force and betrayed beauty of the nouns, or names of the objects, however, that decorate this pretty Florida:

> The tropical rain comes down
> to freshen the tide-looped strings of fading shells:
> Job's Tear, the Chinese Alphabet, the scarce Junonia,
> parti-colored pectins and Ladies' Ears,

arranged as on a gray rag of rotted calico,
the buried Indian Princess's skirt;
with these the monotonous, endless, sagging coast-line
is delicately ornamented.

Not a woman to be frightened by a build-up of predicates, Bishop sets her list of shells down on that "gray rag of rotted calico," and continues unrelentingly to establish her picture of ornament in the face of decay. There is an intermission of white space here, and then the next actors, the buzzards appear—"Thirty or more buzzards are drifting down, down, down,/ over something they have spotted in the swamp,"—and then daylight finishes. The poem works to its grim conclusion.

For the first time, a landscape is full of the specificity and colorful precision that characterise the later Bishop in Brazilian or Nova Scotian settings. It is also the first poem for which Bishop tested some of its images in prose first: an unpublished sketch called "Waiting for the Mail in Florida" ends with the buzzard image opening the second section of the poem. It would not be the last time that Bishop used the elaborations of prose to bring a subject to the mind's surface. Yet one of the effects of the determined anthropomorphizing, the human dress-up that makes birds hysterical, tanagers embarrassed, and turtles helpless and mild, is to call in, once again, the shadow of the allegorical—just as the determinedly allegorical "The Map" subverted Bishop's genre intentions through its material description: genre in Bishop sits on the fence, her ingenuity always teased by latent possibility. In "Florida" we find ourselves asking, are these really only birds and animals that Bishop is talking about? These lines hint at further observations not explicitly spelled out in the poem:

Cold white, not bright, the moonlight is coarse-meshed,
and the careless, corrupt state is all black specks
too far apart, and ugly whites; the poorest
postcard of itself.

Remembering that this poem was first published in 1939, and written during the Depression, it is hard not to suppose it a commentary on more than animal manners, the metaphor of black and white halftone reproduction with its low lighting aimed at something besides postcards. That overwhelmed earth spirit, the "buried Indian Princess," is another oblique support for the theme of "the careless, corrupt state." In the poem's conclusion, with her five distinct calls including "friendliness, love, mating, war, and a warning," the alligator after moonrise turns into a supplicant who "whimpers and speaks in the throat/ of the Indian Princess." An early Bishop primitive forecasting the presence of her Brazilian kin: here merely an original citizen forlornly destined for better things.

In spite of frequent and brilliant aperçus calling on a naturalist's accuracy of observation, in this first collection, the poet is more preoccupied with testing whether or not there *is* a real landscape. There is a clear strain of interrogation: are all landscapes internal? Perhaps in the first flush, or fresh terror, of writing, surface is too little to be trusted to be merely described; we should take seriously the proposition about surface held by "The Unbeliever":

> "I must not fall.
> The spangled sea below wants me to fall.
> It is as hard as diamonds; it wants to destroy us all."

Before we set sail there are truths that we have to know about the sea on which we are to navigate. We are reminded again that in "The Imaginary Iceberg," Bishop says "We'd rather have the iceberg than the ship,/ although it meant the end of travel." Like the Unbeliever locked precariously in his dreams, "This iceberg cuts its facets from within." "Within" needs a great deal of isolated, if abstracting, attention in these early poems. But before the description of that inner space can be completely dared, its boundaries have to be paced and measured from the outside first. It is as if identity itself were so uncertain that each new effort at the presentation of reality called on the need to speak the boundaries over and over, reconstituting them before the shaky self could be trusted to put down foot in front of foot, and know its own name.

For a World
"Minute and vast and clear"

ELIZABETH BISHOP'S work demands that we look at how representation of the people and places of her life were part of her intense concern with representation itself: with drawing correspondences between word and experience, with the curious thingness of language, and with the question of accurate likeness-taking. Bishop's pragmatism, her gifts as an anatomist of appearance and sensation, as well as her treatment of her life as subject, should be firmly linked to the characterization of her work by Jarrell and others as a pursuit of the exact and the descriptive. Such a pursuit led Bishop to a special relation to the visual arts, manifested first as an intense curiosity about surrealism, and then, that interest fading, as an enduring concern with paintings and art objects as paradigmatic of her own relation to poetry.

Quite apart from any role that any single painter can be said to have played in her poetry, her connection to picture-making was direct, intense, and prolonged; she was both a maker and collector of pictures and objects throughout the whole of her life. We can catch glimpses of this involvement through her letters, from the frottages in the manner of Max Ernst that she reports sending to Marianne Moore, to the comic descriptions of herself as painter in competition with her Brazilian cook, on down to the older self that made a box in homage to Joseph Cornell. Various examples of her painting also survive in possession of her heirs, and as covers for her books. Interviews early and late also stress the pleasure she took in finding and acquiring pieces of folk art. Miss Bishop in the world of her hand-worked birdcages, heirloom paintings, antique Bahian gilt mirrors, and beside the carved wood of a large ship's figurehead, was clearly a find for those who believe in the extension of the mental through the material and visible.

The poems are full of movement. Still, there are moments, when through the art of her description, the poems themselves function almost as objects. Set firmly in their spaces, with very few poems attempting to use flashback or sharp breaks in time, they unroll across the unified surface of a map, follow the trajectory of a storm, or curve around a seashore, their canvas of expression unfolding with a strong directional sense, across a landscape or the surface of an object or animal from top to bottom by means of long, steady tracking shots. Bishop relies on enumeration, on stationing her redbud beside her dogwood, her deer beside a fence, or on counting and turning over her successive tropical leaves; she paints with color, indicates size and scale, illumination, and shadow, and depends on a strongly developed sense of the tactile. All of her observations appear in a logical and usually unbroken traverse of the poem's field. While the speakers of poems from "The Man-Moth" on through to "In the Waiting Room" may pause in vertigo, their dizzying homelessness is always at variance with the relatively stable spatial envelope of the poem.

Why this should be so seems a consequence of Bishop's determination to build substance from within the perpetually elusive and insubstantial sign. The ultimate realist, she aims to load and counterweight the always unsatisfactory immateriality of the poem and its inevitably symbolic nature with a vigorous spread of the sensory and immediate: with the goods of observation. Like the painter she occasionally became, Bishop as poet dealt with the problem of illusionism created by the act of reading common to both poetry and painting. The page is a way station, a port. Reading, one wants to fall through the print on the paper, to penetrate its light scrim, behind whose features through some peculiar method of evocation are suddenly located an interior body state, which is literally neither here nor there, but in some spaceless energy of mind, created by mind, off page. Bishop's fascination with objects, with the visual look and feel of existence, again and again calls up this questionable relation between internal and external, between depth and surface authenticity.

A poet generally compelled by mutability, by changing weathers, dissolving landscapes, and flooding memory, her skills are most often revealed in the difficult marriage of physically dimensionless language to a shifting, dimensional world. Like the Man-Moth seeking the moon in Bishop's poem of the same name, writing is a broad investigation of surface to which the poet is helplessly but quite heroically committed:

> He thinks the moon is a small hole at the top of the sky,
> proving the sky quite useless for protection.
> He trembles, but must investigate as high as he can climb.
>
> Up the facades,
> his shadow dragging like a photographer's cloth behind him,
> he climbs fearfully, thinking that this time he will manage
> to push his small head through that round clean opening
> and be forced through, as from a tube, in black scrolls on the light.

The Man-Moth fails, but the black scrolls of the poet are the record of his partial success. As Bishop saw it in "Objects & Apparitions," her translation of Octavio Paz's tribute to Joseph Cornell, both language and object meet in a glancing state of equality in their reflection of the enduring inner world:

> The apparitions are manifest,
> their bodies weigh less than light,
> lasting as long as this phrase lasts.
>
> Joseph Cornell: inside your boxes
> my words became visible for a moment.

Symbol-making, for Bishop, was always both verbal and pictorial.

The firm connection to the visual arts engages more than a single question of influence, a question, for instance, of how she may have dealt at the outset of her career with the surrealist Max Ernst or later with the box-maker Joseph Cornell. Rather, we need to ask first how Bishop treated vision itself. In her work, against what her sharp eyes see, she holds in disturbing and provocative tension what the body feels and what the mind knows and remembers. Two interrelated concerns, the problematic shifts between external and internal realities, and the problem of illusionism, of the relevance of representations of space in the largely nonspatial, nonphysical medium of the lyric poem, haunt her. In her strange man-moths, pulsating weeds, and in the feral activity of her maps, lighthouses, monuments, snails, sandpipers, and paper balloons, she makes stubbornly visible the elusive and strange richness in much of what we blindly label the ordinary and the plainly domestic. In that estrangement of the familiar she invites comparison with the surrealists.

In "Elizabeth Bishop's Surrealist Inheritance," Richard Mullen offered the first, and to date most extensive, treatment of Bishop and the visual arts. Mullen focuses at least as much on Bishop's divergence from surrealist practice as on her apparent submissions to its directives. The most important difference he identifies as Bishop's focus on objects; for Breton and other surrealists, "there were no objects, only subjects. They had no interest in the natural world per se." For Bishop, says Mullen, the "strangeness of our subjective selves, the queer struggle between conscious and unconscious, is projected outward into a world where the 'thingness of things' dominates."[37]

In persuasive detail Mullen shows how Bishop shared with the surrealists a conviction about the importance of the disjunctive relations between our sleeping and waking minds, and a copious use of techniques of dissociation and displacement in description. Inversions and enlargements of scale, sudden and surprising shifts in point of view through personification, and an always subtle, but pervasive emphasis on dreamscape, mark her work from first to last. "I use dream material whenever I am lucky enough to have any," she wrote to Anne Stevenson in March 1963.

Mullen demonstrates at length how two poems drew directly and substantially from surrealist sources. In his correspondence with Bishop, she acknowledged, if a little dismissively, her wide reading of surrealist poetry and prose, including Francis Ponge. In comparing her prose poem, "Giant Snail" with Ponge's "Snails" from Le Parti Pris des Choses, Mullen flags some striking parallels in language and imagery between the two texts. Of her acquaintance with surrealist graphic art, Bishop writes: "I didn't know any of the surrealist writers or painters — I just met 2 or 3 painters, that's all." Mullen points out that she owned an early edition of Max Ernst's Histoire Naturelle; Bishop also acknowledges that the technique of frottage that Ernst illustrates therein produced her poem, "The Monument."

In the process of frottage, or rubbing, which Ernst described as an "optical excitant of somnolent vision," the artist placed paper across wood or other surfaces and objects, and then rubbed away at the paper with blacklead. The subsequent drawing produced the "optical excitant," or object for meditation, which produced further drawings: "the drawings thus obtained steadily lose, thanks to a series of suggestions and transmutations occurring to one spontaneously—the character of the material being studied—wood—and assume the aspect of unbelievably clear images of a nature probably able to reveal the first cause of the obsession or to produce a simulacrum thereof." Ernst invented frottage after a revery into the hours of childhood, when he remembered staring at an imitation mahogany panel across from his bed at naptime.

Bishop, who may have been sympathetically drawn not only by the technique but by the childhood source of it, was soon manufacturing *frottages* at a great rate, and as she wrote to Marianne Moore rather mockingly, "I can turn them out by the dozen now and shall send you one." But her poem "The Monument" offers more direct evidence of this new pastime. Like Ernst's *frottages*, Bishop's verbal exercise uses its wooden sea-surface as springboard into a meditation on the strange space of art's reality, both within and without, penetrable and impenetrable, curiously living and dead, material and immaterial. The poem describes an allegorized object standing in for the artist's relation to the world:

> The monument is one-third set against
> a sea; two-thirds against a sky.
> The view is geared
> (that is, the view's perspective)
> so low there is no "far away,"
> and we are far away within the view.
> A sea of narrow, horizontal boards
> lies out behind our lonely monument,
> its long grains alternating right and left
> like floor-boards—spotted, swarming-still,
> and motionless. A sky runs parallel,
> and it is palings, coarser than the sea's:
> splintery sunlight and long-fibred clouds.

Within the shifting perspectives of the monument,

> The bones of the artist-prince may be inside
> or far away on even drier soil.
> But roughly but adequately it can shelter
> what is within (which after all
> cannot have been intended to be seen).
> It is the beginning of a painting,

> a piece of sculpture, or poem, or monument,
> and all of wood. Watch it closely.

In the play of its altering pronouns, moving freely between singular and plural, and in working out the drama of its dialectical voices, the poem exploits the work of art's peek-a-boo vantages vis-à-vis perceiver, perceived, and the idea of perception itself. Past her twenties, Bishop never did anything quite so programmatically allegorical again.

Mullen puts his finger decisively on the growing causes for Bishop's dissatisfaction with surrealism. There are generally four reasons: first, the surrealist lack of interest in the natural object; second, the surrealist privileging of the realm of the unconscious over the conscious (Bishop records them as fluctuating in dominance but equal in importance); third, their emphasis on the revolutionary impact of disintegrating orders of perception (Bishop concerned herself with a balanced dialectic between associative and dissociative powers of perception); and fourth, the surrealist lack of faith in conventional language and logic.

But we ought not overlook the generally youthful character of Bishop's experiments with surrealism. While her preoccupation with oneiric imagery only deepened throughout a working life in poetry, her eventual resistance to surrealist practice came openly to the surface in several ways. In 1946, in a letter to Ferris Greenslet, her editor at Houghton Mifflin, she rushes in to avert a public association with Max Ernst by way of jacket copy.[38] In some obvious distress she writes: "In the letter that Marianne Moore wrote for me she commented on some likeness to the painter Max Ernst. Although many years ago I once admired one of Ernst's albums I believe that Miss Moore is mistaken about his ever having been an influence, and since I have disliked all of his painting intensely and am not a surrealist I think it would be misleading to mention my name in connection with his."

By the early 1960s, after acknowledging Ernst's role in the composition of "The Monument," Bishop was still busy trying to stamp out all talk of influence. In January 1964 she writes to Anne Stevenson: "You mention Ernst again. Oh dear — I wish I'd never mentioned him at all, because I think he's a dreadful painter." But her general antagonism was already visible in unpublished notebooks of the thirties and forties. In one jotting she writes: "Semi-surrealist poetry terrifies me because of the sense of irresponsibility & [indecipherable] [wild?][39]

danger it gives of the mind being 'broken down' — I want to produce the opposite effect." Somewhat later, in notes about her reading of an episode from Crevecoeur,[40] she says, under the heading of "Tact & Embarrassment": "Why in 'Letters From an American Farmer' does it *embarrass* one when he speaks of the wasp on the child's eyelid, etc.? The whole story of the wasp-nest is fantastic, surrealistic, we'd say now. Is surrealism just a new method of dealing bold-facedly with what is embarrassing? Only for sadism, accounts of atrocities, etc., *embarrassing* as well as horrifying?"

While some readers may want to poke around for a bit longer in that area that Bishop calls the *embarrassing*, regarding her alarmed reticence as embarrassingly close to blind repression, the comments are clear indication of how Bishop's love of indirection and obliquity swerved from the surrealist adoption of those traits. In later years, though, as her own work increasingly risked emotional disclosure both more erotic and more violently painful, we can only guess at the class of judgments that supervened. On June 23, 1950, a brief diary entry still probes at the embarrassing: "Embarrassment always comes from some falsity – the situation, manners, or a work of art – (I suffer from it now so horribly) – & that's why sometimes the strangest little detail of reality – something *real* coming along like a piece of wood bobbing on the waves – will provide an almost instant relief from it." There is a notable persistence in Bishop's attaching morality, and manners, to the real.

"Embarrassing" was an interesting word to apply to the passage from Crevecoeur, probably the following:

> In the middle of my new parlour I have, you may remember, a curious republic of industrious hornets; their nest hangs to the cieling [sic], by the same twig on which it was so admirably built and contrived in the woods. Its removal did not displease them, for they find in my house plenty of food; and I have left a hole open in one of the panes of the window, which answers all their purposes. By this kind usage they are become quite harmless; they live on the flies, which are very troublesome to us throughout the summer; they are constantly busy in catching them, even on the eyelids of my children. It is surprising how quickly they smear them with a sort of glue, lest they might escape, and when thus prepared, they carry them to their nests, as food for their young ones.

With the same bizarre and misplaced love of animal and insect lore that leads the Farmer to fuse both flies, children, and eyelids in the pronoun "them," he then describes the materials of the hornet nest, and goes on with the same thorough zeal to describe the nests of the wasp. Bishop may be uneasy at the nonchalance with which the Farmer offers up his parlor and his children to the study of stinging insects; in this case intellectual curiosity has its sadistic edge, and the unconscious amorality of his study results in something Bishop calls "surreal." Perhaps what she rejects in the surrealist breakdown is a fidelity to unconscious process that is too swiftly unhitched from ethical coding. From this point of view, shame for the species is something that a display of vice evokes; the Farmer, usually an appealing character, is someone whose ethical lapse embarrasses. He lets down the side: an action that an implied *we* must never permit ourselves. These staunch manners are seductive; insofar as they lead to the belief that if we don't talk about things like sadism and atrocity they're very likely to go away, however, such manners are troubling.

Curiously enough, the justification for Bishop's conservative habits, her fondness for conventional, traditional poetic forms, her comfort and dexterity in original deployments of conventional logic and conventional syntactical arrangements, could be found within the licensing procedures of surrealism itself. When Max Ernst looks for those prior forms of nature hidden within the wood grain, which are bidden to rise from it by the collusive mind, he reveals his belief in the fusion through art of the external, objective order and the internal, subjective order of the perceiving mind. He rides the wood grain to arrive at first causes, or at least at a "simulacrum thereof"; when Bishop rides what she was pleased to call the "umpty, umpty-um" of her habitual metric, she no doubt expected the same conclusion. The forms of the conventional sestina, villanelle, sonnet, and the beats of conventional prosody served as the old lumber stacked in the poetry room that a modern practitioner might find useful, much as a surrealist might shred newsprint and old theater programs for his collages. Ultimately, both share the same faith in the congruence and continuity of mind and matter, and the same faith in their homologous structures, although Bishop and the surrealists differed in their opinion of the angle of access at which the body of experience should be drilled.

Anyone looking over Bishop's early drafts for her villanelle, "One Art," would find the same uncanny leap, blooming magically from the mechanical devising of rhymes, that the armature of the wood grain provided for Ernst in his passage from wood to image in his final drawings. In Draft 1 of Bishop's villanelle, there is a sprawling list of items that constitutes the raw matrix of perception. In Draft 2, through the clear urgencies of rhyme, the materials have reconstituted themselves, like the iron filings around a magnet, to follow Ezra Pound's image of creation, forming the rose in the steel dust, or the nearly completed poem. The almost kinetic pressure of the transmuting leap from the emotional tangles of the subjective into the "objective" requirements of the villanelle can be tracked on these two pages. When Bishop stares hard at the fortuitous misprint of "man-moth" for mammoth in a newspaper, and dreams up the strange and marvellous Man-Moth, she seems to respond to the same kind of "optical excitant" that for Max Ernst, staring hard, had produced the ribald drawings of his father from the turns of the wood grain in that fake mahogany panel. For Bishop, the poem that resulted is saturated with other-worldly dream magic, fully as strange and rather more engaging than the more consciously elicited "Monument."

Bishop's frottages, done by the dozens, seem equal to a variety of other experiments, including the one from her Vassar years that involved eating Roquefort cheese at bedtime, or spending half the night in a tree, to produce the right kind of dreams.[41] Bishop's empiricism is the overriding point here: surrealism with its games, devices, and new orthodoxies offered an intriguing field of exploration to a young intelligence discovering and testing the limits of consciousness and interested in lowering the fence between nighttime dreaming and daytime knowing.

For the surrealists, there should be no conscious, directing self boxed within a particular discipline, and overtly controlling the seismograph of the dream, or waking reverie. In explaining frottage, Ernst says:

> The procedure of *frottage*, resting thus upon nothing more than the intensification of the irritability of the mind's faculties by appropriate technical means, excluding all conscious mental guidance (of reason, taste, morals), reducing to the extreme the active part of that one whom we have called, up to now, the "author" of the work, this procedure is revealed by the following to be the real equivalent of that which is already known by the term *automatic writing*. It is as a spectator that the author assists, indifferent or passionate, at the birth of his work and watches the phases of its development.[42]

But the proposed style of Ernst's watching, his frankly erotic passion, seems not what Bishop ever had in mind, nor is his other choice, indifference, any more to her liking.

Ernst's quotations from Leonardo da Vinci's *Treatise on Painting* offer a more promising common line of descent, however. August 1925 finds Ernst musing on the exchanges between Botticelli and Leonardo recorded in the *Treatise*. Speaking with contempt of the "short and mediocre investigation" that produces landscape, Botticelli says "by throwing a sponge soaked with different colors against a wall one makes a spot in which may be seen a beautiful landscape." With ingenuous innocence, Leonardo picks up the stain of the sponge and makes another use of the example: "in such a daub one may certainly find bizarre inventions. I mean to say that he who is disposed to gaze attentively at this spot may discern therein some human heads, various animals, a battle, some rocks, the sea, clouds, groves, and a thousand other things—it is like the tinkling of the bell which makes one hear what one imagines."

The example with its powerful, stimulant synesthesia is wonderful—Ernst mentally tucks away the little scene with its description of projective techniques and finds it erupting for him in his own discovery of the technique of frottage. Yet as he quotes the passage at length, he includes all of Leonardo's cautious injunctions on the need for keen observation based on knowledge; while "full advantage" must be taken of the painter's imaginative ability, from within, to supply form to an external visual stimulus, Leonardo also remarks: "In these confused things genius becomes aware of new inventions, but it is necessary to know well (how to draw) all the parts that one ignores, such as parts of animals and the aspects of landscape, rocks and vegetation."

This respect for the mind's capacity to perceive and record a something out there and apart from us is certainly one Bishop shared centuries later. Yet belief in the mind's kinship with ultimate forms, in a belief that sees the grammar of consciousness as a reflection of the active grammar of being, and one in which flesh and spirit are read correctly as in enduring junction, seems part of a project intermittently but powerfully shared by Renaissance and surrealist painters, and modernist poets alike. In the terms of High Romanticism, it is also the junction that William Wordsworth describes as what we half perceive and half create, in that marriage of self and world which he seized on as the high ground of the poetic mission. A marriage, we might add, in which what the self knows and what the self sees exist in fertile and expansive interconnection.

In a further passage that Ernst quotes from Andre Breton, there is more discussion of what amounts to the union of objective and subjective states of knowing. Speaking of Leonardo, Breton says:

Leonardo's lesson, setting his students to copy in their pictures that which they saw taking shape in the spots on an old wall (each according to his own lights) is far from being understood. The whole passage from subjectivity to objectivity is implicitly resolved there, and the weight of that resolution goes far beyond, in human interest, the weight of inspiration itself. Surrealism has been most particularly concerned with that part of the lesson.[43]

Breton, again as quoted by Ernst, goes on to remark that the new associations of images engendered by poet, artist, and scientist echo Leonardo's original exercise, and use "a screen of a particular structure which, concretely, can be either a decrepit wall, a cloud or anything else: a persistent and vague sound carries to the exclusion of all others, the phrase we need to hear."

It is in the slippages of these examples from ear to eye, from that "either," and the bonelessness of that "anything else," that we come upon the difference between Bishop, empiricist of the senses who would never scant or blur the contours of the enabling agency, and the true surrealist. Breton's next observation about surrealist association, however, firmly connects his thinking to a Wordsworthian romanticism, looking as it does very like Wordsworth's famous "wise passiveness," or John Keats' "Negative Capability": "The most striking fact is that an activity of this kind which in order to exist necessitates the unreserved acceptance of a more or less lasting passivity, far from being limited to the sensory world, has been able to penetrate profoundly the moral world." The sentences that conclude Ernst's quotation are passionately eloquent, as they enlarge upon this point:

Some day, man will be able to direct himself if, like the artist, he will consent to reproduce, without changing anything, that which an appropriate screen can offer him in advance of his acts. This screen exists. Every life contains some of these homogeneous entities, of cracked or cloudy appearance, which each of us has only to consider fixedly in order to read his own near future. He should enter the whirlwind, he should retrace the stream of events which, above all others, seemed to him doubtful or obscure and by which he was harassed. There—if his interrogation is worth the effort—all the logical principles will be routed and the powers of the *objective hazard*, making a joke of all probability, will come to his aid. On this screen, everything which man wants to know is written in phosphorescent letters, in letters of *desire*.

In his seminal essay on the poetry of Marianne Moore, Hugh Kenner disputes the lineage that would move from Wordsworth to

Ruskin; he claims active perception over wise passivity for Ruskin. But whether Ruskin is or is not firmly connected to Wordsworth, he does articulate an alternate literary tradition in English, and one preoccupied with accurate visual description not as a screen but as a map to moral understanding. On the way to Marianne Moore, Bishop's predecessor as a champion describer, Kenner quotes Ruskin:

> The greatest thing a human soul ever does in this world is to see something, and tell what it saw in a plain way. Hundreds of people can talk for one who can think, but thousands can think for one who can see. To see clearly is poetry, prophecy and religion all in one.[44]

In Kenner's transcription of this, perception is "a moral act, and exfoliates legitimately into moral reflections."

As this tradition precedes the exuberant surrealist interrogation of the gazing eye itself, and favors the work of the conscious mind, it clearly offers Bishop, distrustful of the mind broken down or ransacked for perceptual provender, a better rationale for trusting the experience of the eye. Nonetheless, in her latter years, that process of breaking down the self came back to haunt her definition of the poet's job, as she developed her own style for trusting the experience of a self probingly approaching its own dismantling for a better view of viewing. In Bishop's much-cited January 1964 letter to Anne Stevenson,[45] from within Bishop's curious and provocative description of Darwin at his labors, there is a moment of dream life, close to trance, that moves us back into the vicinity of surrealism.

Most readers of Bishop sooner or later pick up this letter, in which a critical fusion is made between sleeping and waking, conscious and unconscious intelligence, and which uses the scientist Darwin as its creator model. "There is no split," Bishop declares, between art and science, or apparently between dreaming and waking:

> There is no "split." Dreams, works of art (some), glimpses of the always-more-successful surrealism of everyday life, unexpected moments of empathy (is it?) catch a peripheral vision of whatever it is one can never really see full-face but that seems enormously important. I can't believe we are wholly irrational (and I do admire Darwin!) But reading Darwin, one admires the beautiful solid case being built up out of his endless heroic *observations*, almost unconscious or automatic – and then comes a sudden relaxation, a forgetful phrase, and one *feels* the strangeness of his undertaking, sees the

lonely young man, his eyes fixed on facts and minute details, sinking or sliding giddily off into the unknown. What one seems to want in art, in experiencing it, is the same thing that is necessary for its creation, a self-forgetful, perfectly useless concentration.

Art and science pour forth from the same dream of reality; they issue from the same cleavage, or sink, or slide from between the dry land of what we already know and the wet depth of what we are about to discover.

The letter also posits for Darwin the same tranced passivity as for Ernst's spectator artist, assisting at the birth of his work. Yet there seems such a distance from the surrealist accoucheur making jokes of probability and casting up those phosphorescent letters of desire. Bishop's "self-forgetful" concentration seems deliberately there to displace narrow self-interest: she premises a "self-forgetful, perfectly useless concentration" on the same mold-shattering, code-breaking experience, radical in its implications, in which the world is revised and reread, but the emphasis is not on seizure, or on mastery of this new world, but on the transformative vision. What Bishop and Moore both seem to reject is the masculine, imperialist process of "interrogating" experience. As Kenner sees the operative distinction between Ruskin and Moore, Moore honors the otherness of her subjects; they are not cannibalized, or subsumed into her objects of knowledge. Bishop and Moore, both marginalized as women, were exempted from a certain amount of that trying on of the vatic mantle. Sideliners in the battle for placement on the heights of Olympus, they were urged less to declare themselves in obedient or antagonistic relation to the forefathers, and toward the products of Ruskin's "seeing" as "poetry, prophecy, and religion all in one." As Helen MacNeil put it recently, "Bishop's necessary distance, not from tradition but from its traditionally male prophetic burden, may partly account for her famously unplaceable style."[46]

Leery of that emphasis on the prophetic self, fearful or skeptical of the rolls and turns of the ego sought for in disintegration, in a "dérèglement de tous les sens," and deeply suspicious of selves promoting interest through a parading of weakness, Bishop increasingly displayed a stubborn allegiance to the physical world and its inexplicable wholeness. Hers is not the poetry of a modernism drowning, or trusting to drown, in its own helpless subjectivity. Sturdily, the work resists narcissism, and being caught within the self's tunnel-blind declarations, reflecting precisely Bishop's faith in the necessary existence of a world of Other, in contact with which the groping subject seeks whatever deliverance from misery is possible.

Memory actively working through the present offers the best perch from which to grasp at a whole reality, especially in the late poetry. Bishop's "Poem" offers us a paradigm of how memory, in company with a painting, helps the speaker, apparently Bishop herself, retrieve a lost, past experience of her Nova Scotian childhood. Once, as Helen Vendler identifies the unfolding action of the poem,[47] through a description of the painting, "About the size of an old-style dollar bill," she retrieves a geography; then twice, through the memory that rolls up through the iteration of the objects of the painting's site, she spells it out anew; a third time, and then the poet's and painter's "visions" coincide, although " 'visions' is too serious a word" and the poet promptly substitutes the deflationary "looks":

> art "copying from life" and life itself,
> life and the memory of it so compressed
> they've turned into each other. Which is which?
> Life and the memory of it cramped,
> dim, on a piece of Bristol board,
> dim, but how live, how touching in detail
> — the little that we get for free,
> the little of our earthly trust. Not much.
> About the size of our abidance
> along with theirs: the munching cows,
> the iris, crisp and shivering, the water
> still standing from spring freshets,
> the yet-to-be dismantled elms, the geese.

Much as our minds mirror and alter objective external reality, art and our mind's work are co-extensive: and that is all, and that is enough.

There is a determination here to fuse the visionary work of artist and scientist, to see the endless heroic and patient efforts of observation as common not only to the endeavors but the goals of each human discipline, as both are seen to advance human vision. But there is also a will to modesty, an effort to thwart the overstated and grandiose, and to cling tenaciously, on principle, to understating, even partly rejecting, the prophetic, or divinizing role of the artist, as either poet or painter. And here we might say that an important influence or graphic analogue for Bishop's poetry might be sought in her long interest in folk, or primitive art.[48]

Bishop's tribute to the Key West folk painter, Gregorio Valdes, opens with this characteristic paragraph:

> The first painting I saw by Gregorio Valdes was in the window of a barbershop on Duval Street, the main street of Key West. The shop is in a block of cheap liquor stores, shoeshine parlors and pool-rooms, all under a long wooden awning shading the sidewalk. The picture leaned against a cardboard advertisement for Eagle Whiskey, among other window decorations of red-and-green crepe-paper rosettes and streamers left over from Christmas and the announcement of an operetta at the Cuban school — all covered with dust and fly spots and littered with termites' wings.[49]

When one remembers that besides her friends Loren MacIver and Wesley Wehr, this is the single painter that Bishop chooses to write and reflect upon at any length, the cluttered details of the introduction appear deliberate in their denial of worldly recognition, in their insistence on a raffish obscurity as a generating or continuing condition of the work of art.

What follows this opening, a dry, comic, but generally affectionate assessment of the artist, concludes in this judgment: in Valdes' art there is "a peculiar and captivating freshness, flatness and remoteness." In the labor of this painting, with its toiling to see, and see exactly, we have a double of Darwin, toiling to see, and see, exactly; a double of the Canadian great-uncle who labored over the dollar-sized, as well as over the "Large Bad Picture" of an earlier poem, and by implication a double of that sophisticated world traveler, Bishop herself. It seems clear, that this and similar passages are, in any case, a rebuke to pretensions on the part of the artist: "the little that we get for free" guarantees our "abidance," which on reflection may be "Not much." In any case, not an amount worth preening over.

The leaning in Bishop's work for comedy over tragedy seems linked to her emphasis on the virtues of modesty, reticence, and understatement. In the writers she admired most unreservedly, in Chekhov and Babel, there is no drawing back from excess of pain and horror. Yet in all of her poetry there is such a pronounced dislike for anything tending to melodrama. And her terror at risking the false through overstatement or blind self-love props up her restraint, as she weighed these brands of untruth against the truths that a more public interrogation and display of self as subject might bring. A poised, mercurial comedy seems her necessity, her tiltpole against nervous collapse, and perhaps these are the qualities decisively turning her from a flatfooted or narrowly literal confessional art. In the Darwin letter to Anne Stevenson she protests sharply against being grouped in any predictable way. She says:

> In fact I think snobbery governs a great deal of my taste. I have been very lucky in having had, most of my life, some witty friends, – and I mean real wit, quickness, wild fancies, remarks that make one cry with laughing. (I seem to notice a tendency in literary people at present to think that any unkind or heavily ironical criticism is "wit," and any old "ambiguity" is now considered "wit," too, but that's not what I mean.) The aunt I liked best was a very funny woman: most of my close friends have been funny poeple; Lota de Macedo Soares is funny.

And after going on to make a list of all the funny people in her life she says "Perhaps I need such people to cheer me up." And then in this letter written to straighten out her habits and associations for the first person to do a booklength study of her work, she writes:

> I have a vague theory that one learns most – I have learned most – from having someone suddenly make fun of something one has taken seriously up until then. I mean about life, the world, and so on.

I cannot begin to guess what specific act may have triggered this remark; it seems so right, though; alert, skeptical, resistant, her head cocked for immediate counter response, the learning that Bishop describes as stemming from such opposition seems the best antidote to dishonest and pretentious emotion, and very deeply a part of the code that she refuses to bring into compartments separating aesthetic from moral, literary from everyday, tragic from comic, and so on.

Still, it will not do to forget that "heroic" is one of the adjectives that Bishop pins to Darwin for his labors. It would be dangerous, too, to suppose that Bishop's work undervalues what art's currency secures. In a comparison of primitive painters with primitive writers,[50] she scolds the "slipshoddiness and haste" of the latter, and praises the

Miss Moore and
Miss Bishop

WHEN SHE was a younger artist, surrealism with its speculative relation to dream material teased and provoked Elizabeth Bishop with models of the interior world, and then the steadying impact of her life with Lota de Macedo Soares somehow made the need for poems sorting out intimate relation less urgent. At the midpoint of her career, Bishop's interests turned more and more pressingly outward, to Brazil itself, absorbing her in the contours of her adopted country. But before I turn to two Brazilian poems for a more detailed account of her developing strategies, a look at two major friendships with poets seems in order. The first of these, of course, was with Marianne Moore, the second with Robert Lowell.

Bishop's placement of the tribute to Moore in her second book as the penultimate poem, to be followed by "The Shampoo," declares homage to the two women who by the time of the publication of *A Cold Spring* in 1955, assumed primacy in her development as poet and person; she lists them in order of their culminating importance, with the poem to her lover and the one to her first mentor now closing this cycle, or period, of her life.

"The Shampoo," whose original title was "Gray Hair," invokes Bishop's relationship with Lota de Macedo Soares and, in the distancing custom of Bishop's published poems centered on intimate relation, the very metaphors of the poem turn the provocative nearness of bodies into something planetary and astral. Full of a disembodied but pervasive tenderness and affection, "The Shampoo" juxtaposes the growth of gray in a dear friend's hair with the growth of lichens on rocks, spreading in "gray, concentric shocks":

> They have arranged
> to meet the rings around the moon, although
> within our memories they have not changed.

The shampoo takes place in a world of long memory, in which "Time is/ nothing if not amenable"; and in the black heaven of her friend's hair, shooting stars appear "in bright formation." In final invitation the poem concludes about that formation,

> —Come, let me wash it in this big tin basin,
> battered and shiny like the moon.

Also an invitation to come closer, like the poem to Marianne Moore, "The Shampoo" presents nonetheless a darker luminosity than the "fine morning" and "white mackerel sky" dedicated to Miss Moore: the moon presides over union with the dear dark-haired friend, even as the gestures seem far more clearly nurturant than amatory. While poems about intimacy like "Four Poems" and "Argument" remain fragmentary and fitfully detailed as ever, "The Shampoo" might be read as a step toward balancing the mood and tone of "Insomnia," the angry and resentful poem also included in *A Cold Spring*. The positioning of "The Shampoo" directly after the effervescent ceremony of "Invitation to Miss Marianne Moore" certainly lifts both poems and book into another tonality of pleasure and equable exchange, pointing to the lifting of spirits evident in the next book, completed in Brazil, *Questions of Travel*.

The brilliance and gaiety of the Moore poem have always seemed wonderful to me, especially in relation to the much more somber currents and streams characterising Pablo Neruda's "Alberto Rojas Jimenez vienes volando," the poem for a drowned poet, curiously enough, which, with its repeated *vienes volando*, or "Come flying," Bishop took as her formal model for "An Invitation to Miss Marianne Moore."

Pablo Neruda was a poet for whom Bishop had only a cautious admiration. In 1942, traveling in Mexico, she had met and liked the Chilean, and written to Marianne Moore, describing how she had attempted to translate Moore's "a glass-ribb'd nest" for him. But she characterized Neruda's poetry as "very loose, surrealist imagery[. . .].

I feel I recognize the type only too well." And after a decent interval she goes on to praise his shell collection. Yet the poem she wrote from a fusion of elements extracted from a poem of his reveals a fairly profitable interchange.

If we put Neruda's elegy for Alberto Rojas Jimenez next to Bishop's poem for Moore, Neruda's tribute seems by its nature so much more somber than Bishop's, his drowned poet deeply buried, definitively dead.[51] In his "new suit and extinguished eyes"—he flies from a truly nether kingdom:

> Under tombstones and under grave plots,
> under frozen snails,
> under the last waters of earth
>   you come flying.
>
> Deeper still, between submerged girls,
> blind plants and rotten fish,

Neruda's drowned poet is heavy with the scent of rot and corruption:

> Beyond vinegar and death
> between putrefaction and violets,
> in your heavenly voice and damp shoes
>   you come flying.

If in this poem there is a life of poetry transcending the mortal, it is nonetheless steeped and stinking in the mortal: finally, there is something terrifying as well as exhilarating in the avian form of this brother poet and his seaborne, aerial triumph, and perhaps as much to duck from as to embrace in his final appearance:

> You come flying, solo, solitary,
> solo among the dead, forever solo,
> you come flying shadowless and nameless,
> without sugar, without a mouth, without roses,
>   you come flying.

Bishop on the other hand chooses a living celebration, as strongly marine as Neruda's, but lighter in both load and tone. If there is another time-traveling and space-exploding literary antecedent for her effort it is surely Whitman's "Crossing Brooklyn Ferry." Bishop has taken Neruda's chanted lists, reduced the repetitions, made them go public and daylight, and prefaced Neruda's vocative with a "Please":

From Brooklyn, over the Brooklyn Bridge, on this fine morning,
    please come flying.
In a cloud of fiery pale chemicals,
    please come flying,
to the rapid rolling of thousands of small blue drums
descending out of the mackerel sky
over the glittering grandstand of harbor-water,
    please come flying.

Whistles, pennants and smoke are blowing. The ships
are signaling cordially with multitudes of flags
rising and falling like birds all over the harbor.
        [. . .]
  The flight is safe; the weather is all arranged.
The waves are running in verses this fine morning.
    Please come flying.

Published in 1948, the poem and its tribute mark the clear end of
Moore's active influence on Bishop's writing. In this public ceremony,
debts are acknowledged, and compliments are paid with a fine teasing
edge, not the less sincere for the edge. After Moore's death, Bishop
declared to R. L. Keller that "I am, after all, an umpty-umpty-um
kind of poet – and I always felt that she had a very different sense of
meter, or rhythm – possibly a physiological kind of thing – than most
poets writing in English."[52] And so in the poem there is a gentle
mocking of these traits; the syllable-counting Moore should come
"Bearing a musical inaudible abacus,/ a slight censorious frown, and
blue ribbons." As a further enticement for the upright Miss Moore,
Bishop adds, "Manhattan/ is all awash with morals this fine morning."
More triumphantly:

Mounting the sky with natural heroism,
above the accidents, above the malignant movies,
the taxicabs and injustices at large,
while horns are resounding in your beautiful ears
that simultaneously listen to
a soft uninvented music, fit for the musk deer,
    please come flying.

With great affection, those "beautiful ears" are saved for an un-
worldly, special music.

Here a reader of their joint correspondence cannot fail to remember Bishop teasing Moore about Moore's inexperience of impropriety,

Elizabeth Bishop in Brazil, 1954. Rollie McKenna.

Elizabeth Bishop as a child.

Gertrude Bulmer Bishop and Elizabeth.

Grandmother Bulmer, Elizabeth Bishop's Nova Scotian grandmother. "My grandmother had a glass eye, blue, almost like her other one, and this made her especially vulnerable and precious to me. My father was dead and my mother was away in a sanatorium. Until I was teased out of it, I used to ask Grandmother, when I said goodbye, to promise me not to die before I came home." (from *Collected Prose*, "Primer Class.")

The Bulmer family home, where Elizabeth Bishop spent her earliest years.

Great Village, Nova Scotia, at the turn of the century.
"A scream, the echo of a scream hangs over that Nova Scotian village. No one hears it; it hangs there forever, a slight stain in those pure blue skies, skies that travelers compare to those of Switzerland, too dark, too blue, so they seem to keep on darkening a little more around the horizon — or is it around the rims of the eyes? — the color of the cloud of bloom on the elm trees, the violet on the field of oats; something darkening over the woods and waters as well as the sky. (from *Collected Prose*, "In the Village.")

Great Village Elementary School, where Elizabeth Bishop attended primer class. "The school was high, bare and white-clapboarded, dark-red-roofed, and the four-sided cupola had white louvers. Two white outhouses were set farther back, but visible, on either side." (from *Collected Prose*, "Primer Class.")

The Bishop home at 1212 Main, in Worcester, Massachusetts. "The old white house had long ago been a farmhouse out in the country. The city had crept out and past it; now there were houses all around and a trolley line went past the front lawn with its white picket fence [. . .] Whenever I could I explored the house like a cat." (from *Collected Prose*, "The Country Mouse.")

John W. Bishop, Elizabeth Bishop's Worcester grandfather: "His thick silver hair and short silver beard glittered [. . .]. He was walleyed. At least, one eye turned the wrong way, which made him endlessly interesting to me." (from *Collected Prose*, "The Country Mouse.")

Elizabeth Bishop as an adolescent.
"She looked remarkable, with tightly curly hair that stood
straight up, while the rest of us all had straight hair that
hung down. [. . .] We called her "Bishop," spoke of her as
"the Bishop," and we all knew with no doubt whatsoever
that she was a genius." (Frani Muser, quoted in Robert
Giroux's introduction, *Collected Prose.*)

Margaret Miller, Quai d'Orléans, 1937
(Photograph identified in Bishop's handwriting.)

Louise Crane and Elizabeth Bishop in New York.

Elizabeth Bishop in Key West, ca. 1940.

Elizabeth Bishop in New York. George Platt Lynes.

Elizabeth Bishop in 1946. *New York Times*, announcement of Houghton Mifflin Award.

Maria Carlota Costellat de Macedo Soares (Lota). At approximately forty years of age.

Elizabeth Bishop, with Sammy the toucan.
"My lifelong dream [. . .] a TOUCAN. He eats six bananas a day – I must
say they seem to go right through him & come out practically as good as
new – meat, grapes – to see him swallowing grapes is rather like playing
a pinball machine." (to Ilse Barker, February 7, 1953.)

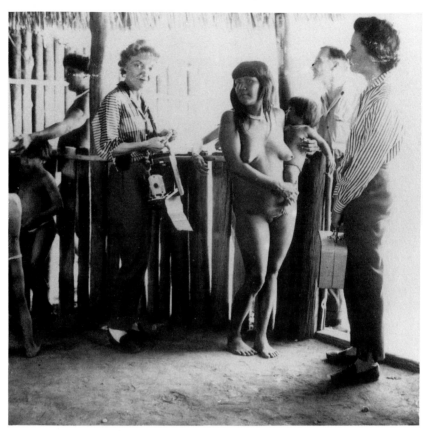

Taken on a trip in 1958 with Aldous Huxley
to the Indian Post of Capitão Vasconceles,
on the Xingú River, Brazil.

Calling in at a river port.
Taken by Bishop on her trip down the Amazon River in 1961.

Brazilian birdcage in Elizabeth Bishop's possession.
"A pity [. . .] Never to have studied history in/
the weak calligraphy of songbirds' cages."
(from "Questions of Travel.")

Fazenda Samambaia, terrace and garden through the glass.
The house designed by Sérgio Bernardes,
which Lota and Bishop shared.
Author's photograph.

Interior of Samambia. Painting by Elizabeth Bishop.

Robert Lowell and Elizabeth Bishop in Rio, 1962.
"We were giving an *abraço*, supposedly, but 2 New Englanders
get awfully gingerly & shy," Bishop wrote to Ilse Barker about
this photograph.

Casa Mariana, in Ouro Preto, in the state of Minas Geraís, Brazil. This structure dated back to the late seventeenth century, and Bishop began restoring it. "The house has the most beautiful roof in town – it is like a lobster lying on its stomach with its tail curled at right angles," she wrote to the Barkers in 1965.

A street in Ouro Preto.
Slide taken by Elizabeth Bishop.

Elizabeth Bishop and Alice Methfessel.

Elizabeth Bishop, Harvard Commencement, 1972.

or ignorance of the risqué. Not for the first time, Bishop dangles a broader knowledge in front of Moore, and then whisks it away before it can really offend. In 1958, long after this poem is written, Doña Alice, whose Brazilian diary Bishop is translating, tells Bishop wonderful stories that "took me right back to Nova Scotia; I'm sure I heard most of them before." Then Bishop adds, "many of her stories would have to be censored for your beautiful ears." Perhaps she needed Moore's prudery as a benchmark to move away from, if only for a measured distance. As Lynn Keller notes, Moore's active period as mentor was extinguished by the nineteen-forties,[53] but Bishop, for the rest of her life, continued to lay flowers in honor of its memory.

The title word "invitation" illuminates the poem's connection to Bishop's complex feelings about Moore. The fact must have lain in Bishop's mind for quite a few years, that there was an actual bridge, even one already commemorated in literature, linking each separate poet in her separate borough, before she made poetic capital of the Brooklyn Bridge as a linguistic and symbolic equivalent of her relationship to the older poet. In 1940, after decisively rejecting Moore's chief emendations for her poem "Roosters," Bishop ends her letter with a conciliatory reference to Klee's *The Moon of Confusion*, a picture on exhibition in Manhattan, and invites Moore to see it: "I wonder if you could be mesmerized across the bridge to see it again with me?"

The poem is an incandescent series of invitations, one more bridge of words thrown down between two women artists parted by age, conviction, and personal reserve, yet nonetheless over a period of years experiencing mutually a profound admiration and affection, each joined to each by a devotion to extraordinary labors in the service of their common trade. Come and do this or that with me, Bishop writes repeatedly, coaxingly over the years, in letters that begin in 1934 and end in 1970, eighteen months before Moore's death. In 1934, "Please don't let me bother you with invitations," and next: "Have you seen the film Son of Mongolia?" Would Moore be interested in a concert? tea afterwards? Will she come to Florida? Spain? France? Even in Brazil many years and thousands of miles later, there is "a favorite daydream [. . .] which is to have you sometime visit us." In Bishop's country retreat in Ouro Preto, in the mountains of Minas Gerais in Brazil, a blue plaque on a yellow door proclaims the house as Casa Mariana, and Moore's picture is up in four places. Bishop kept her sense of Moore as a precious totem to be taken everywhere, Moore's picture, her letters, to be reverently handled. In 1943, before leaving on a journey, Bishop writes: "It was awfully nice to get your letter before I left & I took it with me as a sort of amulet or pass-card." In spite of the frequent teasing as Bishop lightly probed for the limits of her engagement with the older poet, her housing of Moore within her mental life remained permanent.

But the patterns of deference for each are exquisitely organized for advance or retreat. Gifts are showered by Bishop on Moore: rattle-snake fangs, stuffed opossum, Cuban tree snails, Croton leaves, an ostrich feather, an alligator bedside mat, a "special orange papaya elixir," which both Moores, mother and daughter, drank respectfully in concert, and then even a dream book, although the latter evoked a negative response. Bishop writes: "I apologize for the dream book which I'd already sent when your letter came warding it off. But you can just throw it away quickly, without a glance." In November 1943, there is a crescendo of satisfaction from Moore:

> You do out-do yourself, Elizabeth, when giving things to others. You have never sent us anything that I did not feel it was so much the best of its family it was a sin to have it leave you. There is my palm-leaf Moroccan kimono-garden party dress, for instance, which you still have not seen me wear, I think, and my rattlesnake tail that is natural whereas yours was mended. And the ambergris bracelet, and the Florentine pomegranate reddish-pink jewel-box which gets finer in tone all the time! [. . .] the cricket cage [. . .].

Moore lingers next on the act of unwrapping the current present, fingering verbally the very elastic in which the gift is wrapped: so much piercing attention to every phase of the gift-giving ritual, and on the ceremonious rigors attending it, that one almost begins to suspect a parody of attention overwhelming the mere disjunctive object of it.

After a request from Bishop, "please won't you be a pin-up girl?" Moore sends a photograph of herself: "please put it in one of two communicating rooms and look at it from the farthest corner of the farthest room." Moore obviously shared, to a precise degree, Bishop's love of calibrating emotional distance, and understood her language of objects. Moore's letter with a photograph encloses a swatch of fabric, the same discreetly blue stuff of which her dress in the picture is made. The pathos, too, of such tangible objects dropping into the hands of strange readers opening these envelopes is doubtless something both women might have appreciated. Even archives built to measure the vibrations of mind surrender occasionally to substance. The swatch is frayed, and fading, but incontestably there.

So many of their dances of attendance seem intentionally comic, a poker-faced show of determination not to give the high spirits of a nonetheless serious game away by a descent into ordinariness, as in the initial phase of the friendship each woman matched and played up to the other. Here is Moore, in March 1937, volleying a description to her keen-eyed younger colleague:

> the pelicans you describe make me think of one of the most beautiful things I ever saw in the movies—a view of an alligator-farm in Alabama, of alligators [. . .] ascending an artificial bluff, to a shute-the-shute, and sliding down at great speed, only to toil up the rock and do it again.

"Beautiful": we've entered a world of special language, with a special view of endurance and labor, coded and pointed by private ironies and covertly idiosyncratic pleasures.

But the relationship was more than an exchange of charming eccentricities; a large part of the appeal of Bishop's "Invitation to Miss Marianne Moore" rests in its flawless instinct for playful compliment that is neither bland nor blind, and for a voiced affection never servile or mechanical. The rightness of balance also stems, perhaps, from a wish for friendship as pure gift and pure exchange, for that "disinterested 'friendship'" grown in the Arctic climate for which Bishop longed in her letter to Frani Blough. The grandstands irrepressibly appearing, the public roll of drums, the wash of morals, all point to a firm integrity of feeling, a positioning far more openly and freely joyful than the veiled relationships with women that the rest of *A Cold Spring*, or even the rest of Bishop's poetry, will invoke. The juxtaposed tributes to Lota Macedo de Soares and Marianne Moore emphasize for us how the love and friendship surrounding the poem to Moore are silently put in proximity to the love and friendship surrounding "The Shampoo." Nothing seems a clearer indication of why Eros from then on will have to move underground, into the file folders of the not-for-publication, unexposed to the oversight of ladies. The juxtaposition of the two poems tentatively marks a possibility for subject matter, and then declines it for subsequent books.

From here on in, Bishop's work and life enter new thematic and stylistic concerns. The poem for Marianne Moore both evokes the debt of Moore's aesthetic influence, and emphatically marks the closure of its major term. *Questions of Travel* opens after Bishop has assumed her Brazilian residency with Lota de Macedo Soares, and neither of the subsequent books has quite the same buoyancy; yet *A Cold Spring* marked the beginning of a more mature poetry, less exquisite in focus and effect.

In "Invitation to Miss Marianne Moore," literature, and literary form, present Bishop with options of expressive being otherwise closed in her life. The poem provides a particularly delicate and balanced form of the personal enclosed, but also opening, within the literary relation; it is perhaps not disconnected to say that in the main, the more successful poems in *A Cold Spring* concern not Bishop's friendships or love affairs with women, but identify travel and the landscape of childhood as the personal themes now coming on to replace the poems of intimate relation, which will lie dormant until they rise again in *Geography III*. The poem to Moore functions as an unspoken tribute indirectly acknowledging the centrality of that gift: the older poet did, in fact, exactly what Bishop said to R. L. Keller that she did; she directed Bishop to her primary subjects:

> In "North & South," for example, I'd say now that "Florida" shows her influence a lot – possibly "Seascape" – but not many more, or if they do it is more a matter of subject matter . . .

and also affirmed for her a major strength. Bishop remarked:

> We are profoundly different, I think – but a good deal of her subject matter, her insistence on accuracy, and her way of observing, I'm sure did influence me. (I have always been observant, I think – at least they tell me so – but I might not have put this gift to use as much if it hadn't been for Marianne.)[54]

Precise as ever, Bishop acknowledges the benign influence, but then leans to other voices that tell her that accuracy of observation has always been a trait of hers; if influence is present, still, it can only play upon what was embryonically there.

· I ·

As Bonnie Costello, in her sensitive and comprehensive article on the difference between these two poets, presents the major differences between the two poets, she names Bishop "the seeker," and Moore "the gentlewoman."[55] Bishop remains the poet "of moods and mysteries," while Moore represents "the poetry of manners and morals." In characterizing their approaches to description, she writes: "Moore continually attaches value to fact, where Bishop attaches yearning, fear, uncertainty."

It is that yearning which is signally present even in Bishop's title of her account of the friendship in "Efforts of Affection." Her choice of a memoir essay, shows, among other things, one more indication of the limits of candor for her as a literary tool: the memoir will not provide a place for a total assessment either of the differences between their work or of Moore's impact on her own. But her essaying of affection will construct itself from feelings mixed in both conflict and connection, or so the punning title for her memoir might tell us, borrowing as it does from a Moore poem identically named.

Even this much of Bishop's emotional life will not be openly voiced; in the memoir as in life, a move toward a greater consideration of personal themes halts near a junction of the personal and the literary. Somewhere between *A Cold Spring* and *Questions of Travel* in the period including the major weight of Moore's influence, and also during its waning, Bishop was heading toward candid and painful autobiographical material; yet her positioning herself within the model of Moore's gentility finally left no room for development of the powerful drafts and fragments we've seen from the nineteen-forties. Her essay on Moore, never published during Bishop's lifetime, offers suggestive but only partial clues, and partial resolutions to any of these choices.

Bishop was not impervious to the moral judgments that Moore's generation represented. Whatever her differences, there is a freely affectionate respect in Bishop's tone. From the beginning, visible even in the screens of extreme courtesy through which their friendship was filtered, there must have been a stimulating sense of kinship and difference, as well as equality, even through the large difference in their respective ages. At the time that they met, Bishop was still at Vassar, and Moore at forty-six was distinguished, but nowhere near the apex of her recognition. During the early years, Moore is very forthright, according to Bishop, in her condemnation of homosexuality:

I remember her worrying about the fate of a mutual friend whose sexual tastes had already seemed quite obvious to me: "What are we going to do about X . . .? Why, sometimes I think he may even be in the clutches of a *sodomite* . . .! One could almost smell the brimstone.[56]

In her easy urbanity, Bishop in the nineteen-seventies can be openly amused at Moore's perhaps endearing but certainly occasionally exasperating sexual naiveté. But as David Kalstone reminds us, Bishop met Marianne Moore within the year that her own biological mother died in an asylum after years of confinement, and Moore's world "was in part a vanished sustaining maternal world transposed into another key."[57] Bishop was notably struck by the close sympathy emanating from Marianne's relationship with the elder Mrs. Moore. That closeness must frequently have intensified her own sense of isolation, especially as she realized that Moore's ethical code could never have embraced Bishop's own sexual choices, and stirred up old feelings of abandonment, as well as longing.

Moore was not unresponsive to Bishop's loneliness. Bonnie Costello remarks persuasively that

> art and life, aesthetics and morality are deeply linked for both poets. If the nouns of family life (mother, daughter, sister, etc.) do not quite fit, the verbs still do, not the oedipal verb "struggle" which dominates our Bloomian notion of literary influence, but the centrally female verb "nurture."[58]

For Moore, one of the primary facts about Bishop was her orphanhood. In 1963, in correspondence with Anne Stevenson about Stevenson's book in progress about Bishop, Moore quotes Helen Sandison, one of Bishop's Vassar advisers, on her situation as a young woman: "I don't know to whom Elizabeth Bishop might go for summer vacation. Her mother and father have died; she seems compelled to rely for advice and encouragement on herself." After so many years, it was Bishop's special position as an unprotected orphan that Moore makes prominent in giving information about her.

In the early years of their acquaintance, she makes countless suggestions about publication, writes to others about Bishop, sees that she is included in an anthology of young poets, and then writes a memorable and generous introduction for Bishop's contribution. The introduction, titled "Archaically New," is still valid for the chief points of Bishop's work—its reticence, indirection, and paradoxical dependence on tradition within a keen modernity. Her opening summary in its strange negations is oddly reflective, too, of the personal relations between the two poets: "Yet the rational considering quality in her work is its strength—assisted by unwordiness, uncontorted intentionalness, the flicker of impudence, the natural unforced ending." Perhaps Miss Moore has been led, through the offices of the younger poet, to lend approval to practices of whose overpowering worth she is not entirely convinced. Force, wordiness, and contortion are qualities Moore herself wrestled to the ground in her own poetry, often walking them off to victory. Surely one of the greater fascinations that Bishop's work possessed for Moore was its focus on so many of her own subjects and descriptive interests; Bishop's work entered and took likenesses with a familiar reticence, but with unfamiliar rhythms, and through a dramatic and narrative style that challenged her own.

Moore grasped at once the rarity of the younger poet, sizing up that "flicker of impudence" as well as the old-fashioned manners, appreciating very early the "originality," and "the deferences and vigilances in Miss Bishop's writing." As best she knew how, Moore offered to the younger woman's pride the fullest acknowledgment of equality. She praises her "self-respect"; saying, "one feels the sincerity, the proportionateness, and the wisdom of superiority to snobbery—the selectiveness."

It took a slightly sour coaxing on Moore's part to get Bishop even to show her work. In August 1936 Moore writes:

> Maybe you would care to show me what you have been writing? [. . .] I think I recall complaining of having to look at things which were sent me for advice, but I never have complained of writing I *asked* to see. In fact I have rather serious cause of complaint against you for stinginess in this matter.

Bishop maintained a rather desperate insouciance about the exchange. Sending Moore a copy of her fable, "The Sea & Its Shore," she writes to Moore:

> This story is so untidy—worse than that, I am afraid, it is a little CHEAP . . . I was trying to produce an effect something like Hans Andersen but I'm afraid I haven't succeeded in this one. If you don't care for it please don't bother to send it back but throw it out the window or down the elevator shaft.

At least once, Moore pressed too hard with advice, then beat an orderly retreat. As Moore became too close and controlling, Bishop trod a fine line between independence and connection. In February 1937, Moore says: "Your considerateness in wondering how things may be regarding another's choice of occupation is much felt by me, but you should let me see all you do." As Lynn Keller points out, that "should" is unmistakably proprietary.[59] Bishop replies with equally firm politeness: "You are so kind to offer to intercede for me that way – you have a very generous and protective apron and I am not sure how much of it I should seize upon." When Bishop withholds a story from Moore's inspection, and sends it off for publication without allowing Moore to pre-inspect, Moore is pettish: "It was very independent of you to submit your prize story without letting me see it. If it is returned with a printed slip, that will be why." Yet the story was accepted. While neither woman allowed this rather sharp exchange to tilt friendship toward hostility, still, it marked the first occasion of Bishop's open assertion of independent choice in her professional life.

But the older poet also made handsome concessions when she recognized that unintentional criticism had been conveyed. Moore, who was not a great traveler, assumed that Bishop traveled for her asthma. In 1935, in her stately fashion, Moore writes:

> I regard a vacation abroad as a kind of sacrosanctity and although anything you might tell one of it would be a pleasure to hear, do let yourself feel your freedom and forget, if it would be best, your stodgily employed friends on this side of the water. But not, of course, forever.

The idea of being seen as traveling merely for pleasure, in contrast to the hard workers at home, seems to have annoyed Bishop, and by March 1936 Moore is backing off and mollifying Bishop by saying merely, "Travel *looks* like leisure to those who are not doing it."

A week earlier, Moore placidly imagines a Morocco:

> And perhaps you will tell us about camels and date-trees. Several months ago we saw a remarkable film of Morocco, of horses of various types in a race, of high Moroccan ladies doing fancy-work and having tea.

That last vision of the "high Moroccan ladies" may have been one too many for Bishop; hardly able to resist just a tiny perforation of Moore's gentility, she sends back this description of *her* Morocco:

We went to several cafes to see the singing and dancing with our guide, and one of the best things I saw were two very large negroes, very black, one dressed in lavender robes and one in pink, one playing a large lute with a long feathered quill and the other a violin which he held upside-down – the neck on his shoulder – while they both sang as loudly, or shouted, and hoarsely as they could. It looked very much like a parody of the angel in an Italian painting in London. The dancing is of course very improper but sometimes extremely amusing – as, for example, when the lady, to show how still she keeps the top of her head, dances with a tray on it, holding a tea-pot and glasses full of tea. Without spilling any she even lies down and rolls over, and at the end sits on the floor and takes a glass of tea off the tray and offers it to you with her toes.

Moore appears to make no direct reply to this. After acknowledging the receipt of a drawing of the contrasting spirals of a staircase, which put her in mind of the chambered nautilus in a poem she is drafting, she merely says, gamely: "You do extend reference. And you bear the labor while we sit rested, and expand in contemplation."

Indirectly, Moore's poem, "The Paper Nautilus," which was helped into existence by Bishop's gift to Moore of a paper nautilus shell, acknowledges the protectiveness she felt as a style of maternality. In her discussion of this poem of Moore's, Bonnie Costello notes that "The poem describes a careful balance between firmness and gentleness by which the nautilus nurtures her eggs." Within the framework of the poem, "this love is not possessive or narcissistic, it is 'hindered to succeed' for 'the intensively watched eggs coming from the shell free it when they are freed.' " In such an environment, nurturance in action simultaneously withdraws with its own reward, and in Costello's words, "mutual freedom meant an acknowledgement of and respect for difference." [60]

Maternal or filial needs or responses were never openly acknowledged by either woman. Yet the usually unfailing delicacy, the inventive generosity that characterized both women came into play on more than one occasion suggesting reciprocal response to unstated needs. After Bishop's first clear rebuff of Moore's bossiness over her poetry, she found herself in France, in the summer of 1937, writing to Moore about the automobile accident with Louise Crane and Margaret Miller. It takes her nearly a page of offhand description of scenery, defensively placed in another country, in which she can plant an innocuous "how we wished you were along, how well you would go with the Irish countryside" — before Bishop can even work up to the event that has evidently precipitated her letter, and allow her to declare indirectly how strong her need is for an older friend's consoling presence.

The explanatory letter to Moore about the accident and the loss of the painter Margaret Miller's arm is full of stoic fortitude on the part of the young woman suffering the accident as well as on Bishop's. "She began to write with her left hand the 2d day after the accident," Bishop writes. She says of their collective feelings, "to keep 'going' is the main thing." Moore immediately offers the desired verbal comfort, condoling with the young amputee and complimenting Bishop on her courage.

All three young women are required to go through court procedures in France, in which in the interest of the injured girl, the driver of the car must admit fault — the whole incident must have been indelibly painful. Yet all three struggle to maintain composure. Speaking of her friend's skin graft, Bishop writes to Moore, "It is a fascinating process"; and then reports of her friend:

> She is designing clothes for herself, and she insists she wants a "glass hand," like the glass woman in Radio City – have you seen her? – I am afraid this may trouble you, so forgive me. We live with these things and forget how they may seem to other people.

The incident, of course, sank more deeply into consciousness than the light tones allow, and there is a fable scrap surviving in one of the Nemer journals:

> The arm lay outstretched in the soft brown grass at the side of the road and spoke quietly to itself. At first all it could think of was the possibility of being quickly united to its body, without any more time elapsing than was absolutely necessary.
>
> "Oh my poor body! Oh my poor body! I cannot bear to give you up. Quick! Quick!"
>
> Then it fell silent while a series of ideas that had never occurred to it before swept rapidly over it.

On the side of this passage, a note appears: "so this is to be really 'alone in the world!' what it means." Amputation is conflated with the idea of abandonment, and orphanhood. The recent trauma seems to have recombined with the earlier chaotic feelings that Bishop experienced over the loss of her parents in infancy.

It is not surprising to see the urgency with which she reports to Moore; perhaps it is only surprising to see the extent to which good manners tourniquet the flow of intense feeling. Still there is a special need for connection, for assurance of connection in what she sparingly permits herself to say to Moore, a month after the accident:

> Before your letter came I had tried in vain to semaphore myself back into normalcy by putting one of your pictures in the mirror-frame (the one with the fingertips resting on the little heap of "work" – the eyes have the same look as they do in the picture where it says underneath "the 3rd from the right in the group of spectators is the artist herself," or "the artist's favorite child." [...] But your letter which I can never properly thank you for – it represents so much thoughtfulness and actual *work* as well, – has been such a consolation. Things are gradually resuming temporal proportions.

In this world of distress, time distorts and skews, and Moore metamorphoses mysteriously into a child, or into a "favorite child" as Bishop tries to use the votive photograph as a means of restoring her "normalcy." Another key part of that process is the underlined word denoting the little "heap" of writing, or "work," which is the other unifying presence that the picture of Moore, with the metonymic hand intact, simultaneously at rest and at work, can offer. Perhaps most consoling is that within Bishop's sighting of the mirror, Moore's hand is still tangibly connected to the products of language.

Unstated, but deeply at work within her orientation, Moore's example becomes a mothering at a crucial point triggering Bishop's memory of original trauma. Seeing a friend risk losing her own primary work must have restated with special emphasis for Bishop the precarious role that writing might play in her own life, and make specially necessitous a quick assurance from Moore. And Moore apparently gave with a fine and instinctive empathy all that was needed.

·II·

It is interesting to look at the passage that concludes the extant version of Bishop's memoir about Moore. Her final quotation from Gerard Manley Hopkins' letter to Robert Bridges traces the intersection of art, manners, and morals. The quotation occurs after Bishop reports and reflects on her few open disagreements with Moore. "Marianne never gave away the whole show," Bishop opens, and talks about her "decisive intuitions [. . .] as to good and bad, right and wrong;" but "her meticulous system of ethics could be baffling." Bishop notes that they "came close to a falling out" when Bishop told Moore about the psychoanalyst she had been seeing. One can only speculate as to why she introduced the topic to Moore, whose reply was that "psychoanalysts taught that 'Evil is *not* evil. But we know it *is.*' "

At this point, after defending her own "saintly" psychoanalyst to herself silently and to the page belatedly out loud, Bishop closes the subject and moves to invoke Hopkins, who uses some old-fashioned language that she is evidently somewhat embarrassed by. Nonetheless: "I find this letter still applicable and very moving." I give the passage exactly as Bishop quotes it:

> As a fact poets and men of art are, I am sorry to say, by no means necessarily or commonly gentlemen. For gentlemen do not pander to lust or other baseness nor . . . give themselves airs and affections, nor do other things to be found in modern works . . . .If an artist or thinker feels that were he to become in those ways ever so great, he would still be essentially lower than a gentleman that was no artist or thinker. And yet to be a gentleman is but on the brim of morals and rather a thing of morals than morals properly. Then how much more must art and philosophy and manners and breeding and everything else in the world be below the least degree of true virtue. This is that chastity of mind which seems to lie at the very heart and be the parent of all good, the seeing at once what is best, and holding to that, and not allowing anything else whatever to be heard pleading to the contrary . . . . I agree then, and vehemently, that a gentleman . . . is in the position to despise the poet, were he Dante or Shakespeare, and the painter, were he Angelo or Apelles, for anything that showed him *not* to be a gentleman. He is in a position to do it, but if he is a gentleman perhaps this is what he will not do.

What an interesting turn that final *perhaps* takes! A staunch and modest refusal to judge not lest ye be judged seems to be the sense, the essential courtesy, and to overtake and miraculously cancel what is a building momentum, a juggernaut of Victorian morality rolling implacably toward judgment.

In copying this letter to Robert Bridges, whether at the time of writing the memoir or earlier, Bishop picked over and rearranged its sentences so that in her extract Hopkins opens with his remarks about the ungentlemanliness of poets and men of art, although in the Abbott edition these remarks close the letter as an afterthought. Bishop also takes the scissor to Hopkins' explicit Christianity. In the ellipsis which she registers before the sentence that begins "I agree then, and vehemently," Hopkins identifies Christ's "being humbled to death" and dying "the death of the cross," or "this holding of himself back" as "the root of all his holiness and the imitation of this the root of all moral good in other men." This humility, this absolute self-abnegation, was undoubtedly a bit more than Bishop's bred-in-the-bone and heads-up Protestantism was prepared to acknowledge. In reshaping this passage she stresses the ethical rather than the theological underpinnings of Hopkins' argument and concludes: "But I am sure that Marianne would have 'vehemently agreed' with Hopkins' strictures: to be a poet was not the be-all, end-all of existence." Then there is a wonderful coda to her essay, an almost singsong, deliberately childlike and whimsical tangle of sentences that collapse the end of the memoir in a final *seems* both evasive and playful. Bishop finishes:

> I find it impossible to draw conclusions or even to summarize. When I try to, I become foolishly bemused: I have a sort of subliminal glimpse of the capital letter *M* multiplying. I am turning the pages of an illuminated manuscript and seeing that initial letter again and again: Marianne's monogram; mother; manners; morals; and I catch myself murmuring, "Manners and morals; manners *as* morals? Or is it morals *as* manners?" Since like Alice, "in a dreamy sort of way," I can't answer either question, it doesn't much matter which way I put it; it *seems* to be making sense.

Almost as a child does, I, too, find myself repeating the alliterative *Marianne/manners/morals* and by proximity throwing in Bishop's *myself*—repeating it every which way until the terms reduce to nonsense; yet what is the nonsensical sense? The figure in the world that one cuts *matters*. Artists are not different from other people; whereof one cannot speak, perhaps, it is best to remain silent. And yet what is the eventual price paid by the poet when so much of her life lies under heavy guard? The guardedness could be viewed as a tragic evisceration of subject, not entirely a result of free choice made by the poet, but of choices imposed by the manners and morals and muddles of the people among whom one lives and publishes. Finally, if one cannot trust one's own chosen mentor-mother, it must be a very carefully drawn circle that *can* be trusted.

In her own thoughts Bishop mulled over Moore's personal limits. Her candid conclusions surface briefly in the notes for a review of Moore's work that she wrote aboard the *S.S. Bowplate*, steaming toward the tropics. She says:

> I've been thinking about Marianne a lot – trying to finish the review before Santos. I don't think I've ever really given her enough credit for her *democracy* – being put off by the tediousness of her politeness, etc. And yet that is one of her most admirable traits – that absolute refusal to differentiate between people at all – at least I've never seen her. If her manners are too ceremonious at least they are equally so for "Gladys," "Tom," (TSE), or the elevator man. I wish I could quote Pascal's remark exactly, about how all men are *not* counted equal but it is spiritual death if we don't behave as if they were.
>
> I'd also like to get in something about the absolutely wild contrast between her form & her admiration of "spontaneity." [. . .] this *form* is seen in her manners & somehow hitches on to her *guilt*–but the spontaneity is seen in her wit, & in that laugh with which she greets other's witticisms.

Bishop notes the tedium of "ceremonious" manners, but cannot bring herself really to condemn them.

Generally, Bishop effectively strove to maintain a diction poised with extreme nicety between formal and familiar; to resolve for herself the "wild contrast" between a love of form and ceremony and a love of the spontaneity that undercuts them. The balance she achieved seems part of her utter lucidity of style, a style without strain and without affectation. There must have been times, however, when this style, perhaps like all styles too consistently adhered to, began to seem a constraint because it permitted so little variation in dramatic tone and temperature. In a couple of unfinished and unpublished poems, however, coolness gives way to a raffish irony; Bishop acknowledges a seedier reality than usual, and moves toward a more explosive and abrasive language and tone, laced with a disturbing and ungenteel pain and anger. Partly, a poem like the late "Pink Dog" stands out as manifestly different in tone; in spite of its elegantly casual rhyming its humor seems hard and savage in contrast to the subtleties both exquisite and well-bred of poems like the early "The Man-Moth." But both the funny, drunken soldier from "The Soldier and the Slot Machine," a poem that appears in draft form in the nineteen-forties, and the brief cameo of the quarreling, beer-drinking couple from "In a Room in 1936," another early draft, show that Bishop had always had other moods to match "Pink Dog": darker strengths than she was in the habit of acknowledging in print.

Bishop was clearly not a prude, but conventional restraints backed by a beloved but unusually prudish mentor might have tethered her sense of the permissible limit. In the 1940 exchange of letters about "Roosters," which put an effective end to Bishop's period of submission to Moore's editorial ministrations, we have a clear demonstration of the difference between Bishop and Moore on this issue.

Moore evidently disapproved of colloquial color as it stepped out of the house and headed toward the privy. She took a vigorous interest in "Roosters," sitting up an evening over the poem with her mother, in all innocence then returning the heavily-edited and splendidly re-typed and retitled manuscript to Bishop as "The Cock." Bishop replies deferentially to the whole enterprise. She hands over to Moore the initial capitals of her lines, concedes a dropped stanza, accepts one or two other minor changes, but then digs in her heels:

> I cherish my "water-closet" and other sordidities because I want to emphasize the essential baseness of militarism. In the 1st part I was thinking of Key West, and also of those aerial views of dismal little towns in Finland & Norway, when the Germans took over, and their atmosphere of poverty. That's why, although I see what *you* mean, I want to keep "tin rooster" instead of "gold," and not to use "fastidious beds." And for the same reason I want to keep as the title the rather contemptuous word ROOSTERS rather than the more classical COCK; and I want to repeat the "gun-metal." (I also had in mind the violent roosters Picasso did in connection with his GUERNICA picture [. . .] It has been so hard to decide what to do, and I know that esthetically you are quite right, but I can't bring myself to sacrifice what (I think) is a very important "violence" of tone — which I feel to be helped by what *you* must feel to be just a bad case of the *Threes*.

Here is a flurry of highminded reasons beating down Moore's objections. Interesting to see, too, that the more decorous or nonviolent language is felt to be "aesthetically" invoked, an aesthetic from which Bishop separates herself. She sits on the letter for two days, apologizes for being "decidedly *cranky*," but does not substantially alter her text. Most of all, she clings quite determinedly to her own tripleted rhyme, explaining her "rather rattletrap rhythm" as an integral part of her view of the poem's world. Both Bishop and Moore have spoken of rhyme, or rhythm, as being an essential part of the qualities that separated them as poets. For Bishop, in the Nemer notebooks, "*Rhyme* is *mystical* [. . .] a method, of magically interlocking ideas, making associations." Moore, recognizing defeat, merely hung on to the outhouse part of the debate:

> Regarding the water-closet, Dylan Thomas, W. C. Williams, E. E. Cummings, and others feel that they are avoiding a duty if they balk at anything like unprudishness, but I say to them "I can't care about all things equally, I have a major effect to produce, and the heroisms of abstinence are as great as the heroisms of courage, and so are the rewards." I think it is to your credit, Elizabeth, that when I say you are not to say, "water-closet," you go on saying it a little (like Donald in National Velvet), and it is calculated to make me wonder if I haven't mistaken a cosmetic patch for a touch of lamp-black, but I think not. The trouble is, people are not depersonalized enough to accept the picture rather than the thought.

Nothing could provide a more striking illustration of the differences at this point. For Moore, that astonishing "depersonalized," probably written with Eliot's view of the necessary management of an artist's personality in mind and without any consciousness of the totalitarian aura that the word possesses for us, looks as if she were saying that flesh and substance have a penetrating rudeness on which people always fasten. In her opinion, or so I read her sentence, the sanitized "picture," or the verbal idealization, is always to be elevated beyond an inferior reality threatening the uncleannesses of the rebel body. Moore continues:

> You saw with what gusto I acclaimed "the mermaid's pap" in Christopher S. but few of us, it seems to me, are fundamentally rude enough to enrich our work in such ways without cost. If I tell Mother there is a feather on her dress and she says, "On my back?" I am likely to say, "No. On your rump," alluding to Cowper's hare that "swung his rump around." But in my work I daren't risk saying, "My mother had a feather on her rump."

There are those of us who would mourn the banishing of that feather on the rump.

This whole exchange must have tripped a switch; in the 1979 letter to R. Lynn Keller I've already quoted, Bishop briefly summarized her relationship to Moore:

> I showed her my poems up to & including one called "Roosters." She and her mother used to send me criticisms – some amusing, such as objecting to my use of the word "spit" or "privy" – some excellent. After "Roosters" I decided not to show anything to any-one, or rarely, until it was published. Her criticism of that poem wd. be worth publishing – her rewriting of it, rather – if I could find it! – After that I decided to write entirely on my own, because I realized how very different we were.

All the same, it makes one wonder about the kind of coaching by the Zeitgeist to be proper that one Bishop heeded and that another later Bishop might have ignored. In addition to the minor "sordidities" of diction a later Bishop could perhaps have admitted a variety of personal and political topics to a freer range in her poetry. In 1968, when she was brought to a San Francisco party dominated by a younger generation, she spluttered with indignation at the conjunction of love and obscenity in the music and speech she heard; "no use of charm, retreats, the lovely game of love," she commented indignantly in an unpublished journal. In 1966, however, writing to Robert Lowell from her first teaching job in Seattle, she mused about the "more Bohemian friends I have made," concluding a little ambiguously, "Westerners are really different — it took a little getting used to." And then ends, with what explicit meaning it is again hard to tell: "We were so genteel at Vassar, really." There was apparently a limit to which gentility could be shed without peril. Recalling Marianne Moore's defense of "the heroisms of abstinence," however, it seems sometimes a matter of nice judgment to estimate the exact distance that remained in force between Bishop's "retreats" and Moore's "abstinences."

Perhaps what remains most interesting about Bishop's approach in "Roosters," however, is not the firm authority with which she de-fended her "sordidities," her "dropping-plastered henhouse floor," but the covert style of reference to current politics to which she was also committed. In her defense of violent tone in "Roosters," she makes an explicit comment about the bombed territory that was evoked in her mind during its writing, "of those aerial views of dismal little towns in Finland & Norway, when the Germans took over"; it is not the specific landscape of World War II that she calls into the poem directly, however, but that of her more general opposition to "militarism."

On January 22, 1946, Bishop writes to her editor at Houghton Mifflin, worrying about the nontopicality of her poetry:

> The fact that none of these poems deal directly with the war, at a time when so much war poetry is being published, will, I am afraid, leave me open to reproach. The chief reason is simply that I work very slowly. But I think it would help some if a note to the effect that most of the poems had been written, or begun at least, before 1941, could be inserted at the beginning, say just after the acknowledgements.

Dealing with war is something she instinctively avoids. Sharing with Virginia Woolf an opinion of war's terrifying reduction of civilized complexity, Bishop complains of war's "terrible *generalizing* of every emotion." Sometime late in the thirties she transcribes a dream to her notebook:

> many more dreams – almost every night. Tanks, lost in crowds of refugees, bombardments, etc. Last night dreamed I heard cannon and that I was explaining to someone (we were standing beside a plaster-wall covered with bullet-marks) that it sounded exactly like the cooing of doves amplified 2 thousand times and "stretched out" – such & such a degree – and that there was some connection with that and the Peace Dove. (In the movies 2 days ago hardly noticed how the sound bullets make or at least the sound the movies make them make, really gives the effect of young birds starting to sing in spring.)

The whole idea of war is evidently so horrifying that it must be quickly converted to the most innocuous imagery possible.

What emerges in her discussion of "Roosters" with Marianne Moore is not her rejection of overt political reference, but something a little more complicated: her reluctance, perhaps, to engage in a patriotic exercise that will compromise her own anti-militarist opinions. Not wishing to be caught in the ideological fashion of the moment, she dodges easy wartime rhetoric and produces a brilliant, if sidelong, denunciation of the posture. Her adoption of the usual animal mask serves as a classic feint. Reading the poem several decades after World War II, it is easy to see these roosters as both macho and militarist:

> Cries galore
> come from the water-closet door,
> from the dropping-plastered henhouse floor,
>
> where in the blue blur
> their rustling wives admire,
> the roosters brace their cruel feet and glare
>
> with stupid eyes
> while from their beaks there rise
> the uncontrolled, traditional cries.
>
> Deep from protruding chests
> in green-gold medals dressed,
> planned to command and terrorize the rest,
>
> the many wives
> who lead hens' lives
> of being courted and despised;
>
> deep from raw throats
> a senseless order floats
> all over town.

It may be that the audible contempt for both cowed hens and medal-dressed cocks is too evenly distributed to make the poem properly feminist for some readers, but Bishop found herself acknowledging its feminism to George Starbuck in 1977. Speaking of "the way things catch up with you," and "Roosters," she says: "Some friends asked me to read it a year or so ago, and I suddenly realized it sounded like a feminist tract, which it wasn't meant to sound like at all to begin with. So you never know how things are going to get changed around for you by the times."[61] She is still curiously ambivalent about the poem's bolder insights into the relation between the military and the patriarchal, disowning them as "tract."

Bishop's avoidances in "Roosters" resemble in milder form someone like Virginia Woolf's abhorrence of what she felt was the oppressive male point of view on war. Yet those comments to George Starbuck should make us cautious about ascribing a feminist pacifism to her; we could easily make too much of Bishop's extraterritorial, out-of-poem declaration that the piece was inspired by the German occupation of Norway and Finland. Bishop kept this particular reference away from the poem; the "aerial views" she gives as source for her thinking are only tenuously present. An essential and consistent part of her poetry seems to be its resistance to sententiae, or sentiments and causes of all kinds: perhaps its weakness, perhaps its strength. In refusing to come out from behind the rooster, the armadillo, the sandpiper, the moose, or the pink dog, the poet signals her preference for a certain kind of opaque identity; we may be teased to hear her distinctively human voice within that distant animal hide, but we have not been granted a nearer view.

The lack of sententiae brought Bishop a rare general remonstrance from Marianne Moore. As Bonnie Costello points out, "Moore's evaluative turn of mind pervades every aspect of experience, from social etiquette to modern warfare."[62] Such a poet, Moore could write this gentle challenge to Bishop in March 1937, in the virtual dawn of their decades-long relationship:

> a thing should make one feel after reading it, that one's life has been altered or added to. When I set out to find fault with you, there are so many excellences in your mechanics that I seem to be commending you instead, and I wish to say, above all, that I am sure good treatment is a handicap unless along with it, significant values come out with an essential baldness. I hope the *un*essential baldness of this attack will not make it seem that I am against minutiae.

Bishop always held out for image over statement or, as Costello puts it, prefers "moral inquiry" over "moral guidelines."

A year later Moore manages to continue the discussion through the device of a comparison with Bishop and Reinhold Niebuhr. Commenting on Bishop's prose piece, "In Prison," Moore begins, with both cunning and flattering ingenuity:

> You and Dr. Niebuhr are two abashing peaks in present experience for me. Never have I heard an abler man nor seen a more innocent and artless artifice of innuendo than in your prison meditations. The use of immediate experience and of reading is most remarkable, — the potent retiringness, the close observation and interassociating of the circumstantial with the exotic; your mention of the Turkey carpets and the air bubble of potential freedom; the leaves and the inoffensive striping of the uniforms.

Then, throwing down an ever-thicker carpet of compliment, she continues her cautious and interminably qualified complaint:

> I feel that although large-scale "substance" runs the risk of inconsequence through aesthetic impotence, and am one of those who despise clamor about substance — to whom treatment really *is* substance — I can't help wishing you would sometime in some way, risk some unprotected profundity of experience; or since no one admits profundity of experience, some characteristic private defiance of the significantly detestable.

This involuted injunction to openness in its restless turnings no doubt records Moore's own misgivings about her prescriptions. She goes on to worry:

> I feel a responsibility against anything that might threaten you; yet fear to admit such anxiety, lest I influence you away from an essential necessity or particular strength. The golden eggs can't be dealt with theoretically, by presumptuous mass salvation formulae. But I also feel that tentativeness and interiorizing are your danger as well as your strength.

Tactfully avoiding the opposition of *weakness* against *strength*, she substitutes *danger* instead. The letter, a rather wonderful balancing act teetering between advice and observation, and generously maintaining the pride and dignity of both correspondents, closes with a deprecating second reference to Moore's own "baldness":

> P.S. The wrought excellence and infectious continuity of your thinkings — the abashingly as I said above — formidable demureness, disgust me with my own bald performances, and what I have said sounds preceptorial but such clumsiness perhaps is better than the conscientious timidity which kept me from writing.

The letter is a good sample of the complex and productive delicacies of response that ruled both women.

In 1940 Bishop wrote in discouragement:

> I have that continuous uncomfortable feeling of "things" in the head like icebergs or rocks or awkwardly-shaped pieces of furniture — it's as if all the nouns were there but the verbs were lacking —

if you know what I mean. And I can't help having the theory that if they are juggled around hard enough and long enough some bit of electricity will occur, just by friction, that will arrange everything –

For Bishop, the word, or by extension, the image, had to prove adequate, the sentence, or judgment, or precept that Moore looks for, a ruse of implication. Such a belief clearly kept her from Moore's more widely spread sententiae, and from further acquaintance with Moore's own preferred lists of attributes and static predicates, in movement through juxtaposed elements, rather than through the conventional orders of narrative.

Perhaps the broadest difference between the two poets lies in Bishop's steady adoption of a more heavily narrative and dramatic poetry. Speaking of her prose in February 1956, Moore writes to Bishop: "A dry alertness with no over-accented intrusiveness is what I would like sentences to be." Perhaps this is the crux of the difference; in greater possession of the knowledge of her end-goal, Moore foregoes the prickle of being in constant discovery of some unexpected truth along the way. A classicist to the bone, in spite of her modernist disjunctions of subject, Moore was never interested in those baroque possibilities that excited Bishop, the young Vassar student, as she copied out M. W. Croll's description of the baroque sentence that unfolded its truths in the course of speaking them. This interested her:

> how symmetry is first made and then broken, as it is in so many baroque designs in painting and architecture; how there is a constant swift adaptation of form to the emergencies that arise in an energetic and unpremeditated forward movement; and observe, further, that these signs of spontaneity and improvisation occur in passages loaded with as heavy a freight content as rhetoric ever has to carry.

"Dry alertness," and a distaste for "over-accented intrusiveness" have no place in this aesthetic.

In Moore's 1946 review of *North & South*, she makes a public concession to Bishop's point of view, perhaps speaking against her own love of maxim or sententiae by asking, "is not anything that is adamant, self-ironized?" And concludes:

> With poetry as with homiletics, tentativeness can be more positive than positiveness; and in *North & South*, a much instructed persuasiveness is emphasized by uninsistence.[. . .] At last we have someone who knows, who is not didactic.

Finally sensing their key differences, and wishing to try her hand freely on wider populations of response, it is no surprise that, after Bishop's meeting with Robert Lowell in 1947, she became increasingly interested in his more autobiographical work, and a little less interested in the emblematic objects and animals that comprised Moore's more familiar reticences.

Although family nouns are dangerously applied to such changes of direction in development, one might say that Bishop found it time to move from the strictures of the benevolent mentor-mother to the challenges emanating from the brother-poet. But not from too close a positioning: the next significant expansion of Bishop's life and work occurred thousands of miles from either poet in Brazil. Any further discussion of Bishop's Brazilian work, however, must be preceded by some attempt to place the impact of her friendship with the other poet of her life, Robert Lowell.

·E·I·G·H·T·

Skunk and Armadillo

Having discovered the limits of Marianne Moore as coach and model, Bishop found Robert Lowell still provocatively at her shoulder. At first, as she said simply to Lowell in May 1948, he "jerked her up" to "the proper table level of poetry." He was above all her supporter, and quickly then her determined and lasting promoter, even through the occasional rapacity of his admiration, several times plundering her life for poetic subject. His review of Bishop's *North & South*,[63] which was the precipitating cause of their meeting, seemed generous to Bishop, and her response was spontaneously grateful and in no way stiffnecked:

> I suppose for pride's sake I should take some sort of stand about the adverse criticisms, but I agreed with some of them only too well – I suppose no critic is ever really as harsh as oneself. It seems to me you spoke out my worst fears as well as some of my ambitions.

The last sentence is revealing: she grants without qualification that Lowell accurately locates the bottom of her trajectory, but notes that he finds only "some" of her ambitions.

Yet the confidence with which Lowell took the robe as judge, and assigned Bishop the stand as the judged, must have marked their relations for many years, much as birth order establishes the patterns of dominance to be accepted or contested by siblings for the rest of their lives. In this 1947 review, Lowell apportions many compliments, and in tracing Bishop's descent lines from Moore, Auden, and Williams, remarks magisterially that Bishop's admirers "are not likely to hail her as a giant among the moderns," trimming her rank further by denying comparison with Shakespeare and Donne. "Later," apparently having realized the shortfall or bad fit of his measure, he praises her as "one of the best craftsmen alive." Full of shrewd insights about Bishop's early work, the piece is also a model of Lowell's anxiously and rigorously hierarchizing preoccupations.

Bishop clearly passed a kind of test, however. Thereafter, Lowell began the pattern of professional support that lasted throughout the rest of his life, as he tossed reading engagements Bishop's way, proposed her for grants, professional societies, and looked after jobs, appointments, and awards for her, frequently supplying advice and encouragement urging her toward what he saw as appropriate career choices. In 1963, Bishop wrote to Lowell: "To hell with explainers – that's really why I don't want to teach." But in June 1965 when teaching turned up as her best way of temporarily leaving Brazil, Lowell wrote her with lofty but reassuring casualness to explain what he did in a classroom: "Classes are not lectures so much as arranged conversations, and you need do nothing but take things casually and trust yourself to your humor, sense, knowledge and personal interests." Five months later, somewhat admonishingly, but with soothing qualifiers tacked on for better coaxing, he added, "In our society, it's almost a duty for people like us to teach *a little.*"

She had no reason to be anything but grateful to him; in the last years of his life he was still seeing to her needs, arranging the sale of his papers to Harvard, and yet setting aside for her the sum of money involved in the transfer of her letters in that sale. Although her letters to him were legally his, and although he might have profited by them, he returned their price to her. Yet the complex story of their relationship and its mutual indebtednesses needs to be told on several levels: each in the fashion of his or her nature supported the other's career, each was influenced both directly and indirectly by the other's poetry, and each held the other in some inner and inviolable chamber of the mind as a figure for contemplation. David Kalstone sets out the particulars of friendship with all the care that this rich narrative deserves; yet it is interesting to see how indebtedness is largely read by him through the lens of Lowell's accomplishments, still skewing, perhaps, the record of Bishop's more active responses in favor of her more passive refusals and tactical withdrawals.

Bishop's direct response to Lowell's early poetry is never less than respectful; yet at the time they met it is hard to imagine that the poetry of *Lord Weary's Castle* or *The Mills of the Kavanaughs*, Lowell's books up until then, fully engaged her. She made this admission in 1950, close to the onset of their lengthy correspondence: "I find your poetry so strongly influential that if I start reading it when I'm working on something of my own I'm lost." Yet isn't there a barb in this apparent compliment from June 1951, written after she has completed her double sonnet, "The Prodigal": "The Kavanaughs came to spoil my pleasure, because what I can only keep up for twice 14 lines I'm sure you could have kept up for pages & pages."

What Lowell himself deprecatingly referred to as the "big drum" of his unrelenting rhetoric in the weaker poems must have elicited a wary amusement in Bishop, even if at that point she lacked the confidence to reject entirely a work so much more widely accepted than her own. But there is a shade here, the same stubborn self-respect that maintained the younger Bishop steadily afloat beside Moore that strongly suggests to Lowell that what is kept up for "pages & pages" is a kind of mechanical pumping that might well have stopped sooner to its own advantage. Very early in their correspondence, she writes that she has read a wonderful book, the thrilling memoir of a secret agent, and there is a teasing, affectionate mockery of Lowell for his profusion as effusion, as she imagines him turning her good read into poetry: the implication is that Lowell could turn *anything* into poetry, a temptation that Bishop herself would have the wisdom to resist. The whole antiquated, lumbering weight of Lowell's "The Mills of the Kavanaughs," with its histrionic dialogue, need only be juxtaposed with one of Bishop's poems to spell out the difference in tone and stance, which a resourceful Lowell himself was certainly quick enough to see as relevant instruction.

In his first reading of William Carlos Williams he had already begun to shape out his problems. In speaking of the impact of Williams,[64] Lowell says of his earliest work, "Everything I did was grand, ungrammatical, and had a timeless, hackneyed quality." As he describes Williams' strengths, they are his "hard, nervous secular knowingness" as well as a use of forms that made possible "quick changes of tone, atmosphere, and speed." In Bishop he praises "her marvelous command of shifting speech tones," and in virtually the same breath commends "her bare objective language," reminding him of Williams.[65]

Both Lowell and Bishop comment individually on these influences. "Williams enters me, but I cannot enter him," Lowell notes, and the metaphor of masculine resistance fits; Bishop, on the other hand, he found "softer, dreamier, more human, and more personal" than Moore, the lamp he and others always chose to post before Bishop. But perhaps because of her perceived softness Bishop's language marked her poetry as Lowell's point of entry to Williams' homing directness. Yet while Lowell remarks on Bishop's resemblance to Williams, he does not press it. As Kalstone points out, the first open disagreement between them arose over Williams' use of Marcia Nardi's letters to Williams. In a preview of their disagreement over Lowell's use of letters from his former wife Elizabeth Hardwick in *The Dolphin*, Bishop condemns Williams to Lowell for using Nardi's long, accusing and reproachful letters verbatim in *Paterson*;[66] even pseudonymously, Bishop felt that the letters were invasive; furthermore, "They're much too overpowering emotionally" and because of them "the whole poem suffers." Chiefly, she responds with an instinctive protectiveness for the exposure of an emotional vulnerability she recognizes: "maybe I've felt a little too much the way the woman did at certain more hysterical moments – people who haven't experienced absolute loneliness for long stretches of time can never sympathise with it at all." For Bishop, directness and objectivity are not synonymous.

In these early years, Lowell relied on her for a friendly skepticism about his essential sincerity, or weakness for rhetoric, and in April 1952 he writes to her:

> You always make me feel that I have a rather obvious breezy, impersonal liking for the great and obvious — in contrast with your adult personal feeling for the odd and genuine;

And earlier, in January 1949, rather winningly,

> You & Peter Taylor always make me feel something of a fake — so I love you both dearly.

Each poet seems to have relied on the other's opposed tendency for balance, although it isn't until Bishop is a continent away from Lowell's too-compelling personal presence that she begins to ac-knowledge the full force of what she feels she gains from his example. Lowell, always more open and unclouded about influence by his contemporaries, outlines readily the qualities that he feels he must learn from her; initially, Bishop is far more articulate about what she feels she cannot emulate and must avoid.

The differences between them are nowhere more evident than in two early poems with roughly parallel subjects: Bishop's "The Fish," and Lowell's "The Drunken Fisherman." Yet it was obviously the severe plainness of Bishop's narrative description that arrested Lowell. Large of reference and gesture, his poem begins:

> Wallowing in this bloody sty,
> I cast for fish that pleased my eye
> (Truly Jehovah's bow suspends
> No pots of gold to weight its ends);
> Only the blood-mouthed rainbow trout
> Rose to my bait. They flopped about
> My canvas creel until the moth
> Corrupted its unstable cloth.

The understated precision, as well as the emotionally flattened but peaceful surface of Bishop's poem, in which a loose-metered alliteration and anaphora replace rhyme, may have attracted Lowell by the sheer opposition of her means:

> I caught a tremendous fish
> and held him beside the boat
> half out of water, with my hook
> fast in a corner of his mouth.
> He didn't fight.
> He hadn't fought at all.
> He hung a grunting weight,
> battered and venerable
> and homely. Here and there
> his brown skin hung in strips
> like ancient wallpaper:
> shapes like full-blown roses
> stained and lost through age.

In August 1947, commenting on her poem (again characteristically assigning it rank even within Bishop's own work), Lowell says: "Perhaps it's your best anyway. I felt very envious in reading it—I'm a fisherman myself, but all my fish become symbols, alas!"

Whatever violent resentments and fears that intimate relations with women may have evoked at different times in Lowell's troubled personal history, Bishop must have been an intriguing presence for him. So many of his poems appropriate a female vantage point; here was a female vantage point, in the flesh, that wrote its own poetry, and the urge to own it must have been strong. Writing about a group of memorable people from Alice Longworth to Adrienne Rich, Lowell remarked to Bishop in February 1967, "Sometimes I think I would die, if it weren't for a few platonic relations with women." Besides his very genuine affection and respect for Bishop's wit, intelligence, and originality, there is an aspect of her character that must have been for him like the mirror speaking back, or like a captive Other sounding from somewhere inside. Her status as Other, as the feared and desired female, who nonetheless so much resembled him, created a special place filled by no other human relation.

In Lowell's early work, a moment occurs several times in which a protagonist looks with negative results to a mirror to give selfhood back.[67] Within these early images it is evident to him that neither the real taproot of poetry or selfhood has yet been located, although entrance to poetry through assumption of the identity of others is a practice that never lost its attraction. It is interesting to remember that the flood of prose memoir that released the persons and events of *Life Studies*, his breakthrough work, was apparently tripped into being by a reverie in the person of his dead mother, in the years directly before his birth.[68] Ian Hamilton and other sources report that all of Lowell's manic breaks were triggered by, or involved infatuations with women. Searching indefatigably for the prime Other, or attempting forcible re-entry into the lost maternal, or first love, Lowell seems struggling to fill an emptiness or recognition of self not achieved in the first splitting off from the maternal body, performing again and again some helpless iteration of an incompleted Lacanian mirror stage. Among other temperamental affinities, he and Bishop may share their early experience with forms of maternal deficit, each at a critical stage in their poetic careers staring at blank mirrors, Bishop first in "Insomnia," then later again in "Sonnet."

At varying points in this correspondence, he conveys that particular quality of absorption with another as a style of self-definition. In both poems and letters he appropriates her experience, groping for her life as an extension of his. With self-perception he writes in July 1963: "The worst temptations and bad habits are wanting somehow to throw your own shadow on every scene and prospect, that and wanting to ask for a kind of help that no one can give, as if there were another life that could be thrown into your own and remove all its inertia and blindness." In September 1968 he muses: "as I sat on my dry grass lifted above the harbor, and reread your letter, I was almost you." His "almost" does not shift the weight of a need that Bishop doubtless found unnerving. Even if her sexual preferences had been other, or if she had not had her own fragilities and instabilities to contend with, there seems adequate reason for her to have backed away from romantic entanglement.

As Kalstone traces it, the romantic crisis of what Lowell was once pleased to call their "fellowship" took place largely in two separate stages, first, during the summer of 1948, and then nine years later in 1957, when Bishop had returned to visit the Lowells with Lota. Lowell approached Bishop twice for more than loving friendship. In one of the most poignant moments that exists in this thirty-year correspondence, no doubt to be quoted many more times because the language is so haunting, Lowell describes his early state of mind to Bishop. After a fresh outbreak of mental illness has subsided, and after his amorous excitability has disturbed them both a second time, in August 1957 he gives his version of the events of 1948:

> [. . .] all has come right since you found Lota. But at the time everything, I guess (I don't want to over-dramatize), [in] our relations seemed to have reached a new place. I assumed that it would be just a matter of time before I proposed and I half-believed that you would accept. Yet I wanted it all to have the right build-up. Well, I didn't say anything then. And of course the Eberharts' in-laws wasn't the right stage-setting, and then there was that poetry conference at Bard and I remember one evening presided over by Mary McCarthy and my Elizabeth was there, and going home to the Bard poets' dormitory, I was so drunk that my hands turned cold and I felt half-dying and held your hand. And nothing was said, and like a loon that needs sixty feet, I believe, to take off from the water, I wanted time and space, and went on assuming, and when I was to have joined you at Key West I was determined to ask you. Really for so callous (I fear) a man, I was fearfully shy and scared of spoiling things and distrustful of being steady enough to be the least good. Then of course the Yaddo explosion came and it was all over.

It is a marvelously engaging self-portrait; yet it is clear that Lowell's sense of dramatic occasion, of what the situation rather than what the persons might demand, controls action. Bishop is said to have mistrusted the madness hereditary for both of them. Equally, she may have read skeptically the stability of her own and Lowell's affections, and profoundly feared and mistrusted the nature of the physical drive connecting Lowell to her. This, in spite of what was a depth and real constancy of feeling in Lowell's regretful, nine years' assessment of the turns of their relationship:

> No doubt if I used my head better, ordered my life better, worked harder, etc, the poetry would be improved and there must be many lost poems, innumerable accidents and ill-done actions. But asking you is *the* might have been for me, the one towering change, the other life that might have been had.

A large part of her rejection of Lowell's "suit" could have been her sense of the histrionic element of his attachments, of its quality of oversight: Lowell's ability to see the person in the poem he was making of his life and the person in the flesh as but one and the same. As Lowell anticipated in the curious turns of his mid-fifties' essay, "Art and Evil," at some critical junction, Aeneas would leave Dido, "leaving a real woman of flesh and blood to follow the empty abstract fantasy of becoming a figurehead in an epic poem." Lowell says,

> Aeneas, in tearing himself away from Dido, comes to know the full torture of seeming to be, of all but believing himself to be cold, dead, calculating, serpentine. The *Aeneid* is perhaps like Proust's novel, the story of what one must give up to write a book.

Although the myth Lowell chose later in leaving Elizabeth Hardwick followed the contours of the Greek, rather than the Roman, myth, making Lowell into Ulysses over Aeneas, the principle seems the same: what the heart follows is what the eye sees, and what the eye sees is never quite outside of one's inner imaginings, as those imaginings are exalted beyond the merely flesh.

However attracted to him Bishop may have been, and there is a wonderful touch of the schoolgirl crush in her comments to Ilse Barker about Lowell's handsomeness, her instinctive judgment about their incompatibility as lovers were quickly decisive; her feelings during the time that Lowell recalls in the "loon" letter read as markedly different. By August 30, 1948, in a candid letter to their mutual friend Carley Dawson, she is expressing a pungent irritation:

my one feeling just now about our better intellectuals is – *stay away*. It may be some comfort to you to know that I had a letter from C [Lowell] in the same mail & he has already begun to be "mean" to me, try to get "rises," etc. – it began even before he left, of course. He just can't help himself, I guess. I had thought that maybe I was "good for him" – maybe I am, but I think sooner or later I couldn't take any more of that ego-maniacy, or whatever it is – it is too bad, & I do want to remain friends but I think it is going to require great care & fortitude & a rhinoceros-skin into the bargain. One of his recent letters concluded, "Be a good girl & come to Yaddo." And that is all the poor dear knows about how to get along with people!

Bishop's indirect responses to such pressures are whimsically noted by Lowell in January 1954: "We seem attached to each other by some stiff piece of wire, so that each time one moves, the other moves in another direction."

· I ·

As David Kalstone explains the complex genesis of "The Prodigal," Bishop was pushed by Robert Lowell's example into his "grimmer imaginings," a category of composition which eventually allowed Bishop to deal with her own problems with alcohol through the distancing frame of parable. While in a letter to Lowell she admires Corbière's *Le Poète contumace*, which Lowell has sent her in translation, she declines these candors and deployments of the outrageous self: "I can see in them the kind of thing one should try to/could do but half-consciously shie [sic] away from." But prodded perhaps doubly by Lowell and Tristan Corbière to make poetic traffic with images of the unacceptable self, she seizes on her current sense of her life as in drifting and aimless exile from a homelier and sturdier past, and in one of her characteristic gender reversals, pins her mood on the biblical figure of the Prodigal Son.

Notes in one of the journals I found in Brazil for a poem tentatively to be called "Ark of the Covenant" were apparently written in the late forties,[69] or around the time that Bishop was working on "The Prodigal." The sketch of this poem, which overlaps "The Prodigal" in language and imagery, shows Bishop reaching first toward the physical placement of the prodigal's world:

The barns –
    Closing up the barns that night –
The man emerging with the lantern,
The cow mooing, a bat flying around
the barnyard, everything gray & mysterious
    ark-like
lantern-bearing   like the sun setting

clearing, than snowy   the mountains of
dark hay, the strong smells, the bins
of grain

And then there are further notations aligning the comforts of this arklike barn with Noah's conveyance:

[Moon] [Man] [Now] carting off the sun
              taking away "   "

    brute world

gentle & companionable all night

Come back, child, fearfully carrying
the oil-lamp
up the stairs steep as a ladder

In this draft, the poem will be openly autobiographical, and the invitation is to the apparition of a younger self. The mood and tone are much like lines about Nova Scotia that govern the lyric and nostalgic tendernesses of her story, "In the Village"; the draft also touches the mood of reminiscence in patches of "The Moose." The words here run as water from the same well. But jogged by other, riskier possibilities, Bishop finally abandons the strictly autobiographical vein, at least for the moment, and adapts the familiar setting to the biblical story, reaching for the deeper, more abrasive truths of her current position through the fictive shield of parable.

    It is a stunning moment in her work. To judge from the sketch of the poem she has brushed aside, "Ark of the Covenant" seems nearly there; a kind of agreeable sandman, the man with the lantern emerges from the dark of the barn, the maternal cow is mooing, and all is hinted to be well through that probably sweet-smelling hay, as the fearful child represses her dread and with her own oil-lamp mounts the stairs to bed. The projected poem seems a shade on the sentimental side, something close in tone to another Nova Scotian childhood poem, "Manners," pointing to an easy nostalgia for the childhood

self trembling on the threshold of knowledge. It is definitely Wordsworthian, even with that oil-lamp—a prop turning up in other poem
fragments—elsewhere belonging to Faustina, the sinister Key West
figure.

But Bishop rejects the ark of the hayloft covenant as her dominant
motif; instead, setting the parable within the space of her own Nova
Scotia childhood allows her to anchor another better and more unexpected poem in a wealth of detail both lyric and securely naturalistic:

> The brown enormous odor he lived by
> was too close, with its breathing and thick hair,
> for him to judge. The floor was rotten; the sty
> was plastered halfway up with glass-smooth dung.
> Light-lashed, self-righteous, above moving snouts,
> the pigs' eyes followed him, a cheerful stare—
> even to the sow that ate her young—
> till, sickening, he leaned to scratch her head.

This poem decisively abandons childhood security for an iteration of
the adult's malaise and spatial unease. The brutal pig substitutes for
the mooing cow, and the comfortable ark of a hay-loft—"everything
gray & mysterious"—gives way to the dung-plastered sty. When Bishop
talked about this poem to Joseph Summers in a letter written in 1967,
she speaks of its origin in a trip she made during the Forties back
home to Great Village, and makes no mention of childhood; it obviously took her some time to move the poem closer in tone to the
adult visit of later years. She says:

> (I'll tell you, just for fun but please don't use it now – THE PRODI-
> GAL was suggested to me when one of my aunt's stepsons offered
> me a drink of rum, in the pig styes, at about 9 in the morning, when
> I was visiting her in Nova Scotia.)

Yet the complicit rural comedy which triggered the poem in no way
destroyed the word "covenant" as an appropriate figure of the poem's
faith, nor is the ark rejected. In the final version of this effort, sunset
yields to sunrise, and the poem permits the theoretical possibility of
going "home," of a kind of rebirth, even if the Prodigal in Bishop's
poem never quite gets there, or never manages to rouse himself past
the small anticlimax of the final, discordant rhyme:

> But it took him a long time
> finally to make his mind up to go home.

In the early working, it is a "brute world" evidently designed to retire before the "gentle & companionable" ark. Perhaps the child, "fearfully carrying/ the oil-lamp," will be instructed about night's pleasures, but in the moment of the finished poem it is a much more debased domestic reality with which the drunken Prodigal, hiding his pints behind that two-by-four for the shaky morning after, must make his terms. Bishop invokes the comforting figure of "The man emerging with the lantern," but transforms him to the Prodigal's boss:

> But evenings the first star came to warn.
> The farmer whom he worked for came at dark
> to shut the cows and horses in the barn
> beneath their overhanging clouds of hay,
> with pitchforks, faint forked lightnings, catching light,
> safe and companionable as in the Ark.

Here, the evening star comes to warn; if he wants his "shuddering insights, beyond his control" really to touch him into redemption and return, he'll have to get out of that barn, not head mesmerised and nostalgic back to it. It is an interesting reversal here that the solution for the protagonist is to leave the home ground: Bishop senses that the pastoral world of her own childhood will not offer an adequate final station.

Recurrent traits mark this poem as a seminal one: the iridescent flash of sunlight over water appears as her familiar signal for epiphany; there's even a hint of her personal insight-accompanying thunderstorm in those "faint forked lightnings, catching light" in the tines of the farmer's pitchfork. In the final image of illumination,

> The lantern—like the sun, going away—
> laid on the mud a pacing aureole.

that *pacing* aureole resembles the moving target of the moving hunter of her adolescent speculations.

"The Prodigal" is a steep advance in method over the delicate but sturdy playfulness that produced the fantasy figures of "The Gentleman of Shalott" and "The Man-Moth." But while "The Prodigal" may have been the poem that opened up a strategy for autobiography closer to Lowell's practice, finally Bishop was not prepared to descend more than cryptically and schematically into particular folds of her life. Resembling other poems based on deeply disquieting feelings, "The Prodigal" arrives at them by a circuitous, though probably enabling, route through form: the poem is a double sonnet. It is "The

Prodigal's" calling upon a distancing myth that allows Bishop a closer approach to troubling personal material, permitting inspection of drunkenness and helpless drifting. The poem, written in her late thirties, offers a parade example of how the directly autobiographical, even when courted, will never provide for her a more than limited access to the most painful reaches of the authentic self.

·II·

Distance served the friendship well, giving each poet the opportunity to profit in more manageable ways. Bishop, over the years, must have felt Lowell's influence as a steady enlargement of the sphere of the possible subject, loosening her tighter grip on the emotions. In "Gwendolyn," one of the Nova Scotia stories Bishop wrote in 1953, or during the early years of her Brazilian stay, the parents of the sickly Gwendolyn feverishly smother the child with kisses, while the narrator's grandparents are forced to witness the unseemly display:

> My grandmother was disgusted. "They'll kiss that child to death if they're not careful," she said. "Oh lallygagging, lallygagging!" said my grandfather, going about his business.

It was not accident that led an adult Bishop to long residence in a country where the *abraço*, or embrace, is national courtesy. Nor is it a random pattern of development in which these memories of physical reserve in her own upbringing surface explicitly in her work just as her relation with Lota blooms. In this contact with the deepest layers of her own history, at the farthest physical and temporal remove from her northern childhood, Bishop begins to acknowledge its profoundly estranging effects, and this occurs in prose at a period some years before Lowell began writing and publishing the confessional childhood poems of *Life Studies*.

Unlike Lowell, Bishop turned first to prose fiction with its alternate and multiple selving. There are also signs in the texts she eventually chose for translation, João Cabral de Melo Neto's *Pernambuco Christmas Play*, dated 1954–55, and Joaquim Cardozo's "Cemetery of Childhood," commemorating Children's Week, 1953, that she may have been working on these as well during the time that she was concentrating on her Nova Scotian and Brazilian stories. Fiction and translation both were dropping her deep inside childhood and folk consciousness, where the Brazilian primitive represented childhood in another key both detailed and universalized. Where Lowell tended to appropriate women, Bishop was tempted by Brazilians, both also instinctively headed for childhood as the head-waters of significant memory.

It is during these years, when both poets are at the farthest reach from each other and most intensely engaged in the life with their separate partners, that each acknowledges the depth of their relationship. In 1956, Bishop writes: "I think of you every day of my life I'm sure"; and in 1962, five years after his confessional letter to her:

> You have no idea, Cal, how really grateful to you I am and how fortunate I feel myself in knowing you, having you for a friend – when I think how the world and my life would look to me if you weren't in either of them at all – they'd look very empty, I think – I am awfully happy with Lota, odd as it is in some ways, and with living in such a hopeless, helpless country, too – I don't seem to need or enjoy a life of intellectual society – but I certainly need you

His letters continue an almost caressive courtliness, a steady gallantry: in 1958, "I feel that I write only for you and Lizzie"; in 1968, "Dear Heart: This is a name that I use at special times for both Lizzie and Harriet"; and so on.

Baffled by the complex importance of their relationship, Lowell continued to try to fit the friendship into conventionally gendered frames of reference. His first attempt, in "Water," ultimately the first in his series, "Four Poems for Elizabeth Bishop,"[70] is initially drafted as romantic dialogue between a "He" and a "She." In the poems written much later, he struggles to articulate the aesthetic difference so provocative and enticing to both of them. Published in 1970's *Notebook*, "Calling 1970," the third of the series, first emerged in these lines:

> Nowadays painting lives on iron rations,
> never the leisure of Albert Ryder who left
> his landscapes to rot and ripen in the sunlight,
> paint fell off the canvas when the work was perfect.
> But who is destroyed when I destroy myself?
> The Spartans could have marched from Thermopylae,
> instead they rushed into the Persian army,
> dying because they scorned to save their lives.

Elizabeth Bishop is nowhere in sight. But as the poem developed, provisonally titled "Vocation," she entered and the military metaphor for art's rituals of waste and sacrifice of human material in search of truth fell away. As Lowell began sketching the lines that present Ryder's rotting paint as his analogy for Bishop's patient waiting for the emergence of the right word, like the paint exalted through the sun's natural selection, in the final version it is only Ryder's paint which drops, and not the Spartan soldiers. The military metaphor for art stays as a ghost in the now enigmatic single line: "Who is killed if the horseman never cry halt?"

But upside-down, hung like the interceding inchworm itself, a few lines appeared on the bottom edge of a typewritten sheet of another poem:

> Have you ever seen an inchworm crawl up a leaf,
> cling to the very end, revolve in air,
> feeling for something to reach to something?

And in a simulation of the natural process, respecting natural process in Bishop's own way, his poem now completes both thought and image:

> Have you ever seen an inchworm crawl up a leaf,
> cling to the very end, revolve in air,
> feeling for something to reach something? My dear,
> you hang your words in air, years old, imperfect,
> pasted to cardboard posters, gay lettered, gapped
> for the unimagined phrases and the wide-eyed Muse,
> uneasy caller, finds her casual friend.

It won't be until the publication of 1973's *History* that he finds the right last line, waiting patiently like Bishop until the poem has fully revealed itself:

> Do
> you still hang your words in air, ten years
> unfinished, glued to your notice board, with gaps
> or empties for the unimaginable phrase —
> unerring Muse who makes the casual perfect?

In a final tribute, having cleared away the complicating rubble of the earlier lines, Lowell names her not merely friend to the Muse but the Muse herself.

Kalstone poses the differences between the two poets revealed in Lowell's revisions by juxtaposing Bishop's "more submissive mentality" next to Lowell's "irreconcilable energies."[71] Both poets "share the element of risk, but those empty spaces on Bishop's board, empty for years, suggest a moment of rest when finally life and observation will provide the missing detail, the inner premonition will find a confirming external response from a mysterious, enduring, independent outer world." Kalstone's recognition of Bishop's relation to experience is much like Richard Mullen's earlier summation of the reasons for her dissociation from surrealism. In each case, both critics point to her countervailing respect for an objective, outlying, otherness of truth. What is crucial here is not Kalstone's rather limp vision of Bishop's "more submissive mentality," but of Bishop's play on the boundary between self and world, internal and external reality, as the boundary separates, and as the boundary joins. Kalstone sees her patience and her grasp of that negotiating play, and ascribes it implicitly to temperament. I would like to add that the nonaggressive temperament here very likely also represents the hard lessons that gender helped to enforce. Lowell's dropping the Spartan soldiers from "Calling, 1970" is an unconscious recognition of those lessons.

In the late fifties the poems of *Life Studies* continued to nag away at Bishop's sense of the necessary poetic practice, even if the more corrosive examples of Lowell's voyages into his dark interior did not seem imitable for a decade or more. In December 1957 in a letter that came flooding after Lowell sent her the poems that were to constitute the personal core of *Life Studies*, she writes him about poetry, about her responses to people, about how her life in Brazil subverted her shyness and supported intimacy. Uncharacteristically, her response to his poems is almost awed:

> They all have that sure feeling, as if you'd been in a stretch (I've felt that way for very short stretches once in a long while) when everything and anything suddenly seemed material for poetry or not material, seemed to *be* poetry, and all the past was illuminated in a long shaft here and there, like a long-waited for sunrise. If only one could see everything that way all the time! It seems to me that's the whole purpose of art, to the artist (not to the audience) – that rare feeling of control, illumination – life *is* all right, for the time being. Anyway, when I read such an extended display of imagination as this, I feel it *for* you.

"You," the pronoun in use, is quickly taken up by Bishop as referring to her own experience as well as Lowell's; these poems of his have moved her, and work inside her as might her own. This is the closest that Bishop comes to appropriating Lowell's own appropriative style of consciousness, in which life is always tipping over into art. But for her the experience is rare, fitful, and momentary, and still tied both to "control" and "illumination"; her "sunrise" also brings her a measure of immense reassurance. Responding to a compliment of his, she says,

> But "broken through to where you've always been" – what on earth do you mean by that? I haven't got anywhere at all, I think – just to those first benches to sit down and rest on, in a side-arbor of the maze.

In a frank moment she allows herself to face their differing circumstances and name "envy" of what she terms his "luck":

> And here I must confess (and I imagine most of our contemporaries would confess the same thing) that I am green with envy of your kind of assurance. I feel that I could write in as much detail about my Uncle Artie, say – but what would be the significance? Nothing at all. He became a drunkard, fought with his wife, and spent most of his time fighting [. . .] and was ignorant as sin. It is sad, slightly more interesting than having an uncle practising law in Schenectady maybe, but that's all. Whereas all you have to do is put down the names! And the fact that it seems significant, illustrative, American, etc., gives you, I think, the confidence you display about tackling any idea or theme, *seriously*, in both writing and conversation. In some ways you are the luckiest poet I know! – in some ways not so lucky, either, of course.

Bishop makes very plain her own sense of the class division operating between herself and Lowell, a division he tended to blur between them, although Lowell pointed out likenesses with assiduity: in his mind, they both survived on trust funds, and were both New Englanders with Tory ancestors. The passage I've quoted closes with another instance of Bishop's fusing her own feeling with Lowell's, acknowledging the kinship that he elsewhere sounds as a leitmotif of their connection:

> I'm not really complaining and of course am not really "jealous" in any deep sense at all – I've felt almost as wonderful a sense of relief since I first saw some of these poems in Boston as if I'd written

them myself and I've thought of them at odd times and places with the greatest pleasure every single day since, I swear.

Yet the question of what she dares to do in verse rankles:

it is hell to realize one has wasted one's talent through timidity that probably could have been overcome if anyone in one's own family had had a few grains of sense or education... Well, maybe it's not too late!

Even before *Life Studies* came to have its impact on her, Bishop worked on her memoir-story, "In the Village," publishing it in 1953; but it is not until the final decade of her writing life that she picks up prose again, and with amplified confidence focuses on that very same drunken Uncle Artie in "Memories of Uncle Neddy," putting aside the misgivings that she voiced in 1957. Bishop was no more eager to name her alcoholism than her lesbianism in print. But the example of Lowell's poetry of admissions again seems to have edged her to closer and closer inspection of this subject. Close, but not too close: each time an alcoholic raises his head in a poem or story—and it is always *his* head—Bishop makes him a male relative, Mr. Boomer, Uncle Neddy, or, as in "The Prodigal" she interposes a nephew-model between herself and the troubling thirst. It is only in the drafts of "A Drunkard," written around 1960, which Kalstone shows to be written in partial response to Lowell's "The Drinker,"[72] that Bishop assumes the burden of the first person, a dangerous burden saved once again for the unpublished file.

But the obvious indebtedness worked for some further years on Lowell's side. Even as Bishop acknowledged the receipt of these poems with pleasure, she had already been pleading with Lowell to alter "The Scream," his version of her story, "In the Village," with its false implication of maternal violence. (Although fear of the mother never entirely disappears, a fear going beyond simple abandonment. In her 1950 diary, during the year she marked as "Just about my worst so far," Bishop makes these terse notes on November 14: "ghastly nightmare about my mother – outside the closed door, "they"; beating, etc. – 1st time in about 15 yrs - , I think, & wonder why.") "In the Village" recounts the last days in which her mother lived at home, before a final breakdown and her return to the mental hospital in Halifax that became her permanent home, and one in which Bishop never visited her.

"The Scream" is not one of Lowell's better poems; with its eight stanzas, five lines per stanza, it is a reduction of Bishop's complex and psychologically penetrating account; Lowell stresses a static, comfortless violence of feeling and disruption. Bishop's nuance-laden shifts in perspective, moving between a first person angle of vision and a third person proper noun, "the child," become a monochromatic "I" for Lowell: the only first-person lines in dialogue are actually taken from his daughter Harriet, and not very persuasively inserted in the penultimate stanza: "When she went away I thought/ "But you can't love everyone,/ your heart won't let you!" (Earlier, the same truant line strayed into a draft of "The Old Flame.")

Bishop opens "In the Village" with "the echo of a scream," later identified as her mother's final scream of distress and incapacity, as she breaks down before the dressmaker who is to fit her for the purple dress signifying the official end of her mourning for Bishop's father. But Bishop also chose the clang of the blacksmith's anvil as the antithetical balance of that scream, and the scream becomes something considerably fainter than Lowell's horn-blast:

> It was not even loud to begin with, perhaps. It just came there to live, forever—not loud, just alive forever. Its pitch would be the pitch of my village. Flick the lightning rod on top of the church steeple with your fingernail and you will hear it.

In the tiny, dream-submerged and elegiac landscape opening Bishop's story, the remembering speaker can almost take the church steeple up between probing finger and thumb. But Nate the blacksmith's anvil produces "beautiful sounds," and the hope of hearing them again claims the story's last words, despite the lingering burden of the scream:

> *Clang.*
> And everything except the river holds its breath.
> Now there is no scream. Once there was one and it
> settled slowly down to earth one hot summer afternoon; or
> did it float up, into that dark, too dark, blue sky? But
> surely it has gone away, forever.
> It sounds like a bell buoy out at sea.
> It is the elements speaking: earth, air, fire, water.
> All those other things—clothes, crumbling postcards,
> broken china; things damaged and lost, sickened, or destroyed;
> even the frail almost-lost scream—are they too frail for us

to hear their voices long, too mortal?
Nate!
Oh, beautiful sound, strike again!

Each of Lowell's stanzas selects a real bit of the narrative to isolate, yet in the black, heavyhanded outline crayon with which he took up others' stories from Rimbaud's "le Dormeur du val," to Melville's "Benito Cereno" and on through Hawthorne's "My Kinsman, Major Molyneux," he removes lightness of stroke; from Bishop, gentleness as well: Bishop's horseshoes *are* her original "bloody little moons":

In the blacksmith's shop,
the horseshoes sailed through the dark,
like bloody little moons,
red-hot, hissing, protesting,
as they drowned in the pan.

But in Bishop's context extinction is immediately followed by another reference in which extinction, or stinging wasps are part of a generally benevolent and invitingly careful natural world:

In the blacksmith's shop things hang up in the shadows and shadows hang up in the things, and there are black and glistening piles of dust in each corner. A tub of night-black water stands by the forge. The horseshoes sail through the dark like bloody little moons and follow each other like bloody little moons to drown in the black water, hissing, protesting.

Outside, along the matted eaves, painstakingly, sweetly, wasps go over and over a honeysuckle vine.

In Bishop's leisurely narrative, shadow and thing are one. Where Lowell pressed for a blacker human drama, she clung resolutely to another outcome in which hope is as much a human obligation as its opposite. "I don't like *heaviness* – " she remarked to Anne Stevenson in 1964: "It seems often to amount to complete self-absorption – like Mann & Wagner. I think one can be cheerful AND profound."

This temperamental difference is there in the correspondence as well. Lowell, concerned and excited for Bishop's welfare during the Brazilian coup of April 1964, during which Lota was blockaded in the besieged palace, writes to her:

182 · Skunk and Armadillo

I am still reeling as I try to imagine the stir of the last few days and surely the last weeks or months.

As I flew home, there was a clear sky across the Atlantic when we reached it, and I pictured the same moon, thousands of miles south, shining on the same ocean, everything strangely nearer because the sandy shore led like a road to you, and in the mind one might walk it, and be lost as I then thought in conflicting knots of thin helmeted soldiers. [. . .] Do write and tell what has been going on with you, and all that your eye lit on.

In May he urges again:

You speak of the artistic temperament, unsuited to this stuff. But you grasp strongly, and come up with full hands. I am a numbskull in these matters. I wish you could find forms, narrative, description, fiction, poems — to get it out. Maybe this would need time and distance. No eye in the world has seen what yours has. I have a vague image of a sequence of poems through which the Revolution moves — no obvious argument or polemic, but the thing embodied, there in all its awfulness, absurdity — good, bad, real, confused, clarified, in the end judged. I don't mean anything neutral or beyond politics. Rather the opposite, everything rescued from the giddy, hard superficial cliches that the removed give realities, that we all give even what we know well. I am thinking really that the Revolution might give a thread for you to draw together the gathering impressions of your ten years' stay.

But Bishop remained stubbornly proof against urging. Neither war nor politics was ever her ostensible subject. Like Lowell himself, she chose the magnifying lens of the scene, the single episode or image over epic narrative. Her letter describing those days in Rio arrived with almost deliberately understated and domesticated details, the details of a noncombatant:

a nice quick revolution in the rain – all over in less than 48 hours – in fact we felt a weird let-down, having steeled ourselves to live beside the radio & TV, laid in many bags of coffee; I'd *baked*, since there was no bread – etc. – also roasted a leg of pork: since we thought the gas would be cut off. Now we're eating it all up . . . Modern revolutions, I've learned, are funny – everything goes but the telephone because it's automatic – so everyone sits in the dark, unwashed, etc., and telephones their friends all day and night –

And then these final images:

> a real Rio touch – big hairy men in bathing trunks dancing madly, waving wet towels – the whole thing took place in violent rainstorms so all paper stuck – cars, tanks, everything, plastered with wet paper.

Then characteristically choosing an infantilized image to deflect the menace of the siege:

> Another division of marines held the sort of park where Goulart's "palace" is, protecting him – but there are also big apartment houses in it where several of our friends live. They couldn't go out at all for a couple of days. There's a small playground in the middle, and at 2 AM the friend looked out and saw marines (they're the ones that wear the pretty uniforms and Scotch bonnets with streamers) swinging in the swings, "pumping away," he said, to swing as high as possible.

If revolution were to move through Bishop's poetry or prose, it would march to the rhythm of her own tune, and whether rightly or wrongly, the human instinct for violence would never be the dominant sub-text.

·III·

Mindful of Bishop's taste for the "odd & genuine," and obviously intrigued by her use of animal personae, Lowell describes his breakthrough poem "Skunk Hour," as directly modeled on Bishop's "Armadillo." As Lowell himself narrates the genesis of the poem,[73] he says, as ever disarming about his own work, "my own poems seemed like prehistoric monsters dragged down into the bog and death by their ponderous armor." During the period preceding composition, he had been on a reading tour, reciting his own poems frequently six days a week, and often doubling up on a single day, probably not a practice designed to make the poet fond of his own production. Further,

> I was reciting what I no longer felt. What influenced me more than San Francisco and reading aloud was that for some time I had been writing prose. I felt that the best style for poetry was none of the many poetic styles in English, but something like the prose of Chekhov or Flaubert.

Written after his reading of Bishop's stories, his own prose must have permitted him some of the same freedoms that Bishop had experienced. Where Bishop's fiction allowed her a designing of other selves, the bounty for Lowell lay in the assumption of a new language as well as a new terrain for a far more personal subject. He continues:

> When I returned to my home, I began writing lines in a new style. No poem, however, got finished and soon I left off and tried to forget the whole headache. Suddenly, in August, I was struck by the sadness of writing nothing, and having nothing to write, of having, at least, no language. When I began writing "Skunk Hour," I felt that most of what I knew about writing was a hindrance.
>
> The dedication is to Elizabeth Bishop, because rereading her suggested a way of breaking through the shell of my old manner. Her rhythms, idiom, images and stanza structure seemed to belong to a later century. "Skunk Hour" is modeled on Miss Bishop's "The Armadillo," a much better poem and one I had heard her read and later carried around with me. Both "Skunk Hour" and "The Armadillo" use short line stanzas, start with drifting description, and end with a single animal.

Although the extant drafts do not quite bear out this assertion, Lowell claims that his totem, the parading skunks, were the first element of the poem to appear for him, as the poem was "written backward, first the last two stanzas, I think, and then the next-to-last-two." I'll quote them as they conclude the finished poem:

> One dark night,
> my Tudor Ford climbed the hill's skull;
> I watched for love-cars. Lights turned down,
> they lay together, hull to hull,
> where the graveyard shelves on the town. . . .
> My mind's not right.
>
> A car radio bleats,
> "Love, O careless love. . . . " I hear
> my ill-spirit sob in each blood cell,
> as if my hand were at its throat. . . .
> I myself am hell;
> nobody's here—
>
> only skunks, that search
> in the moonlight for a bite to eat.

They march on their soles up Main Street:
white stripes, moonstruck eyes' red fire
under the chalk-dry and spar spire
of the Trinitarian Church.

I stand on top
of our back steps and breathe the rich air—
a mother skunk with her column of kittens swills the garbage pail.
She jabs her wedge-head in a cup
of sour cream, drops her ostrich tail,
and will not scare.

The gender of the mother skunk as well as the litter of skunk kittens were later additions. Finished, "Skunk Hour" set the terminus of *Life Studies* for him, and for anyone reading the collection.

While credit is dominantly given Bishop, it is still interesting to mark the other hands included. Lowell quotes from Annette von Droste-Hülshoff's "Am letzten Tage des Jahres," for "the same shudders and situation," and attributes the peeping scene to an anecdote about Walt Whitman in his old age. Subject is clearly liquid; all streams into the poet's mind, flood-gate up, poets past and present pumping away within the manuscript, reminding a reader, perhaps, of Lowell's own comment about American poetry. In writing of Williams, Lowell remarks that "The subjects of great poetry have usually been characters and the passions, a moral struggle that calls a man's whole person into play." Of "the best long American poems" from Whitman to Pound, to Crane and Williams, he observes "no characters take on sufficient form to arrive at a crisis. The people melt into voices." Lowell's own poems have the same liquidity; perhaps because of this approach to character, neither epic nor dramatic narrative ever seem appropriate genre choices for American poets; the big eye, the one that sweeps over the scenes that should be measured in years as well as miles, in societies as well as persons, seems alien to the national temperament. For different reasons, though both Lowell and Bishop played out hands in narrative, neither moved into those larger rhythms. In Bishop's resolute avoidance of violence and big drum, in Lowell's clinging to Pound's, Williams', and Eliot's high modernist fragmentations, both deeded away valuable powers to prose. Although Bishop tried the expansions of story, memoir, and translation, and Lowell drama as well, each poet stayed well within the lyric's shelter, never crossing over into epic territory. Lowell, in his review of Robert Penn

Warren's prose, focused this sense of contracted ambition indirectly into a Pisgah view of "the fat, populated river bottom of the novel," land evidently unreachable for poets stranded on the high ground.

Ending "Skunk Hour," Lowell is still in conformity with his own use of animals, rather than Bishop's, when he remarked that all his fish turned into symbols: even in the poem for which Bishop stands as the dedicatee, the allegorical, or symbolic attribution is at least as strong, if not stronger than the unvarnished natural fact. In Berryman's description of the poem's opening, "The four stanzas are unemphatic, muted. But their quiet, insistent muttering of the *facts* of an extant world opens towards the danger of its being swept away, into delirium." In the Lowell style, what stands as "fact" is human artifact, a human-dominated "extant world" in which the animal never stands either with or against the human as the element of an unplumbable mystery, to which the human submits in curiosity or any other mood. Lowell as a Miltonic Lucifer, hand at his own throat, still finds that "I myself am hell"; yet those skunks provide the magnificent final disguise for both poem and book: a type of Lowell marching on that moonlit street, a palpable Lowell who "will not scare." (Although John Berryman reads it otherwise: "The last line equals: 'I will, I *do* scare.' ") The person, of course, is an expanded Lowell: "I would call it virtually certain that Lowell had in mind and at heart during this poem not only his own difficulties, whatever they may be or have been, but the personal disorders to which other poets of his age and place have been furiously subject." [74]

An image dominates Lowell's closing thoughts about "How the Poem Was Written":

> I began to feel that real poetry came, not from fierce confessions, but from something almost meaningless but imagined. I was haunted by an image of a blue china doorknob. I never used the doorknob, or knew what it meant, yet somehow it started the current of images in my opening stanzas. They were written in reverse order, and at last gave my poem an earth to stand on, and space to breathe.

In the unending and fruitful dialogue between Bishop and Lowell, it is Lowell who grasps Bishop's fact of the animal to come up with the driving shape of his most mature and memorable poems; yet even in his most powerful tribute to another poet, he submits the lesson to his own point of view. In his poem, nature is a library of human types.

Thinking about the animal that will not scare, about the irrefutably material resistance of that china doorknob, he reached into a poem about madness and self-loathing, about supreme lack of control, and transformed the unmanageable into his symbol for the resistant, imagining human self.

Bishop's respect for the nonhuman animal and material lies deeper; her inclination to measure the world against herself less insistent; her perception of the divisions between a self and a world, a life and a writing more active. In 1962, in a fatigued moment after Lowell's exhausting visit to her in Brazil, she grumbles to Ilse Barker:

> The Lowells, who must have been having a pretty good time, I suppose, decided to stay another month – and that was a bit too long – to think of things for them to do, people to meet, etc. – and poor Cal began to get into the manic stage of one of his breakdowns – from about the middle of August on. They aren't interested in things or places much, just people and books –

Their channeling preoccupations: for Bishop, "things or places"; for Lowell, "people and books." But for one moment, Lowell teases the china doorknob, making it his symbol of the always unyielding material universe before which the mind and its engagement with personality halts. It is a curious choice, that china doorknob, inviting the hand to grasp its rotundity and *open* something, and as Kalstone points out, it is found perching on the top of Bishop's flagpole in "Cape Breton." In an early rehearsal for the extended bus ride in "The Moose," the small bus of "Cape Breton"

> [. . .] passes the closed roadside stand, the closed school house,
> where today no flag is flying
> from the rough-adzed pole topped with a white china doorknob.

A late addition to this poem, the knob has its own extended history for Bishop, where its round, resistant, but milky whiteness bears a resemblance to the wasp's nest which Bishop carries off with pleasure in the late "Santarém": "small, exquisite, clean matte white;/ and hard as stucco."

While Lowell brooms "The Armadillo" and "Skunk Hour" into the same animal bin, Bishop's tough little armored creature lives in another world of reference, its drama foregrounding a creaturely response to the bombardment by fire balloon. Penelope Laurans sees the dedication of the poem as a sympathetic response to Lowell's pacifist objections to the Dresden fire-bombing,[75] but this reading never entirely persuaded me. A simple acknowledgment of the poem's actions as a symbolic rejection of mute resistance to invasive human evil seems sufficient, and really all that is earned.

St. John's Eve, or the holiday that occasions the fire balloons, appeared in an earlier, incomplete, and unpublished poem by Bishop. "St. John's Day" runs in rather Dickinsonian quatrains, with this epigraph:

> *"If St. John only knew it was his day*
> *He would descend from heaven and be gay."* (Old Song)

> A great and early sunset,
> a classic of its kind, went unobserved,
> although today the sun himself swerved
> as far out of his course as he could get,
>
> taking the opportunity
> to see things that he might not see again,
> letting the shadows poke their fingers in
> and satisfy their curiosity.
>
> Now down below,
> the darkness-level rises in the valley:
> in the small tip-tilted town already
> those gold cats' whiskers show,
>
> where six streets lie,
> they shake, almost, to prove
> to that withdrawing, orange presence above
> the power of their electricity.

Then, a little further down the page, and placed as if she weren't quite sure of their order or completeness within the poem, two more stanzas appear:

> the valley's ceiling buckles;
> a golden Roman candle surges;
> down in alleys little demiurges
> crack puff-ball knuckles.
>
> But no, no prayer
> can wake him. Is it cowardice?

> He sleeps, he always sleeps away the solstice,
> If he didn't his party might be gayer.

The quality of light at this time of day continued to interest her, a connoisseur of both those liminal states, sunrise and sunset. In another unfinished sunset poem, she asks:

> We live aslant
> here on our iron mountain. Venus
> already's set.
> Something I'm never sure of, even yet—
> do we shine, too? Is this world luminous?
> I try to recollect, but can't.

In the power of "their" electricity, in the challenge that the rising Roman candles throw up to the lowering, withdrawing sun, even in the question on the iron mountain about our shining, there is a gaiety about all that human voltage, promise sensed through uncertainty. I can only guess at Bishop's reasons for abandoning these poems, the manuscripts which Lowell in August 1963 called "those rich unfinished fragments, such a fortune in the bank"; it is certainly suggestive that the St. John's Eve celebration that she finished and published is much darker than any of these. In "The Armadillo," the "frail, illegal fire balloons" rise toward the same saint, and again are miscible with the larger produce of heaven:

> Once up against the sky it's hard
> to tell them from the stars—
> planets, that is—the tinted ones:
> Venus going down, or Mars,
>
> or the pale green one.

But when the man-sent balloons hit the wrong wind, they become menacing: "in the downdraft from a peak,/ suddenly turning dangerous." The rest of the poem chronicles that danger:

> Last night another big one fell.
> It splattered like an egg of fire
> against the cliff behind the house.
> The flame ran down. We saw the pair
>
> of owls who nest there flying up
> and up, their whirling black-and-white

stained bright pink underneath, until
they shrieked up out of sight.

The ancient owls' nest must have burned.
Hastily, all alone,
a glistening armadillo left the scene,
rose-flecked, head down, tail down,

and then a baby rabbit jumped out,
short-eared to our surprise.
So soft!—a handful of intangible ash
with fixed, ignited eyes.

Yet what seems to have happened in the second crack at St. John's
Eve is that an event, the little drama following from that splashing egg
of fire, moves into the undone stanzas and their matrix of general
observation and general reflection, and transforms a whole new lump
of language and experience into a poem. What might well have been a
simple anecdote in one of Bishop's letters, the story of the time that
the fire balloon fell behind the cliff and then the rabbit and the
armadillo jumped out, feeds the gathering poem instead, with the
result that something less static, lulling and more substantive than the
first attempt I've quoted emerges. Fitting the poem back into a form
of reflection, and into the corner of the book turning on several sets
of events at Samambaia, Bishop adds the final italicized quatrain:

> *Too pretty, dreamlike mimicry!*
> *O falling fire and piercing cry*
> *and panic, and a weak mailed fist*
> *clenched ignorant against the sky!*

Like the italicized lines in "Questions of Travel," which show Bishop
briefly experimenting with the same summary function, these lines
reach for a broader, more comprehensive significance. The weakness
of the head-down panicked armadillo and the baby rabbit echo the
weakness of Manuelzinho and the "weak flashes of inquiry" of the
squatter's children. Like the divisions of *Questions of Travel* that separated the book's two places into "Brazil" and "Elsewhere," these
italicized endings signal Bishop's attempt to bring her book into unity,
and probably to emulate the blaze and finish that excited her in
Lowell's *Life Studies.*

At this point, her solutions turn on uses of narrative. Her immersion in prose has given her rolling, incremental masses of material,

sighting in a range of places for her from Nova Scotia to Brazil, and a freedom to augment detail without sacrificing plot momentum. Additionally, "In the Village" gave her flexibility in shaping a subjectivity with multiple perspectives. Now in this interim book, *Questions of Travel*, in which she is turning over simultaneously both questions of living and questions of writing, her language turns further toward a consciously general discourse, more than it ever will again. But still unsure of her subject matter, casting a still queasy eye at Uncle Artie and all the other events and people of her life, she is not willing to take Lowell's step and reach more prominently into the narrative shaping that openly autobiographical material could offer. She keeps instead the feints of distance within dramatic monologue that she began with "The Prodigal," and marks time, rather magnificently, with her river witch, with Trollope, and with her animal company of sandpiper and armadillo.

Brazilian Choices

Bᴇꜱɪᴅᴇꜱ ᴀɴ experimentation with sestinas, double sonnets, dramatic monologue and translation, Elizabeth Bishop continued her relationship with prose as a means of expanding the resources of her art. In the current university collections of Bishop's papers there are a number of story scraps with Nova Scotian, Key West, and Brazilian settings, many of which were worked on in the fifties and sixties in Brazil. In addition to these pieces, there are the various memoirs, essays, the introduction to the *Diary of Helena Morley*, the early stories and fables published posthumously as *The Collected Prose*, and notes and drafts for a story, novella-size, that Bishop mentioned in May 1953 to Ilse Barker as "my Brazilian one, about worried and peculiar adults." Besides this fiction, another long chunk embarked on and planned as a collection of essay pieces on Brazil, to be called *Black Beans and Diamonds*, and by Bishop's repeated estimate nearly a couple of hundred pages in length before she abandoned it, is currently only to be found in discrete fragments.

Over a long period extending from adolescence it is clear that intermittent fiction, in addition to its utility as a kind of safe house for the identity on leave from its own body, had always offered Bishop some alternate and necessary manipulation of experience. Something in the sheer pour of prose detail jogged memory, loosened and scraped along otherwise unsalvageable particles of living, isolating them, and making their broader patterns and meanings more visible. In looking at the drafts accumulated as background material for the Nova Scotian story "In the Village," there is a palpable groping for and sifting over detail. In an almost sleep-walking intensity, endless tiny accretions noted in ink in the rounded letters of Bishop's early handwriting nudge her memory back to a place and time: a lamp placed just so; the walls of the pantry that particular color; the kitchen matches kept here; the small back bedroom lit only by a skylight; the seasons and colors of an onslaught of moths; the hour of the day at which Grandfather's grog was poured and delivered to the parlor, and so on. The same grounding in a particular territory, the same need to insert the weight of a historical body governs all these pieces, particularly in the two available stories of 1953, "In the Village" and "Gwendolyn." These stories extend the same interest in narrative that brought her to folk ballad and dramatic monologue in the middle years of her work, if not wholly as a replacement for fantasy, then as a substantial addition to her repertory. Prose preceded the most intense immersion in Nova Scotian and Brazilian settings, consuming nearly the whole of 1953 and 1954. When she resumed publication of poems, she led with a mixture of childhood and travel, with the work that would finally become *Questions of Travel*.

As she probed her work, looking for the through-lines that would carry her safely beyond preciosity or exoticism for its own sake, travel, associated with the deeper questions of her location in the world, seemed the promising route through the emerging bogland of the autobiographical. Her published work on the erotic or intimate relationships of her life stopped in *A Cold Spring*, the book of hers which began the work of deemphasizing allegory and fantasy. *Questions of Travel*, with its dedication to Lota de Macedo Soares, reaffirmed the spatial orientation of *North & South* over the temporal focus of *A Cold Spring*. Backing away from the tones that made up either the tenderness of "The Shampoo," or the bitterness of "Insomnia," or the unpublished sotto voce eroticism of "It is marvellous" or "Vaguely Love Poem," her new poems landed solidly in Brazil, making a vivid and broadly territorial commitment.

In their Brazilian setting the poems develop another sensitivity to communal, or historic context. The most direct example of this progression seems the shift from the amused and affectionate condescensions of "Manuelzinho," trained on the firmly quaint foibles of Lota's lovable servant, to "The Riverman." This poem, Bishop's first-person exercise in the voice of an Amazonian *ribeirinho*, transfers her absorption with childhood away from her own pastness, and into a magically other time and place, ruled by that sense of the past that we ascribe to the primitive. Teased as she must have been by Lowell's example, and mulling over the historical and social nuances of *Life Studies* during these years, in 1960 she published "Brazil, January 1, 1502," another and yet more substantial entry in the field of historical connection. This poem, along with the contrasting high-rise and street-level scenes of "The Burglar of Babylon," locates Bishop herself in a historical progression of events, a progression with national, class, and gender connotations. High on her mountaintop, or in the eleventh floor apartment above the beaches of Rio, Bishop simultaneously launched both a systematic engagement with the colors of exile, and a detailed attempt to retrieve her Nova Scotian past. Both efforts, north and south, seem a way of literally grounding her work while extending its inner temporal realities. After some preliminary observation of Bishop's stock-taking efforts in Brazil, two poems, "Brazil, January 1, 1502" and "The Riverman," make the advances of her poetry clear.

· I ·

In enormous uncertainties, but with springing hope for the future in having taken a crucial decision to make a round-the-world journey, Bishop left New York in November 1951, en route for South America. The disastrous months of 1950 were behind her, months during which she had written in her diary:

> I think when one is extremely unhappy – almost hysterically un-happy, that is – one's time-sense breaks down. All that long stretch in K. W., for example, several years ago – it wasn't just a matter of not being able to accept the present, that present, although it began that way, possibly. But the past of the present seemed confused, or contradicting each other violently & constantly, & the past wouldn't "lie down." ([. . .] this was really taught me by getting drunk, when the same thing happens, for perhaps the same reasons, for a few hours.)

It is important to her to note that emotional disruption is both spatial and temporal. A journal entry on board the *S.S. Bowplate* measures the mood possessing her at departure:

> This trip is a "shakedown" trip for me, all right – I know I am feeling, thinking, looking, sleeping, dreaming, eating & drinking

better than in a long time, & when I read something like "The question about time is how change is related to the changeless" – I look around – it doesn't seem so hard or so far off. The warm clouds seem to be moving quite rapidly; those in back of them are motionless – watching the ship's wake we seem to be going fast, but watching the sky on the horizon, we are just living here, with the engines pulsing, forever.

Dreaming on her ship, oddly static in the middle of the ocean, her own life thrusting and suspended in much the same pattern, she watches the water speed in relation to its wake and occasional clouds, then slow in relation to the distant horizon. Taking in the ties between change and the changeless, she fixes the abstract in relation to several forms of the concrete, as is her habit, coming up with a formulation that quickens the past and blends present and future into "the sky on the horizon . . . the engine pulsing, forever." Then her observations glide effortlessly inwards toward an actual shipboard phenomenon altering one's perception of position, and she toys with an image that also reverses the order of perceived and perceiving:

> There are minutes, I've always noticed on shipboard, in one's cabin, when suddenly the ship seems to be *racing*. I don't think it's due to any differences in the sound of the engine, but rather to some slight physical shift of beat in oneself, and I've had that sensation again, because of the one round port-hole, – particularly at night – of being in a box camera, of being "exposed" to the sea & sky. (*Camera oscura.*)

In Bishop fashion, the camera image is endowed with features of scale: on the one hand, the human occupant of the cabin is miniaturized within the camera, on the other hand, a small object blows up to the size of ship, horizon, and sky. Each operation, however, becomes part of the mechanics of a deep look, a taking of one's bearings, and of stabilizing one's present in right relation to the troubling past and a hopeful future. "I wish I had brought '4 Quartets' along" she concludes. And we can only guess at the figures that Eliot's paradoxes of motion in motionlessness, of conflated beginnings and endings, might have generated for her.

Bishop's poems in the first decade in Brazil do more than enlarge her interest in people. The new development in her poetry seems a preoccupation with stationing herself in the flux of time and history, as well as in mapped, geographical space. As she found herself in Lota de Macedo Soares' house in a quasi-familial circumstance, she stretched her poems, against the vivid and emphatic backdrop of Brazil, to more concrete definitions of a national and historic self, intensifying even her early and consistent interest in landscape and geography. Her first two books began to gather pieces on a single unifying ground: in *North & South* the Key West poems make a group; the Paris poems group by hours, days, and rooms. In *A Cold Spring* there is a strong cluster moving outdoors from Key West to Nova Scotia, and a smaller, more diffused group of poems basing themselves in New York, fittingly indoors. In *Questions of Travel,* for the first time, questions of place and identity are buried under the travel theme, sounding explicitly in title and poem, as the book bifurcates into two sections, a quite solid grounding in "Brazil" and then in "Elsewhere." A story, a plot is assembling for Bishop's life in terms of place, even if by contrast the stable unity of the first locale makes the second term of her chosen pair look like an anomaly. Even as "Elsewhere" fails to summarize or differentiate the other varied places of her life, though, the title does point up by contrast the importance to her of having chosen at all, and of having made that choice "Brazil." Thousands of miles away from the people and preoccupations of her past decades, Bishop finds a focus for her poetry both temporal and spatial, and emerges as the naturalist of people and terrain with ever-sharpening distinction.

Perhaps the first poem in which to measure the distance Bishop literally travels away from Marianne Moore's more static description and less dramatic formulation of subjects would be "Brazil, January 1, 1502." Seizing her ground quickly, Bishop dips our faces in a tropical abundance, an exotic abandon; flowers, leaves, and air are all intoxicatingly one and the same, and in the freshness and wonder of the Brazilian scene even time is a matter of seeing double. Her title directs us to Brazilian history: January 1, 1502, commemorates the New Year's day when a shipload of Portuguese colonists first sight Guanabara Bay, and mistaking this body of water for a river, name it for the future city, Rio de Janeiro, or River of January. The contemporary moment when Nature greets "our eyes" and the eyes of the Portuguese colonists fuses in Bishop's opening plural, "Januaries":

> Januaries, Nature greets our eyes
> exactly as she must have greeted theirs:
> every square inch filling in with foliage—
> big leaves, little leaves, and giant leaves,

blue, blue-green, and olive,
with occasional lighter veins and edges,
or a satin underleaf turned over;
monster ferns
in silver-gray relief,
and flowers, too, like giant water lilies
up in the air—up, rather, in the leaves—
purple, yellow, two yellows, pink,
rust red and greenish white;
solid but airy; fresh as if just finished
and taken off the frame.

The precise, but casual description with its determined counting, is self-correcting, a shade self-mocking. This speaker is wary of fussiness; like a good, sophisticated conversationalist, she gives no more than the traffic of attention will bear. Her epigraph, ". . . embroidered nature . . . tapestried landscape," identified as alluding to Kenneth Clark's *Landscape Into Art*, sets the tone. Nature, that delightful custodienne, is at it again; our hostess Earth cannot restrain her prodigal hand. While I acknowledge the justice of Terence Diggory's observation to me that Nature for Bishop is hardly synonymous with the demure embroidress of Adrienne Rich's "Aunt Jennifer's Tigers," still, her representation of Nature imposes a domesticity both admirable and irrepressible.

The second stanza continues:

A blue-white sky, a simple web,
backing for feathery detail:
brief arcs, a pale-green broken wheel,
a few palms, swarthy, squat, but delicate;
and perching there in profile, beaks agape,
the big symbolic birds keep quiet,
each showing only half his puffed and padded,
pure-colored or spotted breast.
Still in the foreground there is Sin:
five sooty dragons near some massy rocks.
The rocks are worked with lichens, gray moonbursts
splattered and overlapping,
threatened from underneath by moss
in lovely hell-green flames,
attacked above

by scaling-ladder vines, oblique and neat,
"one leaf yes and one leaf no" (in Portuguese).
The lizards scarcely breathe; all eyes
are on the smaller, female one, back-to,
her wicked tail straight up and over,
red as a red-hot wire.

The conversational pacing of the poem, even down to the loose assembly of its line breaks, directs us at once to the issue of perspective: when we reach the lizards, Nature's job appears finished, and the time of the poem, which through two stanzas has been indeterminately both Januaries, past and present, now splits decisively to turn to the past, as the third and final stanza leads us to the collision between imperialism and gender.

Like almost all of Bishop's poems, this one has a fairly unified and cut-down space: unlike Moore's much more modernist cutting and jumping from one abrupt place to another in the progressions of her themes, Bishop follows a top-down, left-right orientation where an almost tactile sense of the poem as a made thing prevails. Bishop rarely breaks open the space of her poem in cubist imitation, or in modern juxtaposition, as Moore, or Eliot, or Williams or Pound all do. The Brazil poems opening *Questions of Travel*, although they take place in various parts of Brazil, appear to inhabit similar landscapes of road, mountain, and jungle greenery in a highly conventional narrative space. The only bow to a modernist spatializing occurs as each poem stresses a prevailing mist, or watery dominance through rain or tropical steaminess that threatens our recognition of ground, air, and water limits; yet the canvas of each poem also appears to focus on a given time, in its fluency still observing Bishop's sense of Aristotelian propriety as to temporal and spatial unities.

In the third and concluding stanza of "Brazil, January 1, 1502," a violent historical force erupts against Nature's blending continuum of then and now:

Just so the Christians, hard as nails,
tiny as nails, and glinting,
in creaking armor, came and found it all,
not unfamiliar:
no lovers' walks, no bowers,
no cherries to be picked, no lute music,
but corresponding, nevertheless,

to an old dream of wealth and luxury
already out of style when they left home—
wealth, plus a brand-new pleasure.
Directly after Mass, humming perhaps
L'Homme armé or some such tune,
they ripped away into the hanging fabric,
each out to catch an Indian for himself—
those maddening little women who kept calling,
calling to each other (or had the birds waked up?)
and retreating, always retreating, behind it.

For David Bromwich,[76] the speaker of the poem identifies with those hard, tiny little Christians: a problematic reading because it under-stresses the feminist, antimilitarist point of view of the poem emerging in satire against the imperialist machismo of armored soldiers. And yet the poem resists a too-insistently framed ideology: an identifiable, controlling perspective, coming from a speaker clearly and continu-ously in command of the poem's opinions seems to be missing.

Syntax appears to guide us firmly to the conclusion that we, our eyes greeted by our bit of January, are like the Christians, in Bishop's words, "Just so"; a phrase we might consider as pivotal. But we are neither those little armed men nor the bird women: somewhere be-tween the steady unfolding of the tapestry and the advance of the Christians and the retreat of the Indians, the owner of the voice, too, retreats behind its tonalities, undercutting the neat juxtaposition of then and now, of human and natural, of Europeans and Indians into a shadowy laughter in which female poetry, female Nature, and female Indians take definitive possession of the poem's space through subtle linguistic cues and ambiguous visual presences.

As Barbara Page points out in her perceptive discussion of the poem,[77] by the end of the second stanza the "five sooty dragons" are no longer emblems of "Sin": in the sexual encounter that closes the stanza, they are merely "lizards." In fact, if we contrast the confident, wicked little female lizard in her posture of acceptance with the Indian women in flight from the pursuing soldiers, the "Just so" of the next lines feels ironic: sexual adventure in the natural world is not the behavior of the juxtaposed Christians, is not "just so"; the "corre-sponding" of their vision is a suspect one. The very tapestry that the Christians rip aside looks like the outmoded manufacture of their own

delusion. Yet the question that still needs answering is the full ownership of that delusion.

At the end of stanza one, the visual field of the poem is "fresh as if
just finished/ and taken off the frame." By stanza two, that field
concludes with the lizards; as we begin the third stanza Nature's
embroidery meets the shock of the Christians who counter the fabric
of Nature with one of their own, an "old dream of wealth and luxury/
already out of style when they left home." In this queer new space of
the poem created by the collision of "frame" and "dream," we seem
rushed into a place where the projector shows a blank image and only
the soundtrack is running, as those "maddening little women" bereft
of actual language call and call, or as Bishop's suggestive paraphrase
puts it: "(or had the birds waked up?)." Maybe the women have really
disappeared and we are back only with the "symbolic" birds of an
enigmatic sign system that Nature has never bothered to explain
to any of us. But whether birds or women, Nature or Christian
dream, a force made synonymous with the poem now closing is in
retreat.

It is at this point, perhaps, that we cannot avoid introducing the
puzzling question of Bishop's epigraph for her poem, which reads,
without quotation marks:

> . . . embroidered nature . . . tapestried landscape.

Followed by this attribution: "—*Landscape into Art*, by Sir Kenneth
Clark." How long a piece of the road Bishop meant to go with Clark
is not terribly clear; only the words "embroidered nature" correspond
to Clark's book,[78] even as I look across the accommodatingly broad
ditches of her ellipses. The apposition of "embroidered nature" against
a "tapestried landscape" applies only roughly to Clark's discussion of
either embroidery and tapestry, or nature and landscape. Clark sees
medieval tapestry as decorative and stylized. It is a flat, two-dimensional art frozen into symbol, an inner landscape very crucially not
dependent on close observation; realistic landscape painting can only
develop when the rigid equivalences of medieval allegory surrender to
an acceptance of a natural world conceived as benevolent and as
worthy of observation. "Embroidered nature," as Clark uses the phrase,
"finds expression in the subject of the Hortus Conclusus" or walled
garden, along with the theme of the Unicorn tapestries. While the
"embroidered nature" of the Unicorn tapestries is peaceful, domestic,

and feminine, still Clark attaches no gender significance to either embroidery or tapestry as art forms, for him their importance lies in their particular reading of nature.

It is the passage which precedes the mention of "embroidered nature" which obviously sparked Bishop's poem, and it is typical of her use of Clark that the passage I cite describes frescoes, rather than tapestry or embroidery; what remained of greatest interest for Bishop seems to be the static, two-dimensional, non-vanishing point perspective of all of these forms. This is Clark, on the tapestrylike frescoes of Avignon:

> In these the dark woods of the middle ages are made to fill, with beautiful patterns of leaves and branches, the whole upper portion of each design, while the lower half is richly sprinkled with flowers as the meadows of Boccaccio. There is not a square inch without some delightful reminder of the visible world, all translated into a poetry more real and yet more formal than Spenser's *Faerie Queen*. (p.8)

Bishop's Nature, a lushly clever Needlewoman closely resembling Clark's visual poet, has "worked" a scene of intoxicating pleasures. As she has stitched this world, "Still in the foreground there is Sin:" even though Sin greets our eyes "in lovely hell-green flames," and in two dimensions, each of "the big symbolic birds" can only show us "half his puffed and padded,/pure-colored or spotted breast." (The perspective on the halved birds here may remind us of Bishop's halved "Gentleman of Shalott.") But the perspective can also be seen as an instance of Bishop's insistence, as a sophisticated picture lover, on the limits of the pictorial, as she draws attention implicitly to the baffling nature of visual phenomena. Somewhere between the top and bottom of the second stanza both Bishop as tapestry-maker and Christians as tapestry-makers give way, under the aegis of the sexual, to an unworkable pattern in which flatness, no matter how lovely and fresh, can't quite tell us about everything.

As Bromwich points out, "Sexuality is the most elusive feature of Bishop's temperament" and it is perilous to arrive at too rapid conclusions about the role of sex and gender in a given poem. As Bromwich sees the reading or writing pronoun, "*we* are like the conquistadores in supposing that *we* can make Nature over in a language *we* know" (italics mine), and he goes on to describe the soldiers as rapt in delusion, in that old, out-of-date dream of luxury. Finally, Bromwich backs off onto a *they:* "What they take to be an act of possession is not, therefore, even a successful re-possession, but the enactment of a familiar ritual of self-seduction."

It is not merely Bromwich's cross-gender identification which sticks in the craw, although it is surely the wild, uncapturable female Indians and the female Nature of her text that draw some portion of Bishop's allegiance as a female writer. But the problem as Page outlines it is that Bromwich

> universalizes the love of conquest by describing it as "human," and views the attitude of the poet as analogous to that of the conquistadores, obliging us to suppose that Bishop aligned herself with aggressive masculinity and with intending rapists.

Still we wonder about how identical in property and design are female Nature, female Indians, and female poets; in the stitching of the poem, women, birds, lizards, and soldiers all seem subject to Nature's paradoxically genial, but imperial pattern. Yet the difference between the offering compliance of the female lizard with the "wicked tail" and the brutal stalking of the soldiers seems a measure of actual difference between Nature and Sin, or between uncorrupted Nature and corrupt, fallible human design.

Somewhere between the flat canvas designing of Nature as maker and the false constructions of the Christians is the poet's voice also struggling to be free of the patterning that reads Sin in the birds or Plunder in the women. Both designs are troubling, both ideas of Nature and Christianity break down: for the poet, the symbolic language of the birds is inscrutable and half-formed, and the desire of women can only be named in animal, "lizard" language. It is not only the armed soldiers who find the women amorphous: for the speaker of the poem in the penultimate line it isn't clear that the unseen women haven't dissolved into bird-cries. Like the woman speaking the poem, human female gender is problematic; it tends to go invisible at the point where desire and surrender, with or without forcible compulsion, are invoked.

Language in this poem could turn us both to earlier and later identifications that permit us to read it from the Christians' perspective. We might look again at the pains with which Bishop establishes her scene as both decorous and playful. Against the big symbolic birds keeping quiet, Sin is a trifle programmatically established. And what about those "lovely" hell-green flames? The implicit game of sexual consent—derived, withdrawn, derived, withdrawn—"one leaf yes and one leaf no" in the language of the scaling-ladder vine?

Real power in this scene appears to burgeon from the sexually-compelling female: the only nonstatic dramatic moment in the poem beside the rush and retreat of the third stanza rises from that magnetic female lizard in the posture of acceptance. While the tiny Christians are "hard as nails," and appear to rip brutally into that deceptive fabric, the power of consent actually lies within those "maddening little women," perpetually capable of retreat. The game set-up of the poem, its insistence on its own decorousness, does seem near to accepting a generalized reading of sexual encounter with pursuit and capture as its terms. A brutal capture is suggested as a strong possibility in the stylized picture of this poem, as the soldiers advance humming "L'Homme armé," the tune which begins "Fear the armed man," and which Page points out was "repeatedly set to the Mass, sanctioning the militarist ambition of the Christians." From a late twentieth-century point of view skeptical about the benefits of imperialism, we feel we know how to read the future of these Indian women, which stands ominously offstage in our minds. Yet we should probably avoid readings that overstate the powerlessness of the women, or that give either the tiny soldiers or the little women a role of superior will within the domain of Nature threaded onto Bishop's loom.

All seem within the thrall of the beautifying agency creating and deploying their fresh, tiny and decorative lives across the frame of our Olympian attention. If the theme is dominance, Bishop seems to have given an equal resilience to the women and the soldiers, where in the precise moment of the poem, the power to refuse is as great, if not greater, than the power to force consent. Finally, through the ruling metaphor of Nature the embroidress, Nature saves for herself and the feminine the not inconsiderable powers of beauty, pleasure, and creation.

We have several glosses for Bishop's use of that retreating motion in the final lines ("those maddening little women who kept calling,/ calling to each other [. . .] and retreating, always retreating [. . .]"), each spanning a long portion of Bishop's life. In an adolescent review of W. H. Hudson's *Green Mansions*, Bishop at the age of seventeen closes her delighted review of the book with these words:

> I wished that the book had been twice as long when I put it down, and I was filled with longing to leave for South America immediately and search for those forgotten bird-people. It seemed still unfinished, even more than that delightful region in my mind I told

about, and I felt sure that if I could only find the right spot, the right sun-lighted arches of the trees, and wait patiently, *I would see a bright-haired figure slipping away among the moving shadows, and hear the sweet, light music of Rima's voice.* [italics mine.]

Both language and thought are quaintly sentimental. And yet in that final figure, Hudson's Rima, the Indian girl whose native language resembles birdsong, who stands up on her feet to talk to the sky gods in Spanish, but who bends low to her mother earth in her native song—is still invoked in the poem Bishop finished thirty-two years later. An orphan, and a border figure tying several cultures together, Bishop never forgot Rima. On board the *S.S. Bowplate,* she and Miss Breen confess that the same romantic images have drawn them to the tropics, an early and unforgettable part of which for each woman has been her early reading of W. H. Hudson.

It is initially not *as* Rima but as a *seeker* of Rima that Bishop comes to South America. In all of Bishop's early stories, as well as in many of her later fables and poems, her projected identity is not with the female speaker, but with the male. Love, or courtship *is* seen as a game of advance and retreat. In 1968, her indignation over the San Francisco hippy scene that she has been brought to view spills over at the thought of a too-direct and mechanical sex, and in a notebook kept at the time she complains of lovers that have "no use of charm, retreats, the lovely game of love."

If we look at her own description of the poem, she says to Lowell in February 1960, "I think it is a bit artificial, but I finally had to do something with the cliche about the landscape looking like a tapestry, I suppose." A clue to Bishop's view of the nature of the artifice pursued in "Brazil, January 1, 1502" turns up in a translation done near the time of the poem's writing. Clarice Lispector's "The Smallest Woman in the World" was published in Brazil in 1960 as part of her *Family Ties.* Lispector was an acquaintance of Bishop's, and she may well have seen this story of Lispector's before its publication. In any event, she published her own translation of it in 1964. The story is a fantasy, about a seventeen-and-three-quarters inch pygmy discovered in equatorial Africa, coveted by greedy and heartless urbanites. The wild confronts the tame in Lispector's fable, and the speechless, pregnant miniature woman feels in facing her French captor "a warmth that might be called love."

The probable outcome for Lispector's "Little Flower" is as doubtful for her as for Bishop's miniature Indian women. Bishop's translation contains this passage linking them linguistically. Little Flower is a member of the Likoualas:

> Besides disease, the deadly effluvium of the water, insufficient food, and ranging beasts, the great threat to the Likoualas are the savage Bahundes, a threat that surrounds them in the silent air, like the dawn of battle. The Bahundes hunt them with nets, like monkeys. And eat them. Like that: they catch them in nets and *eat* them. The tiny race, retreating, always retreating, has finished hiding away in the heart of Africa, where the lucky explorer discovered it.

The English verb is the same, the retreat the same. That vibrant female principle of wild, untrammeled native passion is in both texts shrunken and endangered.

Yet there is a danger in overemphasizing the anger with which Bishop contemplated this bitter situation. While Bishop rejected what she called the "exaggeration and pro-slavery feeling" of Gilberto Freyre's *The Masters and the Slaves,* and *The Mansions and The Shanties,* a massive study of the evolution of modern Brazil, she also called it "readable and informative," and put these books in her suggested bibliography in her own book, *Brazil.* Freyre, and other modern scholars, see interracial breeding as part of the strength and diversity of Brazil. Freyre defends the Portuguese occupation by comparing it favorably with other European campaigns. For Freyre, the Portuguese, schooled historically to interracial mixing with Moorish and Semitic peoples, bred with Indians for the creation of a home labor force: an improvement in his eyes over simple extermination. Whatever its early brutal and exploitative record may have been, the resultant strains, of Indian, African, and Portuguese, ultimately constituted an integrated, interracial population without parallel in the modern world.

As Bishop puts this about modern Brazil: "Brazilians take great pride in their fine record in race relations. Their attitude can best be described by saying that the upper-class Brazilian is usually proud of his racial tolerance, while the lower-class Brazilian is not aware of his — he just practices it." Further: tolerance "was not planned; it just happened. But Brazil is now realizing that its history of racial assimilation is one of the country's greatest assets. Racial mixtures can be seen all over the country. With each new census, an increasing proportion of the total population is classified as white."[79]

Her last sentence is problematic, because it seems to imply that the end result of all of this mixing is toward the gradual elimination of blackness, a belief held by early theorists, and hardly one that tends to celebrate mixture. In her book, *Brazil*, as Bishop delineates the history of the treatment of native populations, she balances the theme of exploitation with preservation of tribes. She mentions the work of Orlando Villas Boas, an Indian advocate in the state of Mato Grosso, but she, or the *Life* editors, face the picture of Villas Boas among the Indians with one that shows him fingering the skull of a white victim of tribal hostility. The juxtaposition moves to provide a continuing rationale for a defensive posture toward Indians in relation to other settlers. Bishop is generally dismissive about twentieth century styles of Brazilian machismo, saying of Brazilians:

> They poke fun at their usually bloodless revolutions: "No one fought in that revolution—it was the rainy season." Like the Portu-guese form of bullfighting, in which there is no killing, Brazilian revolutions or *golpes* (coups) sometimes seem to be little more than political and rhetorical maneuvering. A man's speeches, his moral and physical courage, are admired, but actual violence is going too far[. . .]
>
> Jokes tell even more. There is an old favorite, perhaps not even Brazilian originally, about a man walking down the street with a friend. He is grossly insulted by a stranger, and says nothing. The friend tries to rouse his fighting instincts, "Didn't you hear what he called you? Are you going to take that? Are you a man, or aren't you?" The man replies, "Yes, I'm a man. But not *fanatically*." This is the true Brazilian temper.

While we may not be convinced of the adequacy of this assessment of Bishop's, filtered as it may have been through her Time-Life editors, we can still hear this account as part of the context of the poem. Nevertheless, about these jokes on Brazilian machismo, the Bishop scholar Regina Przybycien, herself Brazilian, writes:

> I think they are only jokes and are to be taken as that. The social and political realities are much more complex and dramatic. For example, the last "bloodless revolution" (1964) cost the Brazilians 25 years of military dictatorship, with a lot of repression. Many thousands were

tortured, killed, or "disappeared." A whole generation of Brazilians was not taught to think critically because schools were considered places that generated subversive ideas, and were, therefore, one of the main targets of repression.

It is true that Bishop (like many Brazilians at that time) minimized the coup and even welcomed it, but it was a sad mistake. My point is that these jokes don't tell anything about the Brazilian temper, as Polish jokes don't tell anything about the Poles, etc.[80]

Pryzybycien concludes: "The poem is fine precisely because it balances so well perception and representation, while *Brazil* relies heavily on representations of the quaint and exotic so cherished by Time/Life readers." Yet it is possible to find in the poem's balances the habits of avoidance that lead away from a more emphatic rejection of a victimizing imperialism, or clearer acceptance of a point of view stressing the sameness of gender experience across national or racial lines. Perhaps we should simply be grateful for Bishop's refusal to deny or blur the nuances of her historical position. Still, it is the final image of her poem that seems decisive: held within a prolific and seductively beautiful Nature, the men *are* cruel, narrow, and dangerous; yet as the poem freezes the hunt during the play of female retreat, in their concessiveness, or lack of it, the bird women keep all the power.

·II·

With the large and notable exception of "The Riverman," Bishop's Brazilian poems generally speak from the familiar and career-long habit of distance or occlusion of one sort or another. The tiny soldiers and Indian women, the "speck-like" girl and boy from "Squatter's Children," the broad, delightful canvas of "Arrival in Santos," the "Burglar of Babylon" literally seen through binoculars, even the person-canceling rain and fog of "Twelfth Night, Or What You Will," and "Song for the Rainy Season," — all make of Brazil an opportunity for filtering vision, for juggling persons and sights at a manageable and containing distance from the observer. Yet the grounds for vision have noticeably tightened, sharpened, and unified for Bishop, reflecting a broader set of personal interests. By 1966, she will merely remark to Ashley Brown about the nineteen-thirties, "I was always opposed to political thinking as such for writers. What good writing came out of that period, really?"[81] And she puts herself at some distance from the "popular" Vassar radicalism of her day, saying here and elsewhere that she felt better acquainted with poverty, from her years in Boston with her Aunt Maude, and from her Nova Scotia days with her grandparents, than her wealthy, eventually well-married and placard-carrying classmates. But in 1966, having lived through two major political upheavals in Brazil, from the suicide and fall of Getulio Vargas in 1954, and on through the revolutionary coup of 1964, she concludes to Brown: "I'm much more interested in social problems and politics now than I was in the 30's." We can take this as truth, even if with hindsight we may learn to identify the blind spots of her particular vantage point.

As she is pushed by political events in which Brazilian friends and associates play a part, we can see this interest gaining strongly in her letters; by the nineteen-sixties even her poems have begun to register external historical events differently. Traveling in the isolated and backward country of rural Florida as well as in Nova Scotia, a kind of landscape she was drawn to again and again, she can say fairly, "I had lived with poor people and knew something of poverty at firsthand."

Little of this observation is present in the poetry of her first two books. In spite of her increased interest in "social problems and politics" none of it surfaces with any appearance of intensity, or passion of empathy. Others have spoken with a certain irritation about Bishop's view of the poor. The English poet Charles Tomlinson remarks that "the better off have always preferred their poor processed by style."[82] Bromwich refers to 'poems about squatters and other half-cherished neighbors—efforts of self-conscious whimsy (like "Manuelzinho") or of awkward condescension (like "Filling Station")' as poems "that dwindle as one comes to see them more clearly."[83] I think we can find something better to say about "Squatter's Children," but certainly the judgment holds for "Manuelzinho," and "Filling Station."

Among the poems that she writes in the sixties, "The Riverman" speaks with unique effectiveness both from inside the world of subjective feeling, and from outside, from the apparently greater externality of a particular history and culture not her own. For the first time, Bishop gives us a dramatic monologue fusing fantasy and actual worlds, and making a first person compound of Brazilian legend from within North American diction and feeling. From within its fluent and dreamy water-and-earth venue, the poem touches on central thematic preoccupations, on estrangement and communality.

For Sylvia Plath, a rather different poet set uneasily within a female body, Ariel, or the air sprite, gave the mask and the freedom to explore the anomalies of her position in mythic style. For Elizabeth Bishop, water, the welling, salty element of both birth and tears, provided the medium of release, and it is the figure of the mermaid, whose free tail was given in exchange for crippled speech and female legs, who seems to shade the evolution of her merman. The style that processed "The Riverman" allowed Bishop the articulation of a fairly unique experiment in a point of view intimately both hers and not hers; the feigning of dramatic monologue projected her simultaneously within a problem, and safely at the edges of it, much as myth and cross-dressing protected a core self from grief about alcoholism in "The Prodigal."

Bishop felt unsure of the worth of this poem. In 1960 she wrote to Lowell: "You don't have to like the "riverman" poem – Lota hates it, and I don't approve of it myself but once it was written I couldn't seem to get rid of it." As Bishop explained in letters, Lota's distrust of the poem stemmed from her dislike of Bishop's or anyone's interest in the primitive; an activist in advance of her country's backwardness, she was impatient with what seemed to be her American friend's regressive fascination with Indians, or in this case, the caboclo, or mixture of Indian and European. But Lowell reassured Bishop of her own deeper connection to the poem's subject matter, and told her that "the Amazon poem" was "the best fairy story in verse I know." Later, he connected its themes to the letter that Bishop wrote to him from Maine in the forties, no doubt the one on loneliness in which she fancied herself "a gasping mermaid under one of those exposed docks [. . .] trying to tear the mussels off the piles for something to eat." He had saved her mermaid image himself, using it as the original ending for "Water," his poem commemorating his Maine visit to Bishop in 1948, then moving the stanza to its final, penultimate position:

> One night you dreamed
> you were a mermaid clinging to a wharf-pile,
> and trying to pull
> off the barnacles with your hands.

As Lowell acutely divined, the poem is not simply a remote exercise in describing a shamanic initiation. What makes the poem rich is the exploration of the ironic gap between the pretended speaker of dramatic monologue, and the voice of the poet herself, exploring her own disconnections and powers. The gap, or feint, as it is named in Alan Sinfield's *Dramatic Monologue*, exists at this moment of our reading:

"We experience the 'I' of the poem as a character in his own right but at the same time sense the author's voice through him [. . .] such a speaker has a mode of reality comparable with the poet's but nevertheless teasingly at odds with it."[84] As in any good dramatic monologue, the gap suspends us between sympathy and judgment, where the whole effect of the poem is to be experienced as a doubling of sensibility: the poem's speech and the speaker behind the poem alternately fusing, hiding, and pulling apart at times to separate identities whose differences, discordant or otherwise, are a deliberate harmonics.

In a letter to Anny Baumann, written in 1958, Bishop adopted a sardonic, patronizing tone that also flicked sideways into strange erotic attraction, as traveling with Aldous Huxley, she writes to Dr. Baumann:

> The Indians [. . .] seem very *happy*, quiet, clean, (they go swimming several times a day). Very gentle with their children and each other. They are short and almost plump, a nice dusky color, quite naked except for a little paint – with a small vaccination mark on each nice round behind.

But in "The Riverman," speaking more directly to and for herself as her genre permitted, she came into a much deeper, much more human fusion, into an annexation of the common dream ground between herself and primitive peoples. Ultimately, her poem about a shamanic initiation merges with her own dream of herself as a far-diving and faithful tribal scrivener, aswim in the waters of consciousness of an animate universe. The poem enlarges for us because of her release of the imaginative distance between herself and the Amazonian. Unlike the space of her earlier fantasy poems, in which her projected speaker is suspended above or below or at some barrier before the medium in which a tantalizing and fuller life is being enacted, in "The Riverman" she achieves an entry. In this poem, she is not suspended from the Man-Moth's or the Unbeliever's height, or trapped within the machinery of toy as in "Cirque d'Hiver," or behind the desiccated barricade of "The Monument"; instead, she finally penetrates the remote class of the Other. The narrative of this poem is naturalized, and in Brazilian as well as American voice, the dreamer-swimmer in it deploys his imaginative citizenship differently; in contrast to the tiny figurines seen through the tourist binoculars of "The Burglar of Babylon," "The Riverman" uses the dramatic voice which made later monologues like the child from "In The Waiting Room" and the solitary in "Crusoe in England" possible.

·III·

The poem asks for two sorts of consideration. In the first, Bishop's source, Charles Wagley's *Amazon Town*,[85] invites us to seek the background of the poem's motions. In the second, seeing the riverman as a Bishop double tells something of its expressive place within the figure of Bishop's work.

The poem is prefaced by a bracketed explanation:

[A man in a remote Amazonian village decides to become a *sacaca*, a witch doctor who works with water spirits. The river dolphin is believed to have supernatural powers; Luandinha is a river spirit associated with the moon . . .]

Many of the essential details of the poem are plucked whole from *Amazon Town*, undergoing strange alterations, however, in their transmutation to poetry; from the dry hardpan of the anthropologist's text Bishop has derived a fluent and magical crossing of animal and elemental worlds quite unlike anything else she had ever written or would write in the future. The performance of the poem becomes even more extraordinary when we consider that it was written before Bishop visited the Amazon, and not after.

In *Amazon Town*, Wagley describes his own visit to a local water witch, a *page*. Something about Wagley's wary openness, something about his respectful but alert description of this novice, Satiro—"not a powerful page. He has not been practicing many years"—must have touched something off for her. Perhaps the Wagley text suggested a point of departure in its own poise, its careful balance between responsiveness and credulity. A striking feature of Bishop's poem is its cultivation of a tone of naive humility, its recognition of aspiration and determined longing in the voice of its speaker, a longing, finally, that moves recursively, expressively, to shade the voice of an Elizabeth Bishop speaking her self-imposed barbarian lines.

In Bishop's poem, matching many of the props of Wagley's Satiro, and of other details of Amazonian initiation and enthrallment as Wagley gives them, the spirit of the Dolphin or the Boto calls to the riverman, brings him to the river, and giving him cachaça, or native

rum, and magical cigars, lures him to enter the community of water
spirits, and to turn his back on his wife and his home. A border
creature who lives in water and breathes in air, the Dolphin speaks no
human language; he merely grunts beneath the riverman's window,
hid by a river mist, but still showing up in form as a double of the
speaker:

> I got up in the night
> for the Dolphin spoke to me.
> He grunted beneath my window,
> hid by the river mist,
> but I glimpsed him—a man like myself.

Like a dream, the dolphin materializes at night, when the lines between forms of reality most comfortably dissolve in the mediation of
sleep, as the riverman hovers between earth and sky in his native
hammock. Sweat and mist, body and its environs, both become part of
the miscible boundaries of the poem:

> I threw off my blanket, sweating;
> I even tore off my shirt.
> I got out of my hammock
> and went through the window naked.

Stripped of his sheathing of human culture, naked, unaccommodated
man goes to join a fluent world in which there is no discontinuity
between the human and the sacred, the living and the dead, or the
human and the animal.

While elements of the language of the finished poem appeared in
the very first draft, with a threshold image, a door to the water which
the riverman uses to enter the Dolphin kingdom, it took Bishop an
unusually long time to arrive at these mysterious and beckoning lines:

> I heard the Dolphin sigh
> as he slid into the water.
> I stood there listening
> till he called from far outstream.
> I waded into the river
> and suddenly a door
> in the water opened inward,
> groaning a little, with water
> bulging above the lintel.

The final image somewhat resembles a scrap, an earlier notebook jotting taken down some time before 1945:

> At night the crack under the bedroom door was like a luminous [golden?] letter being slid through.

This image is like the inverted moon image of "The Man-Moth," in which the Man-Moth thinks "to push his small head through that round clean opening/ and be forced through, as from a tube, in black scrolls on the light." The crack, the moon-hole of the Man-Moth's sky, the riverman's door—each is an opening, an entrance, or door penetrated by a pour of substance which is both light and writing. In a liminal state, a threshold of consciousness gives way, and we enter a medium, against the grain of what we accept as ordinary reality, imposing its barrier between us and transcendence. For Bishop, in this poem, many borders were being crossed, and there is a dreamed, uncanny ease to its accomplishments that is all the more persuasive as it knocks against the vividly awkward and unlikely objects and persons of its space.

For most of Bishop's drafts, the central language is usually present from the beginning, and the steady progression forward of the poems is a matter of meticulous tuning and adjusting, with occasional additions of new material only amplifying and extending a poem's original perceptions. Most of her poems have their central ideas complete from their first beginnings on paper. Bishop may have carried around the ideas for poems quite a long time before she began working them out in writing; or, alternatively, when the poems came for her, they must have come with great rapidity and clarity. Her method may contain the explanation for the slowness with which poems evolved. Looking at the dates for journal publications, there were only a few years in which Bishop ever wrote more than three or four poems, and very many for which she wrote one, two, or none. But for the drafts of "The Riverman," we see an unusually high proportion of the maker's decisions in process, as Bishop groped for the right words for her poem's events.

The faux-naif speech of the text itself signals Bishop's anxieties about the ability of language to bear the burden of the magical, or the sacred. Nonetheless, behind the constructed mask of the riverman's speech, a dogged, pessimistic Bishop continues her determined trudging towards the sublime, towards the lift-off inherent in poetic language as it turns to confront the farther reaches of our knowledge of the world. What makes this understated faith in the potentials of language so appealing to so many readers, perhaps, is Bishop's complex refusal to surrender the urgencies of that desire, that ambition to soar, while warding off any grandiose and falsifying representation of the effort, belying its pain, trouble, or accompanying absurdity.

When Bishop describes the riverman's encounter at a party in the river with Luandinha, "a tall, beautiful serpent/ in elegant white satin," the problem of language is prominent:

> She complimented me
> in a language I didn't know;
> but when she blew cigar smoke
> into my ears and nostrils
> I understood, like a dog,
> although I can't speak it yet.

The anthropological grounding of this is impeccable: smoke and fumigation are purifying features of shamanic ritual worldwide; they are other people beside common to the caboclos of the Amazon River. But there is a texture to this moment, both comic and touching, which also resembles a feeling of Bishop's own, at an American distance from the governing language of Brazil. When asked by Ashley Brown in 1966 about the influence of Portuguese on her English she merely replied: "I don't read it habitually—just newspapers and some books. After all these years, I'm like a dog: I understand everything that's said to me, but I don't speak it very well."

And we have one more fusion of the speaker in and of the poem. The words people use about themselves—or indeed about anything—are always revealing: not the paraphrases, or the summaries of their words, but just the very same gritty little language particles that turn up, iron filings around a magnet, again and again reconstating the preoccupying forms of our lives, testifying reassuringly too, perhaps, that there is such form. The riverman travels miles underwater with his new marine escort. Three times, like Christ's three days in the world of the dead, the riverman deserts his family and enters the Amazon, acquiring "a mottled rattle/ and a pale-green coral twig/ and some special weeds like smoke." But his initiation is not complete, and in a passage roughly following Satiro's talk with Wagley, Bishop has him declare:

I need a virgin mirror
no one's ever looked at,
that's never looked back at anyone,
to flash up the spirits' eyes
and help me recognize them.
The storekeeper offered me
a box of little mirrors,
but each time I picked one up
a neighbor looked over my shoulder
and then that one was spoiled —
spoiled, that is, for anything
but the girls to look at their mouths in,
to examine their teeth and smiles.

At this point, Satiro and Elizabeth Bishop again converge: for the North American poet, the mirror on the dresser from the inverted world of "Insomnia," and the Tennysonian mirror on the lake from "The Gentleman of Shalott," all have power to confer not only identity but connection to the larger, sought host of the spirit world. For Satiro, the riverman, and for Bishop, too, the quest is clouded by exasperating images of an intervening humanity. For Bishop and the riverman, the mirror always reflects some troubling Other, always tainting our recognition of self with our recognition of our estrangement from self and our imperfect alliances with others. Yet Wagley's *page* and Bishop's riverman, and no doubt Bishop herself, wish to survive their literal defacements, to escape the exasperating confinements of the body, and to dissolve within a larger community of spirits.

In the Brazilian notebooks, Bishop kept a tiny scrap from *The Harvard Advocate*, an inch of paper clipped from a student interview with John Berryman, familiar to me because I carried around the same interview for years in my own tattering notebooks. The poet is not identified, but the substance is all there: "For whom do you write? For the dead whom thou didst love," is the reply. For the riverman, the longed-for unity remains within the tradition of the sacacas, the great doctors, and for Bishop the writer, within the community of "the dead whom thou didst love." Here the "sincere" ambition of the riverman and Bishop's own personal need appear to merge within similar waters.

Bishop's poem closes oddly for an account of a shaman's initiation,

I have been told by an anthropologist friend, because it does not finish with the traditional, triumphant entry of the shaman into his magical community. Bishop may have been influenced by a sentence of Wagley's that runs: "Perhaps Satiro will even become a sacaca with all the prestige of those great men a generation ago." Like the anthropologist, who has intruded his study onto the living body of a progressive myth, Bishop, too, concludes her poem *in medias res;* her emphasis in the poem is on what the shaman might become; on his earnest, ruminative tone of open possibility:

> Why shouldn't I be ambitious?
> I sincerely desire to be
> a serious *sacaca*
> like Fortunato Pombo,
> or Lucio, or even
> the great Joaquim Sacaca.
> Look, it stands to reason
> that everything we need
> can be obtained from the river.
> It drains the jungles; it draws
> from trees and plants and rocks
> from half around the world,
> it draws from the very heart
> of the earth the remedy
> for each of the diseases —
> one just has to know how to find it.
> But everything must be there
> in that magic mud, beneath
> the multitudes of fish,
> deadly or innocent,
> the giant *pirarucus*,
> the turtles and crocodiles,
> tree trunks and sunk canoes,
> with the crayfish, with the worms
> with tiny electric eyes
> turning on and off and on.
> The river breathes in salt
> and breathes it out again,
> and all is sweetness there
> in the deep, enchanted silt.

For some readers, the opening lines of this passage constitute a break in tone. There seems to be an attempt to rationalize magic, to make a stand at imitating a primitive reasoning process, as if that process were a prelogical and prescientific mode for manipulating environment. In the earnest, slightly pompous practicality of the water witch, we hear the self-betterment program of the upwardly mobile, using tribal magic much as a suburban aspirant to the medical profession might, planning to do well by doing good. Yet I think the break, and this slightly jarring characterization is deliberate on Bishop's part. We might argue that her riverman earns a place in the poem through his refusal to sentimentalize magic, and through Bishop's daring to place his magic within an only apparently prosaic context. What Bishop is doing in the lyric descriptive passages of her poem firmly undercuts a mechanistic rationale for magic, as magic suffuses the strange nouns and prosaic happenings with its own glittering compulsions. The disjunctive weaving of industrial objects with the organic world of the river makes the strange more strange by embedding it within the familiar and homely. Through this tactic the familiar begins to take on the strange, and the strange looks oddly familiar, as categories leak from world to world, keeping the reader offguard, and ready to step into anything.

In the poem Bishop works very hard to avoid the "translated" sound of many renderings of primitive myth. The final stanza of the poem finds a diction that penetrates through both magical and prosaic worlds:

> When the moon burns white
> and the river makes that sound
> like a primus pumped up high—
> that fast, high whispering
> like a hundred people at once—
> I'll be there below,
> as the turtle rattle hisses
> and the coral gives the sign,
> travelling fast as a wish,
> with my magic cloak of fish
> swerving as I swerve,
> following the veins,
> the river's long, long veins,
> to find the pure elixirs.

> Godfathers and cousins,
> your canoes are over my head;
> I hear your voices talking.
> You can peer down and down
> or dredge the river bottom
> but never, never catch me.
> When the moon shines and the river
> lies across the earth
> and sucks it like a child,
> then I will go to work
> to get you health and money.
> The Dolphin singled me out;
> Luandinha seconded it.

Such a poem cannot work its particular magical fusion, its elision of water and earth elements, of the human and the animal kingdom, of the primitive and the developed, of male and female genders in its protagonist, and of the family world of generations, if it camps too much on its essential premises. Belief and identification with the components of the poem must enter, or the poem remains a patronizing acting out, conducted from an unfeeling distance. And it seems to me, that in the creation of this clearly synthetic voice, a voice bridging Bishop's and the Amazon's world, Bishop accomplishes what she set out to do in the poem. In "The Riverman," unlike any of Bishop's previous Brazilian poems, the world of the protagonist actively joins the world of the poet, if only obliquely through understatement and implication.

What helps to give the language of this poem its peculiar fitness is its persuasive junction of prosaic and exotic, so that the tactics of bridging are once more a function of the poem's successes. We recognize the Bishop touch of accuracy in the image of the "primus pumped up high" in that "fast, high whispering/ like a hundred people at once": and it is the homely rightness of such an image that makes the magic of the river all the more haunting. In the intimacy of this detail Bishop domesticates the uncanny, and draws us irresistibly within it:

> There is fine mud on my scalp
> and I know from smelling my comb
> that the river smells in my hair.
> My hands and feet are cold.

If the poem were smoother, missing the strains and lumps of its jarring particularities, it would be less believable; more clearly a remote folk tale to keep at a distance. The industrial objects and analogies of the poem—its primus stove, Luandinha's eyes "green and gold/ like the lights on the river steamers" (an image borrowed directly from Wagley) all weight the poem with a disturbing reality. In the following lines, magic subverts even the clearest signal of the nonmagical industrial world, appropriating its objects for its own superior uses:

> When the moon shines on the river,
> oh, faster than you can think it
> we travel upstream and downstream,
> we journey from here to there,
> under the floating canoes,
> right through the wicker traps,
> when the moon shines on the river
> and Luandinha gives a party.
> Three times now I've attended.
> Her rooms shine like silver
> with the light from overhead,
> a steady stream of light
> like at the cinema.

Bishop's lunar wash reverses the familiar process of reification, in which the mechanical and industrial is said to overturn the natural and organic, so that here the silver screen derives its potency from that subordinating moonlight, and not the other way around. Still, like the reverberating suggestions of loss, change, and retreat from within "Brazil, January 1, 1502," this poem, in its incompletions, poises the riverman between the traditional goal and its contemporary accomplishment.

The last two lines—"The Dolphin singled me out;/ Luandinha seconded it"—point to the source of the riverman's sense of election. They help us to arrive at some indication of how Bishop achieves closure and balance of tone, and how she sets the relationships between speaker of the poem, speaker in the poem, and the auditors of both.

Analysts of shamanic initiation from Paul Radin to Mircéa Eliade describe the shaman's sense of election: one cannot choose to be a shaman; a true shaman can only be chosen.[86] In speaking of initiation, the shaman already speaks from within a community of the elect. Within this context, first person narration is something unusual, literally, something of an alien self-consciousness.[87] If we look at early drafts of "The Riverman," it is clear that Bishop began her poem without the explanatory framework from Wagley. Her poem begins "I got up in the night/ for the dolphin spoke to me." The first person sentence is the earliest element of her poem to arrive, its most secure sense of itself. The second page of this initial draft, though, contains an invocation, an address to its spirit community: "Boto, Father of Dolphins/ River, Mother of Waters." And for several drafts, Bishop plays with this address, placing it in the middle of the poem, then at the beginning, and then at the end: "Mother of Waters, teach me!/ Father of Dolphins, guide me!" Finally, she scraps the open plea for guidance altogether, setting her bracketed explanation in a series of versions at the head of the poem instead, and keeps her final version centered in the ruminative hopes of the riverman. Unusually for Bishop, it isn't until she is deep into a sixth draft of the poem that she reaches her final wording, which keeps election tentative, and sounds almost like an afterthought: "The Dolphin singled me out/ and Luandinha agreed." Unlike the true vatic utterance, in which for the initiate "a thought is thinking me," subordinating her or him to its speech, Bishop's riverman never really cedes his sense of himself as an autonomous speaker concentrating on a learning that goes on inside. Taking imaginative advantage of Wagley's hint—"Satiro is still learning his profession"—Bishop exploits the unfinished process, and creates a breach through which she may enter the poem in her own person culturally as well as mythically.

What she makes is an untypical shamanic initiation story, but a typical Bishop poem. All of her magic and mythic protagonists are caught within choices, suspended within their climactic moments: Unbeliever, Gentleman, Man-Moth, all live within an intensified and foreshortened present time. Within *this* myth, however, Bishop enters a specific culture, and herself an alien, enters as a historic familiar.

A further major change in the story has Bishop realigning the traditional sexual symbolism of the dolphin. As Wagley and other anthropologists see the dolphin in Indian myth, it is an animal possessed of great sexual potency. As Wagley puts it, "The boto, more than any other animal, is 'enchanted,' and the male is a dangerous sexual competitor to man." There are strong hints of this in Bishop's poem: the riverman is forced to choose between his snoring wife and

Luandinha. In the last stanza, however, it is not the bereaved wife that the riverman addresses in his justification speech, but his "Godfathers and cousins" that he hears passing him in the canoes over his head. Adjusting the poem to her own psychological needs of the moment, Bishop adapts the South American myth to reflect herself as orphan rather than as lover or spouse, and it is as a child of a community that the riverman is last seen:

> When the moon shines and the river
> lies across the earth
> and sucks it like a child,
> then I will go to work
> to get you health and money.

Governed by the female moon, and by an image of maternal Nature, the riverman reconciles his election with his membership in the human community.

But whether as sexual emblem, or as powerful parent figure, Bishop's Dolphin attempts to heal the psychic split between man and the animal world, and industrial man estranged from the spirit world. If there is an incompleted portion to the initiation rite which becomes a fortuitous entry of her own person and origin, the breach also records perhaps something sadder which Bishop also felt compelled to record: namely, the decline in the culture of the shamans which her own presence signifies. We are looking at a dying society, and the break in voice that Bishop records, between the mechanistic faith in magic as simply a kind of crude scientific materialism, and faith in magic as faith in the whole inviolable universe of regnant nature, is something that necessarily intrudes into the poem through her own person.

The poem that Bishop writes is on its Amazonian side no simple or naive attempt to appropriate a tradition; finally, the poem succeeds because the poet incorporates her own inability to be the speaker of the poem as part of the poem's beholding. Yet the modifications and representative movements of her own person behind the adoptive persona eventually yield the wide exploration of doubled being, self and other, which is the peculiar domain of dramatic monologue.

Within a solid narrative, the estrangements and suspensions of the poem released for Bishop a uniquely expressive voice, channeling within the banks of its unknown and as yet uninspected river some of her own deepest feelings of solitude and election, distance and commitment. She was asked by Ashley Brown, "What do you think about

·T·E·N·

The Gallery
of Her Glance

AFTER *Questions of Travel*, and during the time that saw the
publication in 1969 of *The Complete Poems*, Elizabeth Bishop continued
to test potential subject, now breaking this way toward Moore, the
genteel, private and largely apolitical, and now that way towards Lowell, amplitude, and exposure. Besides the two prose books, the translation of *The Diary of Helena Morley*, and the Time-Life book on Brazil,
there is in her unfinished and unpublished poetry further tantalizing
evidence of her efforts to broaden the range of her subjects, to tackle
other moods, other modes. These efforts occur even before the large
changes imposed on her life by the death of Lota, bringing on her
permanent return to the United States. Before going on to talk about
the evolution of the work throughout this period, I would like to take
on the two debates between Lowell and Bishop, first in 1961 over the
style of his translations in *Imitations*, the book he dedicated to her, and
then nearly a decade later in 1972 over the verbatim use of Elizabeth
Hardwick's letters in *The Dolphin;* these exchanges show with particular clarity Bishop's evolving sense of the constraints operating between
poet and poetry.

·I·

The debate over translation becomes a sketch of Bishop's working
assumptions about style's relation to subject. As Kalstone details these
events,[88] she drafted several responses to the translations published as

Imitations, in some distress eventually mailing them all off to Lowell to sort out for himself. Some of her corrections of what looked like mistranslations he accepted; in response to her designation of *tartines* as bread and butter, not tarts, he merely stranded the French word in his English line: "At the Green Cabaret, I called for ham, /half-cold, and a large helping of tartines." But the chief difficulty for Bishop seems to be his heavyhandedness; in the Baudelaire and Rimbaud poems, she objects again and again to a forcing of mood and tone. She singles out Rimbaud's "La Maline" for particular objections, where Lowell transforms *brune* into cigar-brown, alters the smell of the dining room from *vernis et de fruits,* varnish and fruits, to shellac and cabbage soup, and everywhere makes things glummer and grimmer. "I just can't decide how 'free' one has the right to be with the poet's intentions," she wrote. Worst of all, the light, deft sexual comedy becomes distinctly sour, as Lowell, taking "La Maline" to mean "A Malicious Girl," rather than the "sly," "cunning," "artful" or "crafty" one, all permissible shades of *maline,* drew fire from Bishop. She found the poem:

> so much more light-hearted than you've made it, and the girl, fussing with plates to make an opening for conversation, is feminine, flirtatious, untidy, by implication young and pretty, "naughty" – but not sordid or dirty.

Rimbaud loosens the girl's neckerchief and gives her an artful hairdo; Lowell sees a slut with "blouse/ half-open, yellow hair in strings." I'd like to point out that for Bishop, it isn't merely that poems are as inviolable as persons. In "Invitation to Miss Marianne Moore," her own "imitation" of Neruda's "Alberto Rojas Jimenez vienes volando," Bishop is quite as free about changing tone: yet in moving openly towards adaptation rather than translation, she builds a higher fence between my poem and thy poem. But perhaps Lowell's lack of ceremony proves infectious. In Vinícius de Moraes' "Sonnet of Intimacy," she makes his closing lines about a back country walk in a cow pasture read like this:

> The smell of cow manure is delicious.
> The cattle look at me unenviously
> And when there comes a sudden stream and hiss
>
> Accompanied by a look not unmalicious,
> All of us, animals, unemotionally
> Partake together of a pleasant piss.[89]

Moraes' final two lines run, "Nos todos, animais, sem comoção nenhuma,/ Mijamos em comum numa festa de espuma." Bishop renders the last figure, "festa de espuma," or "together, in one festival of spray," as a blunt colloquialism, a merely "pleasant piss."

A decade after *Imitations*, she allows herself a certain deft rearrangement of meaning. "It's an interesting fact," she says in her 1966 interview with Ashley Brown, "that there's no word in Portuguese for 'understatement.' How can they understand us? So much of the English-American tradition consists of this. They have irony, but no understatement." Which in her English rendering she supplies here at least in part by down-tilting an edge of quixotic ceremony, perhaps in the interest of maintaining a plainer, unadorned pastoral, perhaps as a subtle snub to the male member. But in the old battle with Lowell of the understater against the overstater, each poet keeps constancy of form in characteristic ways.

Bishop's understatement usually remains a reticence moving toward stoicism and against personal display. In her dislike of Lowell's stuffing his translation with extra words, his tuning of moods into something at once deflationary and exaggerated, she registers her preference as well for a kind of restraint that keeps minds and persons, poems and persons, separate and intact. Lowell's stance crowds her, crowds her world.

·II·

In the account given of her in Ian Hamilton's biography of Lowell, Bishop remonstrates with Lowell about his public use of letters written to him by his second wife, Elizabeth Hardwick, and their daughter, Harriet, in his forthcoming book, *The Dolphin*. Lowell's elderly mentors, like Auden and Tate, had been shocked by this violation of his wife's and daughter's privacy. Lowell appears to offer to himself too tempting an invitation to revise the voices in the transcript, to supply his own version of the dialogue for everybody. In answering Bishop on March 28, 1972, about his use of Hardwick's letters, he says:

> I did not see them as slander, but as sympathetic, tho necessarily awful for her to read. She is the poignance of the book, tho that hardly makes it kinder to her. I could say the letters are cut, doctored part fiction; I thought of it (I attribute things to Lizzie I made up, or that were said by someone else. I combed out abuse, hysteria, repetition. The trouble is the letters make the book, I think; at least they make Lizzie real beyond my invention. I took out the worst things written against me, so

as not to give myself a case and seem self-pitying. Or maybe I didn't want to author them. I promise I'll do what I can to answer your piercing thoughts. I've been thinking of course these things for years almost. It's oddly enough a technical problem as well as a gentleman's problem. How can the story be told at all without the letters. I'll put my heart to it. I can't bear not to publish Dolphin in good form.

At the least one can say he is guilty of mixing his genres: that he confuses autobiography with fiction to the inevitable consternation of his reader and himself. Through the use of "real" names he wishes to claim for his text the truth and authenticity of autobiography, as if one could graft authenticity onto the fictive as a simple matter of coloration.

But in reading the mixed effort of the poems, like a man with a bulky, unmanageable package, we shift uncertainly from belief to its willing suspension and back again, not knowing when or where or how to attach to the text. If only language could be purged of mimetic function. There is no sense in Lowell's letter of his recognition of the goal of a truth standing over or apart from his perceptions of it. Objections are merely about the favorable or unfavorable light in which the participants are cast, nor does he permit any questioning of his judgment about what is "abusive," or "hysterical," or "repetitious." There can be no controversy about the content of these "worst things written against me": Lowell will allow none through his appropriation of all the means of reproduction. He takes out what he judges the worst things: "maybe I didn't want to author them." And politely his good friend Elizabeth Bishop does not question him further about this reluctance. What seems interesting is the degree to which Lowell implicitly rejects adaptation, or interpretation, or paraphrase or translation of the letters as possible linguistic operations: nothing but the letters themselves will do; and yet editorial cuts, or systems of indirection and implication, are in this letter of self-justification not recognized as the powerful interpretive tools that they are.

Nothing in Lowell's letters to Bishop acknowledges this array of problems. On Easter Tuesday he writes again:

Let me re-phrase for myself your moral objections. It's the revelation (with documents?) of a wife wanting her husband not to leave her, and who does leave her. That's the trouble, not the mixture of truth and fiction. Fiction—no one would object if I said Lizzie was wearing a purple and red dress, when it was yellow. Actually my versions of her letters are softer and drastically cut. The original is heartbreaking but interminable.

Then he applies himself to manipulations of sequence in details and passages to obscure tensions between the Lowells over his future happiness with his new wife, Caroline Blackwood, and the birth of their child. Finally, in apparent bewilderment, he says: "who can want to savage a thing. How can I want to hurt?" Quite as if the issue of the truth of partial revelation with peekaboo and altered documents did not exist.

Bishop's stance over whether or not his wife's and daughter's letters should have been used in *The Dolphin* is very firm. After paragraphs of compliments about *The Dolphin*, Bishop writes Lowell this frequently cited letter:

> Here is a quotation from dear little Hardy that I copied out years ago [. . .]
>
> > "What should certainly be protested against, in cases where there is no authorization, is the mixing of fact and fiction in unknown proportions. Infinite mischief would lie in that. If any statements in the dress of fiction are covertly hinted to be the fact, all must be fact, and nothing else but fact, for obvious reasons. The power of getting lies believed about people through that channel after they are dead, by stirring in a few truths, is a horror to contemplate."
>
> I'm sure my point is only too plain . . . Lizzie is not dead, etc. – but there is a "mixture of fact & fiction," and you have *changed* her letters. That is "infinite mischief," I think [. . .] One can use one's life a[s] material — one does anyway — but given these letters — aren't you violating a trust? IF you were given permission — IF you hadn't changed them . . . etc. *But art isn't worth that much.* I keep remembering Hopkins' marvellous letter to Bridges about the idea of a "gentleman" being the highest ever conceived — higher than a "Christian" even, certainly than a poet. It is not being "gentle" to use personal, tragic, anguished letters that way — it's cruel.

What emerges from the letter is first a clear assertion, not at all a qualified one, that one's duties as a poet are not separable from one's duties as a human being. One uses one's life as material, that's hardly avoidable, but there are conditions attached to that use for the ethical.

Once again, Bishop is invoking Hopkins against, or with, a beloved contemporary, ending this phase of their exchange with additional reinforcement by way of both Hardy and Hopkins. But despite her firmness, Bishop closes in a collapsing jumble of objections and irres- olutions, much like the mood governing her dreamy wordplay over much the same issues of living entanglement with text that marked her engagement with Moore. On the one hand, Hardy and Hopkins stand for the writers with whom Lowell ought to align himself; on the other hand there are contemporaries like Mailer, or Dickey, or MacCarthy, whom Lowell ought to shun. She says of these writers,

> I don't give a damn what someone like Mailer writes about his wives & marriages – I just hate the level we seem to live and think and feel on at present – but I DO give a damn what you write! (or Dickey, or Mary ...) They don't count, in the long run. This counts and I can't bear to have anything you write tell – perhaps – what we're really like in 1972 ... perhaps it's as simple as that. But are we? Well – I musn't ramble on any more. I've thought about it all I can and can't reach any more lucid conclusions, I'm afraid.

The finish here is very much like the murmuring tangle, the subsi- dence at the end of "Efforts of Affection." In an effort to be honest at the deepest and not always most self-glorifying levels, Bishop admits to tangled motivation: what we're "really like in 1972" should be kept dark, she says, tentatively surrounding her conclusion with "perhaps." Perhaps the most complete truths are dark ones, that *ought* to be kept from the light. Then she rallies herself again, and a final *But* chivvies away at even that conclusion, before she sternly forbids herself to "ramble" anymore. "What we're really like" dances on one foot; "But are we?" on the other. Her three word question leaves open the possibility that one of the stickier duties of poetry is to represent the selves that we ought to be in preference to the selves that we are.

Her darker ruminations leave doubt as to how much of the truth of ourselves we should tell, but then again, she moves to question if not whether, then at least *how* these truths are even representable in poetry. Poetry's relation to truth she doesn't doubt; early in 1954 she urged Lowell to do autobiography, notes her own satisfaction at doing stories "of that sort," and says:

> somehow — that desire to get things straight and tell the truth — it's almost impossible not to tell the truth in poetry, I think, but in prose it keeps eluding one in the funniest way.

The substitutions and elliptical compressions of poetry allow her to shape a truth to her satisfaction; but in the roomier folds of prose, allowing her ampler narrative, ampler access to detail and drama, the heftier infusions and representations of self are harder to balance, harder to direct, harder to bring in focus. And still it is a curious remark: the most direct and comprehensive of her autobiographical efforts remain in prose, until the last decade of her life. Now in 1972, in a last ditch effort to come up with a definitive position, she tosses Lowell a scrap from Kierkegaard's journals:

> the law of delicacy according to which an author has a right to use what he himself has experienced, is that he is never to utter verity but is to keep verity for himself & only let it be refracted in various ways.

Then she concludes: "But maybe that is exactly what you *have* done [. . .]?"

Little by little, Lowell has wracked her convictions of what it is possible to recover as subject. Bishop in her moving elegy for Lowell can comment feelingly on death as the condition that will forever remove him from literal and literary wobbling and wavering. She says in "North Haven": "You can't derange, or re-arrange,/ your poems again [. . .]/The words won't change again. Sad friend, you cannot change." But if not in this elegy, elsewhere she senses that her own position has its rigidities.

As Lowell's manuscript of *The Dolphin* changed, under Bishop's and others' remonstrance, and through intensive conversation with the poet Frank Bidart, Bishop seems to have reconciled herself more to Lowell's uses of the autobiographical and, by the final decade of her life, to have moved toward a greater sharing of her work with him, and towards a greater acceptance of the painfully autobiographical as subject and focus in her own poetry. In 1963 she muses to Lowell, "this increasing self-consciousness of the human race – its curiosity for some kind of factual knowledge of its own history – surely it will eventually help things – ?" In 1964, finding language for praise, she has clearly put behind her all thoughts of what Lowell teasingly referred to as her dislike of the "obvious" in his work; after receiving *For the Union Dead*, she compares his poetry to Gesualdo, finding "Wild and surprising harmonies, apparently a simple thought but made suddenly so strange and penetrating." A month later, still working on this parallel, she calls the admired quality "That sustaining of the impossible, free, strange or wild, but never disintegrating":

the hardest thing in the world to do – no rules at all – just immense skill and sensibility – and willingness to say something once and *stop*, let it go.

Through all her objections and hesitations, Lowell leaves strong traces in her work. They are there in simple ways: her late poem "Night City," closes with an alternating street light:

> (Still, there are creatures,
> careful ones, overhead.
> They set down their feet, they walk
> green, red; green, red.)

Much as Lowell closes "The Old Flame," in *For the Union Dead:*

> we heard the plow
> groaning up hill –
> a red light, then a blue,
> as it tossed off the snow
> to the side of the road.

And then there are larger and more suggestive debts. "In the Waiting Room" replays childhood, just as "Manners" and "First Death in Nova Scotia" did. Yet here the first person focus is made more intensively inward, and the narrative greatly extended, moving beyond the radical spatial and temporal juxtaposition of scenes which are Lowell's specialty. Bishop also appears to drop the shifting point of view of her more experimentally modernist construction in the 1953 story, "In the Village," as the much later "In the Waiting Room" remains clearly first person. Oddly, though, the perspectives of childhood, and the arrival of a scheme for identity is the largest part of its subject. She takes up the challenge of Lowell's approach, to make a personal record, but sticks with her own sense of narrative positioning, pacing, and timing.

In a rare move, in August 1967 she asks for Lowell's help with "In the Waiting Room":

perhaps you can tell me what's the matter with this poem [...] I really mean it, and say what you think – I'll scrap it, if necessary. I like the idea – but know there's something very wrong and can't seem to tell what it is [...] maybe it should be cut – maybe it should rhyme – maybe it's the fault of the damned METER.

But his influence in this poem is felt long before she turns to him for suggestions. In a climactic scene from "91 Revere Street," the prose memoir from *Life Studies*, a preadolescent Lowell pictures himself in bed at home, overhearing his mother's hysterical complaints to Admiral De Stahl, who has forced Lowell's father back on duty at the Navy base on Christmas Eve. The hapless senior Lowell is caught between allegiance to the Navy and allegiance to his wife, and unable to put his body in two places at once, has submitted to the admiral's orders. Throughout the memoir, a subtext has been the formation of Lowell's masculine identity; his timid father and overbearing mother have left him with inadequate and distasteful gender models. Images in the Lowell passage that I will quote obviously owe something to the bedtime polar atmospherics of Randall Jarrell's "90 North"; but whatever its mingled sources might have been for Lowell, the whole of the passage must have sunk deeply into Bishop's consciousness:

On our first Revere Street Christmas Eve, the telephone rang in the middle of dinner; it was Admiral De Stahl demanding Father's instant return to the Navy Yard. Soon Father was back in uniform. In taking leave of my mother and grandparents he was, as was usual with him under pressure, a little evasive and magniloquent. [. . .] Later that night I lay in bed and tried to imagine that my father was leading his engineering force on a surprise maneuver through arctic wastes. A forlorn hope! "Hush-hush, hush-hush," whispered the snowflakes as big as street lamps as they broke on Father—broke and buried. Outside, I heard real people singing carols, shuffling snow off their shoes, opening and shutting doors. [. . .] I imagined Beacon Hill changed to the snow queen's palace, as vast as the north pole. My father pressed a cold finger to his lip: "hush-hush," and led his surprise squad of sailors around an altar, but the altar was a tremendous cash register, whose roughened nickel surface was cheaply decorated with trowels, pyramids, and Arabic swirls. A great drawer helplessly chopped back and forth, unable to shut because choked with greenbacks. "Hush-hush!" My father's engineers wound about me with their eye-patches, orange sashes, and curtain-ring earrings, like the Gilbert and Sullivan pirates' chorus [. . . .] Outside on the streets of Beacon Hill, it was night, it was dismal, it was raining.

It is not hard to hear in these words the lines that end "In the Waiting Room":

> The War was on. Outside,
> in Worcester, Massachusetts,
> were night and slush and cold,
> and it was still the fifth
> of February, 1918.

Not difficult to recognize, either, in Lowell's snow queen, the germinating seed for the frosty royal retinue of Bishop's "First Death in Nova Scotia." But the reasons for the passage's burr-like hold on Bishop's consciousness lie further than verbal echo. Lowell's narrative continues:

> Something disturbing had befallen the familiar and honorable Salvation Army band; its big drum and accordion were now accompanied by drunken voices howling: *The Old Gray Mare, she ain't what she used to be, when Mary went to milk the cow.* A sound of a bosun's whistle. Women laughing. Someone repeatedly rang our doorbell. I heard my mother talking on the telephone. "Your inebriated sailors have littered my doorstep with the dregs of Scollay Square." There was a gloating panic in her voice that showed she enjoyed the drama of talking to Admiral de Stahl. "Sir," she shrilled, "you have compelled my husband to leave me alone and defenseless on Christmas Eve!" She ran into my bedroom. She hugged me. She said, "Oh Bobby, it's such a comfort to have a man in the house." "I am not a man," I said, "I am a boy."

Refusing to be seduced into premature manhood, and shaped into cannon fodder for the ruthless domestic war against his father, Lowell sticks to his problematic boyhood. It is possible to speculate, too, that the breathy, choppy phrases of that nighttime catalogue of sounds — bosun's whistle, women's laughter, doorbell — also owe something to the treatment of sound in Bishop's "In the Village." Debts were always two-way in this relationship. Bishop takes up the subject of gender anxieties for her poem, but of course explores the discomfort and disquiet of female identity; like Lowell's memoir, her narrative poem turns on anxious connection to the family. In both cases, a child faces down and passionately denies the necessity of joining the adult world in the gender role to which the child is being forcibly assigned.

·III·

While she could not take on Lowell's challenge to register the political upheaval of the coup of 1964 which Lowell urged her to see as uniquely her field of vantage, Bishop did not automatically reject the incursion of the more broadly political into her work. If she came to childhood, loss, and the traversable boundaries between human and animal as her principal subjects in the last years of her life, it was not through having failed to test her own limits. The stories that she published, the translations and prose poems that appeared in *The Complete Poems* published in 1969, her 1972 *Anthology of Twentieth-Century Brazilian Poetry* in company with Emanuel Brasil, all point to a continuing preoccupation with Brazil, even as she made a variety of unsuccesful efforts to keep her hold on that country. The absence of Brazilian material from the poems of *Geography III*, published nearly a decade after Lota's death, yet only three years before Bishop's own death, becomes a late mark of the definitive end of her life in that country.

No one should underestimate this loss of both a person and a world for Bishop. In concentration on the development of her work it is easy to focus on her relations with other poets, and to ignore Bishop's less publicly documented nonliterary friendships. Given the conventional preoccupations of either heterosexual or male readers it may be all too easy to discount the power of loving relations between women, also in monolingual and typically North American fashion to slight the full impact on Bishop of her life in Brazil. If in this discussion I have not fully prevented my own monocularities from obscuring questions, I hope at least I have made clear the need for a certain wariness. In Bishop's letters there are outbursts to show that her voluntary exile had its increasingly doutbtful moments. Decades of Bishop's faithful and copious letter-writing must have been part of an effort to keep her English alive in the daily streaming of Portuguese around her. Returning slowly to Brazil on the *S.S. Brazil Star* in 1964, she writes to the Summers about the effects of a recent visit to the Barkers:

> I wanted to visit my old friends and TALK ENGLISH – which I did, to excess. It was wonderful to have one's mildest pun caught, or one's half-finished phrases – and to be able to talk without thinking if you knew the words first – just let it come!

"For about a week I didn't think I could ever make it – thought I'd just leave my bones in Brazil – " she writes to Lowell, after going to Rio after Lota's funeral. About the funeral itself, which she did not attend, she had written to the Barkers,

> There was even a military escort to meet the plane. . . And 3 governors, and an ex-governor, and the ex-head of the Supreme Court [. . .] I get full descriptions, of course. Over 200 people, and more at the 7th day mass . . . and the headlines just say "Dona Lota dies in N Y" – and 2 of the articles are just headed LOTA – she had become so famous, my poor darling Lota . . . Only our maid, Joanna, carried on, and howled in the good old proletarian way, apparently, *coitada*.

But as she tells Lowell the story of her actual visit, she can't bring herself to move into detail:

> I'll skip all the Brazil stay; it was really too awful to speak about – not only the packing-up, dreadful as it was – but the behaviour of people I had thought were my friends for almost 16 years. I suppose it can be explained – Anny [Baumann] explained it as reactions to great grief – but I felt more as if I were being used as a sort of scapegoat – without exaggeration – and think now that Lota's death left everyone feeling somewhat guilty and then I appeared and was unconsciously used in this way.

Her severance from Brazilian ties even after Lota's death was complex, long-drawn out, and physically and emotionally wrenching; it wasn't until severe illness forced a retreat from her house in Ouro Preto in 1971, however, that she finally began to consider leaving Brazil altogether. By March 1972, after one of the last attempts to live in her house in Ouro Preto, she writes Linda Nemer in discouragement:

> I arrived there when I was already too old, with nearly everything, as to work and my life, already done – and as a tourist, or an expatriot – [. . .] I think O.P. is very bad for me now because of the solitude: it's too isolated, and life is too difficult – difficult also here, but not as much – and when I'm still older – O.P. lacks good doctors, servants, etc etc . . . It's not a place for me –

And then again more explosively to Lowell, once more from within Ouro Preto in July 1972:

I've really HAD Brazil – I can barely endure reading the newspapers with all of the same old idiocies they've printed for 20 years – plus the newer, and much more sinister ones . . . (the town is full of police – 3 cars, paddy wagons, parked permanently in the *praça* – and more around town – barred, grilled, armored, etc . . .)

There are many signs indicating that her years in Boston held their measure of happiness. Repatriation offered deep pleasures, not the least of which was a return to her own language; but if one looks at the directions taken in her work, it is still like tracing the fault lines of earthquake damage, or a passing of hands over old scars, touching the signs of healing over rupture and disconnection.

Poems in the limbo between the publication of *Questions of Travel* and *Geography III*, marked by the intervening appearance of 1969's *Complete Poems*, are much more various than the ten poems of the final book would suggest. Yet much of Bishop's interest in political detail underwent the same sort of pressure toward speech, and then retreat away from it characterizing her interest in the intimately erotic. The new life with Lota, beginning in the early fifties, saw an end to Bishop's efforts to deal publicly with the agonies of personal relationship. After *Questions of Travel* there is a decisive break away from anything resembling what she described in Emily Dickinson's work as that annoying "constant insistence on the strength of her affections," that clinging to the female topic, love. In the fifties and most of the sixties, from her voluntary exile's post in Brazil, she asked her naturalist's eye to cast its beam over more than the animal and vegetable, to include urban as well as pastoral or village life among its landscapes. In these years, portraits of servants like "Manuelzinho" and "House Guest" grow in detail and depth, and there is a paradigm shift in her vision of the outsider, as she locates herself in "The Riverman" and lifts the more diaphanous garments of a fantastic Man-Moth or Gentleman of Shalott onto the rags of an actual *ribeirinho*, or a Burglar of Babylon Hill. But if personal affections are not her chosen subject, her moves in the fifties and sixties nevertheless show a need to find a poetic brace in the dust of the worlds around her. Yet the years that saw her immersion in Brazilian life come to a tumultuous close, as Bishop struggled to survive the impact of Lota's death. By the time that she returns to the United States, there is an end to her poetry's involvement in the more directly social and political, and an even greater convergence with the kinds of topics — memory, childhood and other personal losses, relation to poetry—that Bishop shared with Lowell and other American poets of her era whose experience was considerably more conventional than her own.

As I've shown earlier, "Going to the Bakery" picks up a variety of politically sensitive judgments about living in Rio. Yet historical reporting of the kind Lowell pressed Bishop to make had begun abortively when Bishop attempted a poem on the suicide of Getulio Vargas. This event in 1954 was obviously a critical one in her Brazilian life, since both Bishop and Lota de Macedo Soares were then friends and neighbors of Carlos Lacerda. Lacerda, who had been wounded by Vargas' gunmen as they attempted to shoot Lacerda down in an effort to stop his press reports, was said to have been part of the motivation for Vargas' suicide, through his steady coverage of this and other scandals of Vargas' administration. But Bishop's unfinished poem deals directly with none of these events.

Hers is the same eye and ear that in 1961 backgrounded the American Civil War to a page "From Trollope's Journal, [Winter 1861]," foregrounding Washington's foggy bottom instead, reducing the onset of war to the civilian mire that produced it and kept it going. The poem might be seen as not only a commemorative gesture, but as a determined American equivalent to the Brazilian scene that she has mounted earlier in "Brazil, January 1, 1502." A double sonnet, "From Trollope's Journal" is also another dramatic monologue:

> On Sunday afternoon I wandered—rather,
> I floundered—out alone. The air was raw
> and dark; the marsh half-ice, half-mud. This weather
> is normal now: a frost, and then a thaw,
> and then a frost. A hunting man, I found
> the Pennsylvania Avenue heavy ground . . .
> There all around me in the ugly mud
> —hoof-pocked, uncultivated—herds of cattle,
> numberless, wond'ring steers and oxen, stood:
> beef for the Army, after the next battle.
> Their legs were caked the color of dried blood;
> their horns were wreathed with fog. Poor, starving, dumb
> or lowing creatures, never to chew the cud
> or fill their maws again! Th'effluvium
> made that damned anthrax on my forehead throb.
> I called a surgeon in, a young man, but,

with a sore throat himself, he did his job.
We talked about the War, and as he cut
away he croaked out, "Sir, I do declare
everyone's sick! The soldiers poison the air."

In war or out of it, nature's images are primary; the problem of the human will to extremes of violence is still not Bishop's even during wartime; the Washingtonians are suffering this war as they might a disease. It is the same sensibility that later brings out the Scots bonneted Brazilian Marines pumping their legs in the park swings during the coup of 1964.

The three stanzas of her aborted poem, "Suicide of a Moderate Dictator," begin:

This is a day when truths will out, perhaps;
leak from the dangling telephone earphones
sapping the festooned switchboards' strength,
fall from the windows, blow from off the sills,
– the vague, slight unremarkable contents
of emptying ashtrays; rub off on our fingers
like ink from the un-proof-read newspapers,
crooking the way the unfocussed photographs
of crooked faces do that soil our coats,
our tropical-weight coats, like slapped-at moths.

The poem cannot get underway, or lift up from under the load of its descriptive details. Somehow the edge of incongruous domesticity that gives a fermenting, surrealist chop to other worlds in other poems isn't working here. The last attempted stanza concludes:

This is a day that's beautiful as well,
and warm and clear. At seven o'clock I saw
the dogs being walked along the famous beach
as usual, in a shiny gray-green dawn,
leaving their paw-prints draining in the wet.
The line of breakers was steady and the pinkish,
segmented rainbow steadily hung above it.
At eight two little boys were flying kites.

Those paw-prints Bishop saves for another, more peaceful occasion: they show up again, in grander form, in "The End of March." But the poem cannot break through to its subject. Bishop's prose notes on the same subject are considerably more successful, demonstrating again the usefulness to her of prose as a strategy for opening up subjects not yet accessible to poems. Entitling this section SUICIDE OF A (MODER-ATE) DICTATOR—A REPORT IN PROSE AND VERSE, she treats the subject frontally, beginning with what must have been the televised footage of Vargas' funeral. The corpse is tightly jammed into the coffin, "none of our puffed silk, pillows, etc.," and Bishop follows it down the avenue, to the airport:

> The coffin is carried off, apparently by the crowd, like a log tossing on a flooded river, but always with the head-end tilted upwards. Thousands and thousands of people surging rapidly, always, along the avenue by the waterfront to the airport – the coffin apparently on a small bier of some sort – how they kept it on it one cannot see or imagine. Thousands of soldiers by this time, too, but no "disorder" just all silently surging surging, and cries and shrieks – weeping men and women – sobbing, howling men and women, clutching their limp long stemmed lilies – like the palm trees that shoot up languidly but rapidly occasionally in the backgrounds – A long long look deep into the eyes of a Negro girl, glistening blankly. Women sobbing in each others' arms. Then the women start fainting. Then the Wreath makes its appearance – an enormous circle of lilies and greens mysteriously floating along, too, bobbing along, like a giant frilled life preserver – first here then there – where & how – Up it goes – sidewise it slips – it can never reach quite the side of the floating up-ended mystic black feather that the Pres. has become, but it seems struggling to reach his side and never catches up. But those are people underneath. And underneath the people are the flowers. The avenue is littered with them now. Motorcycles, soldiers, [. . .] like a released dam – a flash flood. How fast the coffin goes!
>
> At the airport things start getting rough. Will they let the feather join the mystic bird or not? The soldiers start using their clubs. Ambulances close in and women are tossed on stretchers left and right. And there's the Wreath. How did *it* get here? Now it's over at the right – no – it's fallen behind – no there it is, tipping up on a crest. But it never tips over. It is a patented life-preserver. It is buoyant as the coffin. The coffin reaches the plane door – the worst moment – tipping and swaying, almost writhing, push and pull, they get it in somehow – the camera heaves a sigh.

We see the wife, supported by two very plain female relatives – black glasses – her mouth twisted. Hands try to reach her – a girl kisses her wrist – she murmers something. Back to the plane, that makes a neat quick take-off through the bright haze, past the water and the hills of Guanabara Bay – Off and up and off – oh assumption! Where is your Wreath?

As in so many of Bishop's poems, the objects of this scene have displaced the human actors, and carry their own grotesque, comic-melancholic subversions of human actions. The tone of this sketch resembles the group of animal prose poems that Bishop published later on in 1967 as "Rainy Season; Sub-Tropics," and to which she added the mordant early piece of 1937, "The Hanging of the Mouse," in which the same cool, mocking observation, the same gift for wrenchingly accurate comparison appears in the sentence relating the mouse's demise, after the hangman's son springs the trap: "His whiskers rowed helplessly round and round the air a few times and his feet flew up and curled into little balls like young fern-plants." The simile here, like the nineteen-forties spring birds/ movie gunfire comparison, seems an automatic deflection of the too-malignant charge of the human events.

Almost mechanically, Bishop figures the natural world of the non-human as a buffer against human cruelty, and in the ironic substitution of feather for coffin, she calls on the irreducible materiality of even the lightest things against the terrifying flux of human life. But whether from temperament, or from the insoluble puzzle of redefining her use of the lyric, the leap from imagined to actual public event, the move from the fancied to the historic somehow was not possible. Self-conscious and uncomfortable within the openly historic, Bishop closed this theater of operations along with the erotic, declining a too-close inspection of the body in transports of love or of pain.

Not only travel, but the manipulation of degrees of distance remained her poetics. In a letter to Joseph Summers in October 1967, we can register the deflection from politics or history back to geography that will dominate the image-making of her late poems:

There's a sentence in Auden's book – is it an "Airman's Journal" (something like that), and I can't remember the figures now; I shd. know it by heart. "If recorded history is – years long and the world is – miles away from the nearest planet, then geography is – times more important to us than history ..." That's all wrong but the general idea. I didn't read this, however, until after I'd begun publishing poems – so can't say I was "influenced by it" – I just thought, that's a silly notion, but I think I agree with it ...

She recognizes the attractiveness of this spatial expansion of temporality, and though its dismissal of anything closer than planetary connection might seem dangerously "silly," she has not been able to put the insidious notion aside.

But there are still wild plunges and starts of connection. In a draft of a poem called "Belated Dedication," begun perhaps in the mid or late seventies when she was seeing more of Anny Baumann, and recording images of slatestone angels to friends as she walked past the Harvard Yard cemetery, or the Copps Hill graveyard in Boston, she links two open stovelids, a two-seater privy, tears, and two blue eyes in dizzying symmetries. Picking through a typescript gives a rough indication of this stillborn poem:

> I looked down through
> two open stove-lids
> and saw the flames below,

> I looked down, through
> the graveyard angel's eyes
> blind circles without lids
> as in the past I'd stared

> down through the identical eyes   [shameless eyes]
> of the privy   [shameful muck]
> at the sad muck   [littered papers]

> The blue tides had withdrawn
> and left the red-veined mud carved into flames
> The gusts of rain lifted only to show
>   Avernus

> outwards, outwards and down,
> in pairs like tears

And then within a further litter of unfinished lines:

> Under the rainbow's caress.
> Its colored fingers are kind.
> within it is the clean honest blue of your eyes

Bishop in these startling analogues struggles toward a poem incorporating her gratitude to Dr. Anny Baumann for having helped to pull her through both emotional and physical distress. It is a Dantesque linkage of graveyard statuary, privy muck, and cookstove in a visionary downward and inward spiral of shame and self-disgust that we glimpse burning through Bishop's sense of what it is that Dr. Baumann's "clean" blue eyes have helped her to see and survive; but the feelings become too strong and chaotic to allow either analogy or poem to complete itself. Teasingly, provocatively observant, the drafts stand as signposts to a might-have-been. But for a woman who had the patience to wait a quarter-century for a poem like "The Moose" to swim into focus, and then to make a triumph of it, there's no reason not to believe that given a decade or two more she would have drained the honey from these bones.

Geography III

To BEGIN a little perversely, with last things first, I'd like to recall the last two lines of *Geography III*, from the poem "Five Flights Up," concluding the volume: "—Yesterday brought to today so lightly!/ (A yesterday I find almost impossible to lift.)" These lines, bristling as they do with orthographical qualifications of their discouragement, referring backward to other poems in the book, and to other poems in other books, point to Bishop's increasing interest in architecting book as well as poem, and now in her sixties, in terminations and continuities.

After reading John Berryman's *His Toy, His Dream, His Rest,* and Lowell's on-going "14-liners," she writes to May Swenson in November 1968: "I wish I could find a *form,* like them, but perhaps it is more my style to stick to diverse small forms." Speaking from an identifiable set of themes, and a unified perspective, in *Geography III* she contemplates relations between poems more systematically, and settles comfortably down in roomier and roomier poems. Imperceptibly over time, she has discarded the practice of the almost geometrically examined complexities of allegory in poems like "The Monument" or "The Unbeliever" and their free-standing nature; as if each exploratory tour, each reading, could be conducted behind the hedge of the poem and the gate of its title: each figure—monument, weed, sleeper—mounted securely within its separate paper park. In *Geography III,* even her very title will be an on-going member of an unfinished series.

Childhood is one of the more crucial examples of a continuous, interlocking subject. In her last poems, Bishop finally attributes femi-

ninity to the child now fully identified as "an Elizabeth," who without
a specific gender has haunted her poetry since, in chronological order,
"Over 2,000 Illustrations and a Complete Concordance," "Manners,"
"Sestina," and "First Death in Nova Scotia." All three books, *A Cold
Spring, Questions of Travel*, and *Geography III*, with their respective
closing homages of one sort or another to Moore and Neruda, then
Trollope and Pound, finally to Octavio Paz, and posthumously to
Robert Lowell, emphasize Bishop's growing preoccupation with positioning herself with respect to a tradition of writers. It seems no
accidental convergence that as primary identifications like gender and
nation solidify, the poet also strengthens her sense of membership
within the tribe of artists. Through her accumulating responses to the
multiple phases of her identity Bishop is assembling a literal or lettered
or contextual body for her own work. This seems another function of
her reduced interest in allegory and her heightened interest in naturalistic narrative, and actually, in geographic, social, and historical deter-
minants.

Geography III, where the need to look beyond the lyric's self-suffi-
ciency truly asserts itself, is the most carefully put together of all of
her books. Clearly mindful of sequencing and position, the book
carries a little overture, or commentary on the old themes, as an
ostensible instruction on how to read it. *Geography III* begins: *From
"First Lessons in Geography, Montieth's Geographical Series, A. S. Barnes
& Co., 1884,"* and poses a series of questions which appear to be a
continuation of an earlier title, *Questions of Travel*, although the artless
italics do not assume the more sophisticated tones of the earlier poem's
adult speaker. "What is geography?" and "What is the Earth?" and
"What is the shape of the earth?" the unseen monitor asks, his official
questions reduced to "VI" and "X," the whole extract fading into a
series of italicized questions on the facing page. As if Bishop were now
obliging us with a school figure, a pedagogical chalk or benchmark to
guide us more carefully onward in the new book. The implied Geography I and II, as well as Monteith's omitted lessons I–IV, and VII–
IX, seem deliberately to convey that all general sequences are gapped,
all abstract discourse a piece of an always intermittent and only partially visible scene.

Even if, as John Hollander alleges,[90] the questions were the poet's
own invention on the geographical theme, rather than "strict" quotation, the impulse, or need to do this is telling: the contents of the
book are subject to a codification, as each of the ten poems reveals its
time, place, and style of boundary. Each of the ten, including the

translation of a poem by Octavio Paz, conducts an investigation of a terrain, mythic, literal or both, which is often in motion, the survey itself often interrupted. In only one case is a trip concluded: the hike taken at "The End of March" is a round trip, for instance; but the visit to the dentist stalls "In the Waiting Room," "Crusoe in England" flashes back to his island for most of the duration of his monologue, "Night City" starts at the plane's landing, the bus is followed only partway to Boston, stopping short at "The Moose," and the rest are more or less stationary scenes in which the major traveling is temporal, and internal. "Poem" moves back through Nova Scotia with the help of a landscape painting held in the hand as an aid to memory, "12 O'Clock News" broadcasts from the terrain of a desk enlarging in the beholder's eye, and "One Art," initially planned as the last of Bishop's poems in the book, and the piece the most global in circumference of all, surveys the lost objects, places, and persons of the writer's life.

In the final two poems in the collection as it stands, the translation of Octavio Paz's "Objects & Apparitions" stations us inside Joseph Cornell's boxes, in which a doubled speaker's words become visible for a moment. By now this gesture of homage to other artists, crossing not only national and linguistic boundaries, but also gender and genre boundaries, becomes a signature closing gesture for a Bishop book. Additionally within this poem, however, the contemplation of the artist's rendering of internal and external space are made valedictory as well. In the tenth poem the traverse is purely temporal: darkness moves to dawn; the despair scarcely muted, but the vantage point a final, elevated "Five Flights Up."

Each of the poems fixes for us the integrative or disintegrative force that memory and emotional engagement impose spatially upon our experience, and maps with both pleasurable and painful exactitude the varieties of distance that alter feeling and mood. Bishop does not depart from this format in *Geography III*, even where, as in "One Art," a qualified counterforce exerts itself, in the singular art of writing come to memory's aid, against the processions of loss wiping out house keys, random hours, personal mementos, rivers, continents, cities, houses and people—evenly and overwhelmingly.

Loss, and surviving loss, appear the main custom of the book. Each further place, person, or object devising strategies for surviving loss helps to build the augmenting massive weight of loss, a loss that by the time we reach the final poem of the book seems a virtually insupportable burden: "(A yesterday I find almost impossible to lift.)"

Following in the quaint remoteness of Monteith's time, the opening poem, "In the Waiting Room" revisits Bishop's childhood. But instead of the pastoral elegizing of "In the Village," where each heavy repetition of the mother's scream is balanced against the clang of the comforting blacksmith, and his enormous horse (its "rump. . . like a brown, glossy globe of the whole brown world. . .the cloud of his odor. . . a chariot in itself."), this later poem sets its child protagonist down in the dentist's waiting room, and frightens her with uncensored and estranging pictures ("The inside of a volcano. . .spilling;" "those awful hanging breasts"). This time, it is the child herself who voices an unmediated grief and fear:

> Suddenly, from inside,
> came an *oh!* of pain
> —Aunt Consuelo's voice—
> not very loud or long.
> I wasn't at all surprised;
> even then I knew she was
> a foolish, timid woman.
> I might have been embarrassed,
> but wasn't. What took me
> completely by surprise
> was that it was *me:*
> my voice, in my mouth.
> Without thinking at all
> I was my foolish aunt,
> I—we were falling, falling,
> our eyes glued to the cover
> of the *National Geographic*,
> February, 1918.

It is not Aunt Consuelo crying "*oh!*"—but the surprised little speaker: "it was *me:*/ my voice, in my mouth." The poem turns on that moment of awareness that in the six-year-old child enforces her terrified submission to membership in the human race, stripped of the comforts of the animal and natural, and clinging to a ledge of time. But geography in the context of that cover is national, familial, and entrapping:

> But I felt: you are an *I*,
> you are an *Elizabeth*,
> you are one of *them*.
> *Why* should you be one, too?

Unlike the allegorical selves of "The Weed," or "The Gentlemen of Shalott," who represent a splitting off and away for a species of autonomous identity, the figure here, in all of its tense realism, multiplies, and multiplies in bondage to an engulfing world.

The terror of this identification has not been easy for Bishop to arrive at; the poem is the first full admission of these fears. The poetry has been a witness for the potential malignity of the maternal long before in the waves of the seas at the fishhouses and in the flickering malice of Faustina's care. But this is the first frontal exposure, done too, in the person of the poet herself. In Draft 1 of the poem the breasts of the women "filled me with awe"; this phrase was rejected, and in subsequent versions, with unusual tentativeness Bishop substitutes one synonym for frightening after the other, finally settling on "horrifying." The initial image of the spilling volcano is also quite old. In the Walnut Hill School's *The Blue Pencil* an eighteen-year-old Bishop uses the volcano imagery for the unknowable self in a far more reassuring context: "the whole interior of the world is filled with molten, seething lava," she remarks; "we," however, "have in ourselves, not the boiling lava of the earth, but a kind of burning, unceasing energy of some sort that will not let us be finished off [...] This energy, this fire, is always there, ready to explode or to burn fretfully, to show itself surprisingly in our work, our games, our looks and actions." Nor is the concern with "family voice" new: a similar phrase, "the family yell," is what helps a character back from an emotional abyss in "Into The Mountain," another juvenile piece from 1929. What is new is the nausea in identification, the bitter malaise that has taken the adult poet over fifty years to acknowledge as her own. She observes rather quietly to Anne Stevenson in March 1964:

> The next to last Bishop, an aunt, died last year aged 86 or 87 – I'm the last, actually, of that short and undistinguished line. I never fought with what family I had, never to "rebel," etc. – I was always on more or less visting terms with them, and I feel that has had a profound and not altogether good effect on me – it produces passivity, detachment, etc – on the other hand making one's friends one's family, really. But from the age of 18 I have always been independent and gone where I wanted to.

The grown-up child of this history says of her present life in Brazil that she is "very happy here, except for this recurring sense of anxiety and loss." More than fifty years after having experienced herself as on tour within her biological family, this last descendant sets to right the shuddering vibrations of that connection, in the most expansive presentation of a personal self Bishop has yet devised in her poetry.

The answer to the question, what is the shape of the Earth, is that it is something you are in danger of slipping away from:

> . . . sliding
> beneath a big black wave,
> another, and another.

This is unlike the earlier description of such slippage, the epiphanic moment where Bishop imagined what it was like to be Darwin, thinking up evolution; for Darwin, strangeness is merely strangeness, and vision itself is not essentially estranging:

> the beautiful solid case being built up out of his endless, heroic observations, almost unconscious or automatic — and then comes a sudden relaxation, a forgetful phrase, and one feels that strangeness of his undertaking, sees the lonely young man, his eyes fixed on facts and minute details, sinking or sliding giddily off into the unknown.

Bishop continues:

> What one seems to want in art, in experiencing it, is the same thing that is necessary for its creation, a self-forgetful, perfectly useless concentration.

But in this later moment under the wave, one is a tiny child facing a skewered and bound human body, with its ominous suggestion of cannibalism: "A dead man slung on a pole/ — "Long Pig," the caption said." And phrase and picture topple her into a precarious, terrifying, and vulnerable junction. The language of the later epiphany mirrors the earlier language, but this time blackly.

The next exploration of loss and slippage follows in the narrative of the castaway Robinson Crusoe. In "Crusoe in England," the longest and most complex of Bishop's dramatic monologues since "The Riverman," once again a male protagonist enacts for Bishop another drama of the endangering losses embedded within human attachment and detachment. Like Alice after an over-indulgence in mushrooms, a childishly querulous and outsize Crusoe perches glumly on top of one of his "fifty-two/ miserably small volcanoes" and says:

> I'd think that if they were the size
> I thought volcanoes should be, then I had
> become a giant;
> and if I had become a giant,
> I couldn't bear to think what size
> the goats and turtles were [. . .]

Wholly enclosed within his own isolation, Crusoe experiences a dislocation of physical scale, and an analogue of the nausea of connection and disconnection overtaking the child in the waiting room.

A repeating theme, the dislocating dizziness has overtaken a younger Bishop, looking down at the sands of Sable Island, during the nineteen-forties. In a draft of a prose piece called "The Deadly Sandpile" she writes:

> there was almost nothing on the beaches – a sand-ground bottle or two & once a few small-sized dead sharks; but here & there I noticed the white vertebrae of larger fish, heaped up or scattered. I found myself staring down at them, like an aeroplane up ten thousand feet, say, over the ruined columns of a Greek temple [. . .].

Here, a vertiginous view of death's embrace of an empty nature also stops short in beach sand, as in her mind Bishop wills herself to cover exposed bones with the fig leaf of culture, even if a maimed culture. But in the later invention, Crusoe, standing with his feet in a cloud dump, or something that looks like a home-made, washed-up Heaven, or perhaps a purgatorial waiting room, clearly loses his bearings through involuntary isolation. The child of "In the Waiting Room" washes away after experiencing the unwelcome, involuntary bond.

For Bishop in the seventies these are two horns of the same dilemma: no matter how inviolably alone we appear to be, or wish to be, sanity comes from making accommodations with others. At first, before Friday, there were:

> nightmares of other islands
> stretching away from mine, infinities
> of islands, islands spawning islands,
> [. . .] knowing that I had to live
> on each and every one, eventually,
> for ages, registering their flora,
> their fauna, their geography.

Without human company, it is not that the mind's stock shrinks, but that the unstoppable proliferation of experience garnered through memory, and cut loose from affect, acquires a deadly momentum. For Crusoe, nightmares cease at Friday's coming into the poem. By implication, the death of Friday renders even Crusoe's triumphant return to England sterile.

Bishop acknowledges in interviews that for the description of the island, she took Darwin's notes on the Galápagos, backed up by her own visit to the premises. But in addition to any personal elements contributing to the poem, Fiona Shaw, in an unpublished doctoral dissertation for the University of York, persuasively gives a number of antecedents, including both Charles Darwin and Randall Jarrell. As Shaw points out, much in the language of the poem echoes Darwin rather than Defoe, and many of the departures from Defoe are as interesting as the parallels. Randall Jarrell's dramatic monologue, "The Island," may also have planted the idea of the poem subliminally, at the same time, it seems to me, showing Bishop what to avoid: the very bravura of Jarrell's heroic Crusoe might have pushed Bishop toward her flat, laconic castaway, as a distinguishing gesture.

In the first draft of the Bishop poem, a dispirited Crusoe watches turtles, turtles, and turtles in his solitude. The proto-poem then concludes in lines that very much resemble the "Sandpiper" of a decade earlier. "Sandpiper" has a beach that "hisses like fat"; its closing lines also end with a view of a blankly spilling shore life which the sandpiper is condemned to learn much as Crusoe has to learn his islands:

> Poor bird, he is obsessed!
> The millions of grains are black, white, tan, and gray,
> mixed with quartz grains, rose and amethyst.

Their beach scene is quite similar: in "Crusoe in England" the island turtles hiss like teakettles, and the folds of lava also hiss. Turtles and islands both appear to multiply in the same discouraging way, although in the first draft the islands have not yet made their appearance. The poem stops at these lines, finishing with a clean couplet:

> The beaches were all lava, variegated,
> black, red, and white, and gray;
> the marbled colors made a fine display.

And for the time being, there Bishop stuck. She was back even to the very colors and textures of the sandpiper poem.

How to find the next stage? Bishop's shore-bird shares the dilemma of the fracturing world of the illustrated concordance of childhood, "Everything only connected by 'and' and 'and.' " But before the poem on Crusoe could advance in new directions, the poet needed the reference of a more complex emotional world. She built it in two ways: her new protagonist is human rather than bird, and his situation is enacted within the ampler folds of dramatic monologue. My own guess is that this occurred when Bishop picked up the unfinished poem again after Lota's death.

As David Kalstone has observed, the figure of the sandpiper is not unlike the poet herself. We might say further that in shifting to a human protagonist, Bishop is of course approaching the more or less subliminal tensions of autobiography. Behind, or within the figure of Crusoe, we feel the pull of Bishop's own narrative; if her poem does not foreground her life, that life cannot help but inform the larger figures of what we are reading, in the book, the work, *and* the life. In speaking of this early poem's more general effects Kalstone says:

> The bird, on the one hand, is battered and baffled by the waves, the misty "sheets of interrupting water"; on the other hand it attends and stares, is preoccupied, obsessed with the grains of sand, a litany of whose colors, minutely and beautifully distinguished, ends the poem [...] Bishop lets us know that every detail is a boundary, not a Blakean microcosm. Because of the limits they suggest, details vibrate with a meaning beyond mere physical presence. Landscapes meant to sound detached are really inner landscapes. They show an effort at reconstituting the world as if it were in danger of being continually lost.[91]

In the new poem loss is less an abstraction, and in Robinson Crusoe the swimming vertigo of the sandpiper approaches nearer to the problems of Elizabeth Bishop, accessible now in human terms and recognizable as in part at least the study of her connection to people as well as things.

While he continues to be the feverish compiler, imaginatively reconstituting violet-blue tree-snails as beds of iris, Crusoe's main consolations disappear in a dense loneliness:

> —well, I tried
> reciting to my iris-beds,
> "They flash upon that inward eye,
> which is the bliss ... " The bliss of what?

What else does the insertion of that anachronism do for the poem but once again illustrate how exactly limited is the medicinal value of art, a question *Geography III* will worry in other ways subsequently. Crusoe cannot verify that *solitude* is bliss until he returns to human society.

But his plight is worse than this. In England once again,

> I'm old.
> I'm bored, too, drinking my real tea,
> surrounded by uninteresting lumber.
> The knife there on the shelf—
> it reeked of meaning, like a crucifix.
> It lived . . .
> Now it won't look at me at all.
> The living soul has dribbled away.
> My eyes rest on it and pass on.

Disconcertingly, Crusoe discovers that the misery from which he so willingly fled was the chief stock of his life; the relation with Friday, a test of love. At the point at which love is openly recognized it is lost and irretrievable, gone in the relentless swim-off of detachables that seems to characterize our backward-looking but onward-moving lives.

Thematically, "Night City" continues to name and locate the losses of the traveler in a corrupting and unstable urban environment, closely resembling the American cities to which Bishop was returning, like Crusoe, from her own species of cultural isolation. Here, unlike "Arrival at Santos," there is no interior that is fit for penetration: "No foot could endure it/ shoes are too thin." Suspended, *"From the plane,"* above a nightscape inhabited only by flaring acids, silicate rivers, and bituminously weeping tycoons, this blurred, rather strung-out poem recovers energy, perhaps, in the last stanza, in which a touch of Bishop's whimsy revives in the binary flash of the stoplight:

> (Still, there are creatures,
> careful ones, overhead.
> They set down their feet, they walk
> green, red; green, red.)

If we compare this poem with "From the Country to the City," the earlier poem can be seen to deliver its similar message with both a better grace and a better clarity. In late poems when Bishop nears the allegorical or fantastic the freshness of the impulse fades quickly.

Instead of concentrating on landing by plane in the city, with the trip behind us, Bishop now takes up the other end, traveling this time by bus, and concentrating on departure in Nova Scotia, rather than arrival in Boston. Maybe the placement of "Night City" before "The Moose" tells us something about the proper order of observance: like Crusoe, we find once more that the best thing is to have been, or to be going, but certainly not to have arrived. What completes "The Moose" is not the accomplishment of Boston, but the intrusion of moose, and our welcoming, self-abnegating acceptance of the natural and nonhuman world. All land crossing, all traverse, can be valid only as it slips through, or breaks into such deeper alignments of feeling and value. Adult now, the speaker of *Geography III* begins to assemble comfort from other parts of the earth's surface for the little girl in the waiting room, even if comfort is largely retroactive and differently speciated.

Bishop began thinking about "The Moose," the oldest poem in *Geography III*, in 1946. She wrote to Marianne Moore about the trip that triggered the poem:

> I came back by bus — a dreadful trip, but it seemed most convenient at the time — we hailed it with a flashlight and lantern as it went by the farm late at night. Early the next morning, just as it was getting light, the driver had to stop suddenly for a big cow moose who was wandering down the road. She walked away very slowly into the woods, looking at us over her shoulder. The driver said that one foggy night he had to stop while a huge bull moose came right up and smelled the engine. "Very curious beasts," he said.

In this letter all the critical details of the moose encounter are there. Looking over the decades of drafts which Bishop compiled in the writing of this poem, it is tempting to stop and try to elicit from these papers why it halted, why it was so difficult to finish, and which were the movements that might have made its completion possible. "I could never seem to get the middle part, to get from one place to the other," she merely says to Elizabeth Spires in 1978.[92]

In going through the driest and most age-darkened piles of the drafts for this poem, and holding up what must have been the first sheet, I was struck by the almost patchwork nature of the assemblage. Unlike most of Bishop's drafts where there seems a swift, immediate certainty as to each stage of the poem, however intermitted the stages might be, in this poem, each major piece took much going over for each element of its descriptive narrative. At least half the central verbs and qualifiers have been placed and re-placed many times in the twenty-six years between the first jottings and the final publication.

The short, largely three-stress, six-line stanzas came together like chips in the flood of memory being balanced, tested and set; each facet of description, the tidal meeting of bay and sea, each detail of flower, tidal river, road and house, each stop, each aspect of the moose's appearance are unusually fussed over, with many alternate descriptive words proposed and rejected. This degree of revision is contrary to Bishop's usual practice, where only late key phrases betray these hesitations. The short lines of the poem, as well as their number per stanza, however, were early decisions, and while rhyme wanders in and out like the moose at will, first drafts worked deliberately with clear rhyme pairs. Occasionally, lines are numbered and left blank, with only rhyme words showing in place. At late stages, stanzas are numbered, with blanks replacing the stanzas that Bishop evidently felt sure were to come.

The biggest halt in forward momentum occurs in the middle of the poem, where Bishop is contriving the passenger's entry aboard the bus. There are no notes about the trip from inside the bus, no sketches for what the passengers are doing until the moose steps in. The details of sighting the moose were there from the beginning as closure to the poem's experience. In the first run-through, before the poem has even acquired the eventually discarded title "Back to Boston," Bishop sets up the first stanza, very much as it remained for the next decades until the poem was finished. Immediately off at the right, though, perhaps even before finishing the second stanza, she is fiddling with the closing stanza, counts off its lines as seven, and can't quite get her rhyme for *gasoline*, in both the forties and seventies the poem's last word. In short, the beginning and the ending of Bishop's longest poem were virtually complete at the moment of the poem's inception, with a lot of middle that took her a tad longer.

It was also an early decision to elide the driver's mention of the bull moose encounter and to take his "curious beasts" to refer only to the cow moose at hand, changing only the wording to the alliterative and perhaps friendlier "creatures," over beasts, and making explicit the poem's embrace of a benevolent female Nature.

But the largest obstacle seems to have been the transition from inside to outside, and without forcing the issue, it seems to me that the problematic balance of entry into inside and outside states also represents Bishop's struggle to find the proper course of the autobiographical in her narrative. She must have put the poem aside after the trip in 1946, and then obviously packed it along to Brazil: the probable first sheet has crumbled, browned and dried in the manner of several of the books in her library there, and before the librarian and the menders took hold of the page to prevent its complete dissolution, there were pinholes where insects had made their own editing contributions. The drafts were taken out on many occasions over the years; on the reverse of one of the pages there is a sketch for "Song for the Rainy Season," a poem Bishop first published in 1960.

We cannot guess as to whether the final working-out came in a rush or rushes, but it certainly took a measurable while before Bishop figured out where to put herself, and the detail of hailing the bus by flashlight. In the first pile of Bishop's working pages, after roughly assembling the contents of the first six stanzas, she apparently sets out to recopy the poem, gets the first stanza out, and once more off at the right tackles what seems a problem: six lines are numbered; the third, fourth and sixth give her a rhyme, and a leg up onto the next stanza: "as the red sun sets/ behind the rim of firs,/ a lone passenger gets// aboard the passing bus/ leaving a relative/ waving at the passing window." Nothing more is seen of this passenger, probably Bishop herself, for quite some while. At one point the passenger emerges, this time doing the waving to an aunt and uncle. But it isn't until the close of the poem's evolution that we get the full sweep of the opening six stanzas, only one sentence in length, and ending with a collie's supervision. The poem takes as its next, crucial syntactical breath, a "Goodbye": "Goodbye to the elms,/to the farm, to the dog." And a near-final goodbye to Nova Scotia itself for Bishop.

There is terrific juggling going on over what will occupy stanza six or seven, or the place up to "goodbye": seven is the final niche for the passenger, Bishop. But the answer to the poem's perspective apparently lay in not putting herself in at all, except as her usual, hovering, invisible, and disembodied voice. By the time the entrance into the bus is effected, and the poem moves inside the bus, taking up the passenger perspective firmly, we do it via the third person of the elderly woman with the market bags; the assumption in the final version is that "we" have been there observing all along since line 1, somehow watching, and somehow getting on that bus. Once again,

Bishop chooses to privilege a more general narrative, subduing the autobiographical reference considerably.

A smell and a sound precede the assumption of the inside perspective. At the side of one of the original sheets, the bridge "trembles"; the line is not yet contained in any stanza. But as the poem completes itself, the swim of the red lantern, the "pale flickering," "the smell of salt hay," the dog's one bark, and the trembling of the bridge fuse in a burst of near synesthesia, building up to entry:

> A pale flickering. Gone.
> The Tantramar marshes
> and the smell of salt hay.
> An iron bridge trembles
> and a loose plank rattles
> but doesn't give way.
>
> On the left, a red light
> swims through the dark:
> a ship's port lantern.
> Two rubber boots show,
> illuminated, solemn.
> A dog gives one bark.
>
> A woman climbs in
> with two market bags,
> brisk, freckled, elderly.
> "A grand night. Yes, sir,
> all the way to Boston."
> She regards us amicably.

From here on in it is moonlight, and we're looking out the windows. The sound of the bridge, a loose detail worrying the structure like a terrier at a bone, has bridged a transition for the poet herself, and has become consoling, and steadying; "a loose plank rattles/ but doesn't give way."

Both subject and narration then begin a slow, natural elision to a dream state that allows Bishop to fuse the elderly people in the back of the bus with her own grandparents, and this time she openly makes her way into the poem. Here is the start of that dreamy process:

> The passengers lie back.
> Snores. Some long sighs.
> A dreamy divagation

> begins in the night,
> a gentle, auditory,
> slow hallucination. . . .
>
> In the creakings and noises,
> an old conversation
> — not concerning us,
> but recognizable, somewhere,
> back in the bus:
> Grandparents' voices
>
> uninterruptedly
> talking, in Eternity:
> names being mentioned,
> things cleared up finally;

The sound of that bridge signaled Bishop somehow that *sound* was going to be important; something auditory was "trembling," needing embodiment, and there is an almost preternatural quality, a sitting up on edge in the darkness, peering forwards, and listening for sounds in the cave of one's head. After the woman with the two market bags clambers on, the moonlight takes over, and under her sign we penetrate the New Brunswick woods, and into the hard-fought middle passage of the Grandparents' conversation that precedes the entrance of the moose.

The importance of this conversation has been clear from early drafts: speech "not concerning us" has been there almost from the beginning. And before we can get to the moose high as a church and safe as a house the Grandparents' relation to eternity must be spelled out. Like Bishop, they are also not quite there in the body, existing nameless and dark as they do only in the poem's dream state. Touched into existence by the gleam of the lantern, set into sound by the rattling of the iron bridge, they have come over into speech not by fidelity to the conventional relation of personal narrative, but by deep attention to the sensations that are prior to that in a poet's hearing and seeing. If we read the drafts attentively they will tell us why any true lyric that concentrates exclusively on verbal gestures does so to its peril.

The poem also seems a paradigm of the evasion of the personal to arrive at the personal in the most luminous and compelling way:

> If you should dip your hand in,
> your wrist would ache immediately,

> your bones would begin to ache and your hand would burn
> as if the water were a transmutation of fire

Bishop says of the absolute clarity of the waters of Nova Scotia. Here in this poem both diction and event have that extreme transparency; limpid, simple, cool and burning. Very little in twentieth-century poetry has ever given us this combination of brilliance and simplicity. A stripped narrative of the poem could be chanted by a six-year-old: "We were on the bus. It got dark. We met a moose. She was big, but I didn't get scared." And yet from the opening lines, moving as they do in their strange, rocking recursive motion from sea to bay, in the shock of river to tide, and from the iridescent interconnections of sea and land within a steadily dropping sunlight, the poem pushes us along its westward journey: from day into night and from life into death we go, the poet offering us only the comfort of a speechless animal presence and the stoicism of the aged.

Yet Bishop means us not to misunderstand how much comfort that is: the drafts brighten when we get to the Grandparents: they are noticeably newer. And yet without having solved the problem of where to put the narrator—that is, where not to put her—getting the right dialogue for the grandparents, and naming the significance of the moose might not have been possible. Much painstaking work continued to go into getting the descriptive details of the countryside right, even getting the dented bus in position, its flank yet another friendly extension of the sustaining animal:

> a bus journeys west,
> the windshield flashing pink,
> pink glancing off of metal,
> brushing the dented flank
> of blue, beat-up enamel;

Yet after this blocking is finished, the dialogue emerges: "what he said, what she said," and then:

> "Yes . . ." that peculiar
> affirmative. "Yes . . ."
> A sharp, indrawn breath,
> half-groan, half acceptance,
> that means "Life's like that.
> We know *it* (also death)."

Bishop has practiced the indrawn breath before. It is the indrawn breath of the seven-year-old in the dentist's waiting room. It is also in her 1940's Sable Island piece, "The Deadly Sandpile":

> Anyone familiar with the accent of Nova Scotia will know what I mean when I refer to the Indrawn Yes. In all their conversations Nova Scotians of all ages, even children, make use of it. It consists of, when one is told a fact–anything not necessarily tragic but not of a downright comical nature,–"yes," or "yeah," while drawing in the breath at the same moment. It expresses both commiseration & an acceptance of the worst, and it occurred to me as I walked over the fine, fatalistic sands, that Sable Island with its mysterious engulfing powers was a sort of large-scale expression of the Indrawn Yes.

In "The Moose," the indrawn breath signifies a stoic, commiserating acceptance of death, of "the worst"; but here, nature in animal form tips that acceptance into a mysterious counter affirmation. At this point in the poem, Bishop makes the switch into her own grandparents:

> Talking the way they talked
> in the old featherbed,
> peacefully, on and on,
> dim lamplight in the hall,
> down in the kitchen, the dog
> tucked in her shawl.
> Now, it's all right now
> even to fall asleep
> just as on all those nights.

It is precisely after the reiterated "now" of safety and peacefulness, when Bishop in the voice of the invisible narrator brings on the moose:

> — Suddenly the bus driver
> stops with a jolt,
> turns off his lights.
>
> A moose has come out of
> the impenetrable wood
> and stands there, looms, rather,
> in the middle of the road.

Working in further dialogue from the passengers who exclaim in whispers "childishly, softly," Bishop underlines, climaxes the mood of safety and sweetness she has invoked with this explicit stanza on how to read this intrusion of animal presence:

> Taking her time,
> she looks the bus over,
> grand, otherworldly.
> Why, why do we feel
> (we all feel) this sweet
> sensation of joy?

In its tortuous evolution, in which these small six-line chips have been endlessly, patiently, thrown about, floated and re-worked, the poem has fixed, clarified, and taken its final shape, here in the middle of the book as "joy," the word in the poem itself, like wisdom, late-blooming.

While the book's bus never gets to Boston, the book's author does, and this is probably the last trip in which joy, childhood, safety, and Nova Scotia are all there and present. The poem's pleasures are valedictory, and the remaining poems struggle to balance the gains and much more perceptible losses that the completion of a westward journey always signifies.

"12 O'Clock News" continues to deliver bulletins from the urban front. Like "Night City," the poem seems to draw with fatigue from earlier Bishop stylistic preoccupations. "12 O'Clock News" is notable, though, for the open interest it signals in writing as subject. Set before "Poem," Bishop might have intended the piece as a warm-up for the next poem's more substantial reflections on art. In this little prose piece with its magnified and rather self-consciously alien objects, the very tools of the writer's trade seem immitigably distant, like the temple bones on Sable Island, and like the daylight of "Five Flights Up," almost too heavy to lift. In the piece's midnight perspective the darkened world of the poet's desk is lugubriously still: the light from the gooseneck lamp is poor, the scaly keys of the typewriter gleam only faintly, the pile of manuscripts a soil of "poor quality," and the sheet of paper in the typewriter as easily an airstrip as a cemetery; in the ashtray, the paper uniforms of the dead cigarettes/soldiers give proof of "childishness and hopeless impracticality" or of "sad corruption" in the management of their leaders. From this "superior vantage point" the comedy of mistaken identity seems thin and unremittingly premised on the writer's insignificance and unproductivity: the "joke" is too close to morose complaint. A single flick of the page, however, improves the outlook.

"Poem," the next of the ten poems, begins with the inspection of an object, a painting "About the size of an old-style dollar bill," and steadily turns the painting into a general metaphor for art. But the argument of "Poem" as to art's durances, put so explicitly and powerfully as it is, dispels some of the shadows cast in "12 O'Clock News." In the glum confines of dead desk country, like the Crusoe whose mind swells in his isolation out of any natural contact with landscape — the indefatigable, but pointless registrar of an endlessly islanded flora and fauna — it is possible to gain a prospect of art's value far more shrunken than that in "Poem." "Poem," however, concludes: "how touching in detail — the little that we get for free,/the little of our earthly trust." Perhaps the inclusion of "12 O'Clock News" means to tell us that within the overall perspective of *Geography III*, although Great-Uncle George's dollar-sized painting touches us in detail, detail is still potentially the frantic, nightmare accumulation of Crusoe before the coming of Friday, a Crusoe spawning worlds of atomized and nonhuman island realizations that sweep our feet out from under us. Without love grounded in a human, natural, and continuously civil and domestic environment, art does not transfigure experience; in the sinister moonscape of disconnection the writer's pen proves only a reed to lean upon.

"Poem," in the deliberate modesty of its choice of exemplary artist, offers Bishop's strongest statement yet that memory fused with vision not only transfigures, but offers us the closest alternative to resurrection that we have. As the poem's voice tells over the details of the painting, speech soars to become sight, touch, and hearing; yet even beyond the comfort of this, the words assert the power of words, as memory's agent coils and recoils into and out of the body of "life itself":

> art "copying from life" and life itself,
> life and the memory of it so compressed
> they've turned into each other. Which is which?
> Life and the memory of it cramped,
> dim, on a piece of Bristol board,
> dim, but how live, how touching in detail
> — the little that we get for free,

the little of our earthly trust. Not much.
About the size of our abidance
along with theirs: the munching cows,
the iris, crisp and shivering, the water
still standing from spring freshets,
the yet-to-be dismantled elms, the geese.

Still, this is "Not much": even more than in "The Moose," the living and tenderly delicate world is all past and animal, vegetable, or mineral.

If any weight lifts at all it rises bodilessly in language. To move beyond a poem-by-poem reading of *Geography III*, and to read in the whole order of Bishop's poetry, we might say that if we put Great-Uncle George Hutchinson's effort in the very early "Large Bad Picture" next to its late evocation in "Poem," we have to revise his stature upward, and very probably Bishop's own estimate of the worth of her occupation. In the early poem, the painted landscape of Bishop's attention never moves beyond the world of paint, or even of writing: the birds hang in their banks of n's; the small sun congeals on the painted plane of its "perpetual sunset." In this fixed space, painting or language has no power to move us.

Within "Poem," however, we move confidently out from the world of paint into something resembling an unmediated space that language and memory free from the domination of time. Within "Poem's" conclusion, experience is literally current, everything paradoxically arrested in print, but running within the immediate, fresh, and volatile: the cows in their gerund are still "munching"; the crisp iris shivers; the water "still standing from spring freshets" is there at the base of elms which are only to be dismantled in the time this poem holds at bay, its last words simply, "the geese." It is as if their very being needed no construction, no explanation, and no defense.

While "One Art" confronts the death of Lota de Macedo Soares with understated but searing directness, Bishop drew on this personal relationship for her art only through extreme compression and ellipsis: once at the beginning for the astral tenderness of "The Shampoo," once at the end for the stark notice of "One Art." Yet within this poem, a global experience of loss is containable by the practice of writing, even if only barely so. Within "The End of March," loss is spatialized, metaphorical, and impersonal; but once again, as in "Poem," Bishop concludes with a dominant natural image that defies loss.

In "One Art," "Loved houses" and "lovely cities" have both disappeared; in "The End of March," after a cold walk along the beach, where "Everything was as withdrawn as possible," the "proto-dream house,/my crypto-dream house" is boarded up. No more than Crusoe's actual, returned-to England, the dream house won't do. We wanted to get to the house, our empty paradise, but we couldn't. First our faces froze on the one side, then the other. On this trip, as for the passenger of "Night City," for Crusoe, and for the Boston traveler of "The Moose," there isn't any homecoming. The dream of ultimate satisfaction stays remote, just as urban reality or inaccessible pastness closes out the other voyagers from return. Nevertheless, the poem ends on the positive exposure played out between the tide, the "lion sun," and the bezeled stones set "high enough," and the contents of satisfaction are changing subtly.

The goal of the roundtripper, the proto-dream house, has many things about it that seem as unlivably "dubious" as the forbidding climate of "Night City" or the poet's desk in "12 O'Clock News." If we look at the modifiers for the dream house, moving from proto to cryptic to dubious, something interesting emerges in that devaluing sequence, pulling together all the protagonists of the book in a common dilemma with a common solution. Just as the little girl in the waiting room is yanked back into history, and Crusoe is made to face England, and the master loser practices the terminations of her one art, writing, the hiker in "The End Of March" seems compelled to yield up her fondness for "dubious" and "impossible" dream houses. The renunciation of this dream house might constitute a denial of what the poet recognizes as dangerous solitude, possibly wrapped in alcoholic haze. The poem explores the possibility of this denial, as it fingers the lovely, seductive aloneness it proposes and then dismisses:

> (Many things about this place are dubious.)
> I'd like to retire there and do *nothing*,
> or nothing much, forever, in two bare rooms:
> look through binoculars, read boring books,
> old, long, long books, and write down useless notes,
> talk to myself, and, foggy days,
> watch the droplets slipping, heavy with light.
> At night, a *grog a l'américaine.*
> I'd blaze it with a kitchen match
> and lovely diaphanous blue flame

would waver, doubled in the window.
There must be a stove; there *is* a chimney,
askew, but braced with wires,
and electricity, possibly
—at least, at the back another wire
limply leashes the whole affair
to something off behind the dunes.
A light to read by—perfect! But—impossible.
And that day the wind was much too cold
even to get that far,
and of course the house was boarded up.

The alcohol-fuddled Edwin Boomer, the Prisoner, all of the looking-glass proto-selves that dreamt of such houses are wryly being put aside. Bishop also redirects a style as well as a subject: twice in this poem there are moments that invite the fantastic personae that bloomed in her early work as Man-moth, weed, sandpiper, Giant Toad, and so on; but in this late poem the cluster of feeling and insight that would have urged the creation of such beings flames up suggestively, "diaphanously," and then like gas from that rejected stove turns down, subject to other controls. In the line of the tide,

lengths and lengths, endless, of wet white string,
looping up to the tide-line, down to the water,
over and over. Finally, they did end:
a thick white snarl, man-size, awash,
rising on every wave, a sodden ghost,
falling back, sodden, giving up the ghost. . . .

The white, foamy strings of the lapping tide relate distantly to the wiry rain streaming down the birdcage of "It is marvellous." Only here the tidal strings are flaccid, snarled, and "sodden." The image also calls up the earlier shore of "Florida":

The tropical rain comes down
to freshen the tide-looped strings of fading shells:
Job's Tear, the Chinese Alphabet, the scarce Junonia,
parti-colored pectins and Ladies' Ears,
arranged as on a gray rag of rotted calico,
the buried Indian Princess's skirt;
with these the monotonous, endless sagging coast-line
is delicately ornamented.

For this northern coast, at "The End of March," the "lion sun," a wild spirit near kin to the Indian Princess, presides over the closing lines. But in sober, pulled-back language, and in tone rather firmly identifying her image as a speaker's whimsy placed at the outskirts rather than the center of the magical, Bishop launches her ending:

> The sun came out for just a minute.
> For just a minute, set in their bezels of sand,
> the drab, damp, scattered stones
> were multi-colored,
> and all those high enough threw out long shadows,
> individual shadows, then pulled them in again.
> They could have been teasing the lion sun,
> except that now he was behind them
> —a sun who'd walked the beach the last low tide,
> making those big, majestic paw-prints,
> who perhaps had batted a kite out of the sky to play with.

To prefer "Florida" to "The End of March" may be as arbitrary as preferring age to youth or vice versa. The later poem simply urges us into the wintry sunlight, its large and vital company preferable, finally, to that of the dubious dream house.

Very lightly, it seems to me, one is being nudged by Bishop to look more steadily at her world of poem-making, and to consider her place as artist, as place in this metaphoric sense begins to substitute for Bishop's more usual literal preoccupation with geography. At the close of her career, as "One Art" indicates, she must "practice losing farther, losing faster:/places and names, and where it was you meant/ to travel." In *Geography III*, Bishop settles at least partially for a home in the exercise of her art, harnessed alongside others of her kind.

The poems have moved to the autobiographical; teased by Lowell's adoption of the confessional style, and aided by her ventures into prose, Bishop openly inserts the figure of the poet, as well as the figures of poetry. In "Poem," familial, ethnic, and cultural background merge; she, Nova Scotia, and Great-Uncle George are at one in art's abidances. The job of the final two poems is to enlarge the frame even farther and place Bishop within the world of childhood as well as the adult world of the present containing her last years at Harvard. Years, we might note, in which increased recognition for her work, her assumption of a professional position as teacher, as well as the end of her Brazilian exile, coincided.

"Objects & Apparitions," the translation of Octavio Paz's poem in homage to Joseph Cornell, in its own maverick way, doubles the affirmations of artist and artist's community in "Poem." In the final vision of the home scene in "Poem," the fused vision of painting, place, and memory kindles for us with Great-Uncle George and Miss Bishop remembering in illuminative communality. Just so in "Objects & Apparitions" the doublet of Paz/Cornell becomes a triplet, fusing with Bishop's wonderfully empathic translation. Yet further intensifying this participative art through translation and transpeciation, these final lines echo with their forceful resonance through the medium of several containing boxes — language, person, book, and poem:

> Joseph Cornell: inside your boxes
> my words became visible for a moment.

If Bishop had invented the original poem herself it couldn't have fitted more neatly into *Geography III*. In her near literal translation, "Objects & Apparitions" begins much as Bishop did in "Poem," with an object representing miniature landscape:

> Hexahedrons of wood and glass,
> scarcely bigger than a shoebox,
> with room in them for night and all its lights.

"Objects & Apparitions" is a much more somber evocation, however:

> Monuments to every moment,
> refuse of every moment, used:
> cages for infinity.

Caged, manipulated refuse. Here the objects are far closer to the outlook of "12 O'Clock News," than the gentler currency of "Poem's" dollar-sized painting. Yet in these boxes — "where things hurry away from their names" — Bishop's own lifelong fascination with miniature and its radical transformations of meaning through scale and disrupted context is validated, made congruent through the practice of other artists in other languages and in other art forms.

Rightly, Gaston Bachelard in *The Poetics of Space* names miniature as "the refuge of greatness"; "refuge" seems the right word, too, for the artist whose talent Paz named as "reticence" — or the power to satisfy "a double thirst: thirst for reality and thirst for marvels."[93] The maker, too, in the words of Paz's tribute, of poems whose powerful lens "plays with distances and presences"; in which "The juxtaposition of spaces and perspectives makes the poem a theatre where the oldest and most quotidian of mysteries is represented: reality and its riddles." Or in Paz's Spanish, as refracted by Bishop's English, the world of Joseph Cornell, too, in which from "Minimal, incoherent fragments" we derive:

> Theatre of the spirits:
> objects putting the laws
> of identity through hoops.

It is still a bleak version of existence that Bishop/Paz/Cornell are claiming: "the opposite of history, creator of ruins,/out of your ruins you have made creations"—which seems a cool distance from the cheerier "abidance" of a few pages before. The spirit of this box theater resembles our survivor, Crusoe, looming disconsolately over his spent volcanoes, not much prospect given for an itinerant fabulist of the real. Here is the traveler for Paz/Bishop:

> The reflector of the inner eye
> scatters the spectacle:
> God all alone above an extinct world.

Although the next and final lines flare with something that resembles the mood of "Poem" 's "little of our earthly trust," they are sized, as "Poem" is, for brief abidance:

> The apparitions are manifest,
> their bodies weigh less than light,
> lasting as long as this phrase lasts.
>
> Joseph Cornell: inside your boxes
> my words became visible for a moment.

The translation demonstrates how the geographer's, or the mapper's, urge to delineate place, and secondarily thing, serves to project personal history. In the Paz translation, two scales of measurement converge: the scale that enlarges small objects and magnifies their properties into emotional affiliation; and the reverse scale, which contracts bodies into toy and doll counters—displacing, distorting, and skewing the orders of our responses as the world of thing and person, or subject and object, intersect in alternately diminishing and enlarging forms.

Appropriating these scales to point toward her book's themes, Bishop nonetheless retains her own characteristic preoccupations, fitting them with enormous subtlety, box within box, inside the architecture of her book. For Paz, "bodies weigh less than light." Bishop's bodies, even in their dizziest slides from the spinning globe, retain their live weight through a canny enumeration of particulars. In *Geography III*, the scope of the assigned feelings fleshes all of her people, her watchers, with the weight of character. Weight, a dawn weight which is "ponderous" and "meticulous" in "Five Flights Up," thus becomes a junction, a fusion of spirit and matter. Weight, here given enormous potency, severely qualifies the light-bearing properties of art, however participatory, in this poem which concludes *Geography III*.

"Five Flights Up" opens: "Still dark." Yet even in this uncomfortably suspended scene poised before motion, a poem above its field of action, it is the natural and animal world which proves redemptive or enabling. The village life, which has provided the connective root or contravention of human paralysis and sterility, is absent; it exists only desultorily as a scolding voice, bringing in irrelevant and cheerless guilt:

> The little black dog runs in his yard.
> His owner's voice arises, stern,
> "You ought to be ashamed!"
> What has he done?
>
> He bounces cheerfully up and down;
> he rushes in circles in the fallen leaves.
>
> Obviously, he has no sense of shame.
> He and the bird know everything is answered,
> all taken care of,
> no need to ask again.

Dog and bird here echo the guilty cat ("in his mouth's a moth") and bird of "Sunday, 4 A.M." way off in the world of *Questions of Travel;* but this time, faith for the speaker lies a little further off. Some things are the same: the predations of the animal world are a necessary consequence of animal relationship, and light proceeds. But in the earlier aubade, light is about to come, in the later, gray light is

> streaking each bare branch,
> each single twig, along one side,
> making another tree, of glassy veins . . .

This exquisite, eerily beautiful invocation makes light only a shadow of substance. Where earlier in "Sunday, 4 A.M." things are set going by the bi-valent bird who "arranges/two notes at right angles," in "Five Flights Up" it is existence that blurs, divides, and finally withholds its lightest self. Questions of travel have crossed into questions of distance and disconnection. While travel, or the business of stopping and starting is still prime motivation in *Geography III*, it has become harder for the speaker to get started again, reconnecting light to light, and sustaining the voyager's buoyancy:

> —Yesterday brought to today so lightly!
> (A yesterday I find almost impossible to lift.)

Much sadder than any of Bishop's previous books, almost as if someone had gone around and let the air out of the tires, the book withdraws from none of her previous themes. In fact, most are amplified, especially in *Geography III*'s frugal recall of most of their unique stylistic habits and pleasures. But beyond Bishop's increased experimentation with autobiography, with extended lines and extended narrative, there is a new feature: the achievement of a book with a figure as book, as well as a collection of poems recombining with previous poems to make a figure for the work as a whole.

But the figure leaves us with a reading problem: if we accept the terminal position of "Five Flights Up" as an act of definition, it puts the more positive reassurances of "Poem," the hard-won and stoical control of grief and longing in "One Art" and "The End of March," at some variance. As a planned dramatic moment, that morning pause at the window in "Five Flights Up" seems a performance of anticlimax, nearly a stall of helplessness, with "almost" as the sole bit of active yeast for the future. The best we can argue is that we have to read against the sequence of the book, the sequence of the poem itself. Bishop asks us to superimpose over the discouraged but not downed parenthesis, the irrepressible frisking of the little black dog, even while the poem continues to wheel forward: the weight of her "almost" for us, too, almost impossible to lift.

·T·W·E·L·V·E·

Last Poems

I F WRITERS' lives only followed their work more exactly, there would be an end that could tidily be read in sequence, single file like the lines and pages of their books. In which case, lastness could be defined as the last word published, and unpublished work could scintillate posthumously, a little red-eyed, as if it slept long and woke late. With few exceptions, nothing published or republished after Bishop's death quite measures up to the little group of poems that appeared in *The New Yorker* from February 20, 1978 to October 29, 1979. Emerging as cleanly as water poured from a well-bucket, and with the same sense of inevitable flow, the four poems do not represent the planned choices of *Geography III*, yet each of the group of four has its own brilliant consistency of style, tone, and theme.

"Santarém" and "North Haven" bring together Bishop's emblematic south and north in their respective Brazilian and New England town settings. Both of these poems, one for herself and one for Robert Lowell, sound the late theme of death, touching as it does for two artists on achievement, arcing upward on ambition as well as downward on resignations and stoical acceptances. The final poems advance in range of inquiry within the general angst and disappointments explored in individual poems in *Geography III*, now and newly in "Pink Dog" sounding a note of pain, despair, and cold anger vividly unlike "In the Waiting Room," and within the narrow but resonant chamber of "Sonnet," perhaps proposing a final, tonic chord for all of Bishop's questions of gender, sexuality, and personal isolation. Or, in Adrienne

Rich's phrase, her "own last word on division, decision, and questions of travel."[94] The first two, "North Haven" and "Santarém," are largely elegiac; the second two, "Pink Dog" and "Sonnet," should be considered directly with the other poems that might be said to prefigure their concerns.

· I ·

The wash of color and light in both "Santarém" and "North Haven," stressing landscape and larger view, is lovely; the details of the language are painterly in ways that belong to all the best of Bishop's poems. Working on our sensibilities in tandem, the flower-filled summer hazes of "North Haven" combine with the golden, late light of "Santarém," its dazzling properties repeatedly invoked. The sensuous abundance of detail seems a late phenomenon. In a poem of mid-career like "Questions of Travel," sunset is a fold of cloth, flowered trees are "noble pantomimists, robed in pink"; but in "Santarém" the light is a spilling richness permeating every corner: figure and personification do not distance us from the full impact of its physical presence. The dashed, qualifying phrases at the beginning and end of this passage undercut the mood and question the memory:

> Of course I may be remembering it all wrong
> after, after—how many years?
> That golden evening I really wanted to go no farther;
> more than anything else I wanted to stay awhile
> in that conflux of two great rivers, Tapajós, Amazon,
> grandly, silently flowing, flowing east.
> Suddenly there'd been houses, people, and lots of mongrel
> riverboats skittering back and forth
> under a sky of gorgeous, under-lit clouds,
> with everything gilded, burnished along one side,
> and everything bright, cheerful, casual—or so it looked.

Yet the light paints everything the same elegiac gold. Like the wash of sunrise along the tree in "Five Flights Up," light, always in human terms a dialectic of light and shadow, provides two options: the first an enhancement, the second a cancelation or limitation of experience, which Bishop's dashes respect. After naming the poles of this dialectic, first in the two-sidedness of its physical effect, then second in posing the metaphorical underside of brightness and cheer as a matter of ephemeral appearance or how things "looked," the poem continues to evoke its strong yellow. Golden light is ultimately carried from top to bottom, from golden evening to "one house faced with *azulejos*, buttercup yellow," on down to a street that is "deep in dark-gold river sand/ damp from the ritual afternoon rain," through to

> The zebu's hooves, the people's feet
> waded in golden sand,
> dampered by golden sand

Five repetitions make it a fairly deliberate effort, one might say, to render a precise lighting as essential to the scene.

Similarly, the cool wash of salt, light and water in "North Haven" as well as "The Moose," and the freshets, wave spills, and cold skies of "Poem" and "The End of March," all point to a greater domination of land by light, less mediated by metaphor, more direct in observation, and more tied to temporality than to sweeps over distance. In the skies of these poems, we're on the ground experiencing them around us or above us; we're not up there at the top of the poem's canvas, getting our aerial look down, as we are so often in earlier poems like "Florida" or "Sea-scape," or "Little Exercise." Late in a life of work, the poet plants her feet on the ground, and makes a habit of speaking *in propria persona* visibly and materially; in these poems, she looks up at the heavens, rather than down through them. Unlike the landscape of "Cape Breton," which gives one the same lively tumble of detail, and which, seen from Bishop's miniaturizing and distant vantage point, starts impersonally from the cliff-top, and gradually moves with the mist down onto "the small yellow bulldozers," "The little white churches" and "the small bus," "Santarém" identifies its perspective immediately and definitively as the poet's own, and marks it as first-person memory. In earlier Bishop poems, it is often the landscape that dreams—the brook, the sea, the hills or the mist—but this time the dream has human ownership: it contracts to fit the poet's mind, it is not projected or diffused over external space. The pace of traveling over the field of the poem slackens, too, and the new naturalistic skies seem to allow light to dominate mass, to condition weight through light and time.

In fact, calling on vision more frequently as they do, the poems make a curricular move toward history and literature and further away from geography: perhaps the naming of her topic as *Geography III* in the previous book enabled Bishop, paradoxically enough, to go beyond the bounds of that subject. At the peak of her powers, she is to realize the lines of connection that bind the study of the earth's surfaces inevitably to study of the earth's depths, and to assert the bonds that enclose the human population within those surfaces and depths. Temporality, or that lingering over surface and sequence, seems to happen inevitably when a line takes a walk and becomes a circle or a cube, and we watch extension become duration. Finally, perhaps, temporality becomes a greater compulsion, a greater interest than the mere massing of planes, a temporality qualified by the way that our growing attachments to people, or our grief or anger soak or striate or otherwise shape our sense of time's passing, beyond the mystery of tangibility.

"Santarém," like "The Moose" and others of Bishop's trip poems, is an unfinished journey, representing Bishop's tour of this tropical city of a million souls sitting at "that conflux of two great rivers, Tapájos, Amazon." Nowhere else in the poetry do we meet a place where Bishop the traveler voices the desire to go no farther, even if in the concluding lines she says: "Then—my ship's whistle blew. I couldn't stay." And if longing, unslaked, but full of resigned acceptance, has a color it is probably the gold of "Santarém." The heart of the poem is an extended narrative of river and town life, recounting the flux of events in the long ago golden evening. What apparently frames the evening for Bishop is the initial reading of the geography of Santarém and its two great rivers as emblem of division, or dialectic, in Bishop's own life. There are lines full of separations and voluntary exiles, as people embark and disembark, nuns wave gaily, and then there is a brief whiff of pathos:

> — off to their mission, days and days away
> up God knows what lost tributary.

But the about-to-be lost nuns are immediately counteracted by female comic union:

> Side-wheelers, countless wobbling dugouts [. . .]
> A cow stood up in one, quite calm,
> chewing her cud while being ferried,
> tipping, wobbling, somewhere, to be married.

Then after a progression of further details on "Two rivers full of crazy shipping—people/ all apparently changing their minds," we touch land, and let hearsay give the miracle of the providential absence that saved the priest from a lightning bolt that cracked his church's tower and struck his very bed. Then we are onto a final episode: the poet's acquisition of a souvenir wasps' nest.

The wasps' nest, like the two rivers of the city, elicits just another pairing of essential difference: admiration from the narrator, and disapproval from Mr. Swan. How does this object connect to the rest of the poem? If we look at the passage that deals with the dialectics of the city's position, it springs from the idea of choosing or not choosing to go on:

> I liked the place; I liked the idea of the place.
> Two rivers. Hadn't two rivers sprung
> from the Garden of Eden? No, that was four
> and they'd diverged. Here only two
> and coming together. Even if one were tempted
> to literary interpretations
> such as: life/death, right/wrong, male/female
> —such notions would have resolved, dissolved, straight off
> in that watery, dazzling dialectic.

The lines bespeak a further deep division, of a reality beyond our individual ideas of it, or of a reality as we choose to imagine it. It falls to the poem to reconcile these choices, so that going on becomes a necessity in either the language of simple being or the language of choice, and probably preferably in both.

Somehow, seeing that river gets Bishop back on board in the face of her fellow passenger's resistance to her prize:

> In the blue pharmacy the pharmacist
> had hung an empty wasps' nest from a shelf:
> small, exquisite, clean matte white,
> and hard as stucco. I admired it
> so much he gave it to me.
> Then—my ship's whistle blew. I couldn't stay.
> Back on board, a fellow-passenger, Mr. Swan,
> Dutch, the retiring head of Philips Electric,
> really a very nice old man,
> who wanted to see the Amazon before he died,
> asked, "What's that ugly thing?"

Mr. Swan's desires and judgments have no less dignity than the poet's; his opposed way of seeing is acceptable; he is "really a very nice old man." Just as Bishop relinquishes all crude complementary pairings like "life/death, right/wrong, male/female" as beside the point, as mere "literary interpretation," just so she is able to keep her notion of the wasps' nest's worth in the face of Mr. Swan's opposition. On that river full of crazy shipping, with its people changing their minds, the speaker, too, can return to her northern home, clutching her wasps' nest and keeping its beauty intact as knowledge within her. "What's that ugly thing?" reverberates as the last judgment of the poem, but the words are indeed a question and not an answer; the answer lies in the poem's unfolding, and contravenes the question. More and more, Bishop's last poems toy with endings, abandoning strong closure, forcing us backward against the linear thrust of reading into the more open circuits of her texts.

The wasps' nest vibrates as emblem. Its hard stubborn whiteness suggests its affinity to that strange object in Bishop's other lost landscape, "the white china doorknob" topping the rough-adzed flagpole and opening the heavens over the empty schoolyard of "Cape Breton." But the nest also fits Brazil itself in Bishop's life: something beautiful, now empty, once full of potential sting; a home of absent pain, both pain and home having to be relinquished.

"North Haven" presents yet another relinquishing, as Bishop writes her farewell to Robert Lowell. Again she grapples with relations to another artist, composing a poem with literary reference whose personal intensity has not been matched since "An Invitation to Miss Marianne Moore." Although this poem, too, like the Moore tribute, is another harbor scene, embodying yet another waterfront town. But quite another size on quite another continent from either Santarém or New York, "North Haven" keeps the late manners of "Santarém": it, too, adopts a perspective which is firmly the narrator's vantage point. The italicized opening lines, while they scan a far prospect, are nonetheless first person:

> *I can make out the rigging of a schooner*
> *a mile off; I can count*
> *the new cones on the spruce. It is so still*
> *the pale bay wears a milky skin, the sky*
> *no clouds, except for one long, carded horse's tail.*

Like Santarém, this ground is light-shot and sensuously expressive in Bishop's late manner.

The lines convey her happiness at being a New Englander again, returning to home ground. A key bit of description first appears in a January 1978 letter to Loren MacIver about winter, not summer, and about Boston Harbor, not Maine:

> Yesterday and the day before were beautiful here – lots of snow (12 inches while I was away), but sunny and not too cold and the harbor a pale, pale milky blue. – 7 ducks seem to be wintering here. I walk [. . .] along the waterfront – yesterday I walked back the long way, around by "Copps Hill" graveyard – very ancient and very beautiful, all the faint, slatestone angels eying one, out of their depths in snow. I'm afraid I do like Boston – better than New York.

A parallel for the mermaid on the wharf piling, the slatestone angels eye one from out of their depth in snow, but Bishop is "afraid" nonetheless that she *does* like Boston, as the compass circle of her life completes itself to run north-south-north. As much as death, the poem's subject is change within an order of the nonchanging. Speaking to Bishop's old shipboard musing, " 'The question about time is how change is related to the changeless,' " her new poem opens: "The islands haven't shifted since last summer," and the first line of the next stanza invokes change in nature as a kind of human fancy:

> The islands haven't shifted since last summer,
> even if I like to pretend they have
> — drifting, in a dreamy sort of way,
> a little north, a little south or sidewise,
> and that they're free within the blue frontiers of bay.

The wished-for freedom is a human imagining; the islands of nature, at least in our lifetimes, won't shift, and freedom of movement of that kind is something we only dream of having, although change is still something within which we live. The next stanzas establish the seasonal flowering on the island which is "our favorite one"; like the months, the same flowers return to the island. The next bit of repeating nature belongs to the birds: "The Goldfinches are back, or others like them,/and the White-throated Sparrow's five-note song,/pleading and pleading, brings tears to the eyes."

The impulse to check and qualify, to note that these may not be the very same Goldfinches coming back to us, and that nature's grasp on the distinctiveness of individual lives may be tenuous, becomes part of Bishop's habitual qualifying. Almost obsessively, she still clings to her double-check, her need to float the first assertion within sight of its modification, to keep turn and counterturn part of her faithful habit.

But as the five-note song rises, a very understated grief makes its presence known in the tears of this stanza, rising ostensibly through the pleading of the White-throated Sparrow, always in my experience a rather brash, piercing, and frequently seven-noted cry. But here the iteration of the song becomes a reminder of what will not recur, of what is different from non-human nature, of the death that cannot be revised or undone. The stanza closes in another outbreak of italics:

> Nature repeats herself, or almost does:
> *repeat, repeat, repeat; revise, revise, revise.*

While Bishop repeats, she revises, and nature does, too, tacking and shifting like the poet, who enters after these italics, alive in memory.

In the unrepeating human past, North Haven was part of Lowell's sexual awakening, "that classic summer" in which he " 'discovered *girls*'/and learned to sail, and learned to kiss." But in parenthesis, the stanza closes: "('Fun'—it always seemed to leave you at a loss . . .)" And with that ellipsis the elegy drifts to closure:

> You left North Haven, anchored in its rock,
> afloat in mystic blue . . . And now—you've left
> for good. You can't derange, or re-arrange,
> your poems again. (But the Sparrows can their song.)
> The words won't change again. Sad friend, you cannot
>   change.

A part of the sadness becomes the futility of certain changes, given what we know of the darker constancies of human life, like the islands, only apparently free, by a mental effort which in time will come to its cessation.

There is no bitterness in this poem. The limpid stillness of its opening, the recursive buttercups, the burning Hawkweed, the "incandescent stars" of the Fragrant Bedstraw, the five-note birdsong, all point in spite of death's human terminations to what largely continues and modifies, revising our endings. Much as the towering moose brought its benevolent presence to the losses of *Geography III* that memory constantly dredges up for the poet, North Haven havens; even if eventually we are able to do nothing further for ourselves.

This resignation is something Bishop sounded, in a note of good-tempered admonition, in one of her last letters to Lowell; on January 16, 1975, she writes:

> I am now going to be very impertinent and aggressive. Please, *please* don't talk about old age so much, my dear old friend! You are giving me the creeps . . . The thing Lota admired so much about us North Americans was our determined youthfulness and energy, our "never-say-die"ness – and I think she was right! In Florida my hostess' sister had recently married again at the age of 76, for the 3rd time – her 2d marriage had been at 67 – and she and her husband also 76, went walking miles on the beach every day, hand in hand, as happy as clams, apparently, and I loved it [. . .] Of course – it's different for a writer, I know – of course I know! – nevertheless, in spite of aches and pains I really don't feel much different than I did at 35 – and I certainly am a great deal happier, most of the time. (This in spite of the giant oil tankers parading across my view every day . . .) I just *won't* feel ancient – I wish Auden hadn't gone on about it so his last years, and I hope you won't.

Within its tenderness and deep feeling, there is a hint of the same admonishing in this elegy, a sense of something almost Victorian in that faint reproof for people who *won't* enjoy themselves, who "de-range" their poems, unable to leave well enough alone. Or, in the words of her March 11, 1963 letter to Lowell, praising Gesualdo: "just immense skill and sensibility – and willingess to say something once and *stop*, let it go."

·II·

"Pink Dog," published in 1979, but by Lisa Browar's calculation written in 1964,[95] introduces a different mood. Each of Bishop's books has featured animals and objects, streets and houses. Each book has had its resident animal, with the possible exception of *A Cold Spring*, where perhaps "The Prodigal" in his pig sty will do in the customary role, just showing a little more baldly than usual how poems about animals are always deeply allegorical about human beings. Besides Marianne Moore, I do not know of any modern or contemporary poet

who pushed the animal masquerade quite as hard and effectively as
Bishop; even her small prose poems in "Rainy Season; Subtropics" are
saturated with the pain of the grieving human animal working the
microphone behind the poem. Nothing is so savage and hurt as "Pink
Dog," with its almost unbearable Swiftian irony, where the speaker
rises almost inevitably in our minds, moving in a ghost duet with the
trotting miseries of the naked little bitch with scabies:

> You are not mad; you have a case of scabies
> but look intelligent. Where are your babies?
>
> (A nursing mother, by those hanging teats.)
> In what slum have you hidden them, poor bitch,
> while you go begging, living by your wits?
>
> Didn't you know? It's been in all the papers,
> to solve this problem, how they deal with beggars?
> They take and throw them in the tidal rivers.
>
> Yes, idiots, paralytics, parasites
> go bobbing in the ebbing sewage, nights
> out in the suburbs, where there are no lights.
>
> If they do this to anyone who begs,
> drugged, drunk or sober, with or without legs,
> what would they do to sick, four-legged dogs?
>
> In the cafes and on the sidewalk corners
> the joke is going round that all the beggars
> who can afford them now wear life preservers.
>
> In your condition you would not be able
> even to float, much less to dog-paddle.
> Now look, the practical, the sensible
>
> solution is to wear a *fantasia*.
> Tonight you simply can't afford to be a-
> n eyesore. But no one will ever see a
>
> dog in *mascara* this time of year.
> Ash Wednesday'll come but Carnival is here.
> What sambas can you dance? What will you wear?
>
> They say that Carnival's degenerating
> —radios, Americans, or something,
> have ruined it completely. They're just talking.

> Carnival is always wonderful!
> A depilated dog would not look well.
> Dress up! Dress up and dance at Carnival!

In another context, "they" could be wrong about the ruined Carnival; in these lines, though, ruin seems all too likely and a scolding, black desperation clings to both speaker and dog. In contrast, Bishop's earlier "Sandpiper" seems a creature of hope:

> The roaring alongside he takes for granted,
> and that every so often the world is bound to shake.
> He runs, he runs to the south, finical, awkward,
> in a state of controlled panic, a student of Blake.

The gibe at Blake is quite goodhumored.

Yet the very explosion of this bitterness into print marks a further advance in subject: this is only the second major female animal emblem allowed into Bishop's work, and an eye interested in looking for a fuller spectrum of emotions could balance the recent appearance of the benevolent and potent moose against the ill and damaged mother dog, perhaps as well as against that ferried cow in "Santarém," on its wobbly, tippy way to be married. For most of her work, at least overtly, Bishop says little about the world of female possibility, but if we look at what is enacted in animal terms there is a richer field of discourse. In "Roosters," the wives of the rooster, perhaps other wives as well, lead lives "of being courted and despised." Occasionally, Bishop's animals are allowed what her people are not: pity accrues for the scabious mother dog with her dangling teats, where the black mothers of the *National Geographic* "with those awful hanging breasts" remain an object of childish horror.

One might say that from 1944's "Songs for a Colored Singer," which Thomas Travisano notes[96] as Bishop's first female protagonist, Bishop has always struggled to find the right place for the female body in her writing. It is only in the last published poems that she fully succeeds: by then, animals, people, the poet herself—all move to a more open concern with femininity, after the little girls of the fifties' prose work have made their points. Tracking from the miniature entry of the female lizard and the retreating bird women of "Brazil, January 1, 1502," and on through the gendered kingdom of chickens in "Roosters" with its not entirely flattering portraits of either sex, Bishop is uncomfortable with female gendering, finally allowing herself to register that discomfort openly in poetry in 1971's "In the Waiting Room." In the late work, moose, dog, and child are refracting powerful statements that ensnare the poet herself more openly in their deployments. We might also say that the stoical restraint which Bishop advocates in "North Haven," and the genial acceptances of difference in "Santarém" were something far more fierce in "Pink Dog." In the painful ironies of this poem the feminine game of dress-up, the injunction to dance, comes cruelly to the sick and wounded for whom society has no other or kinder commands.

The stripped sonnet that follows "Pink Dog" is a much more ambiguous affair. In this poem which published a few weeks after her death, an almost geometric opposition opens and balances the sestet with "Caught—" against the concluding octave that begins the turn of the classic sonnet with "Freed—." This pairing of opposites then seems to resolve, in a pattern of turn, counter-turn, into a final stand, as "Caught—" and "Freed—" synthesize in the last word of poem, work, and life, in that almost defiant "gay!" A tiny but hugely suggestive poem, this is the sonnet in its entirety:

> Caught — the bubble
> in the spirit-level,
> a creature divided;
> and the compass needle
> wobbling and wavering,
> undecided.
> Freed — the broken
> thermometer's mercury
> running away;
> and the rainbow-bird
> from the narrow bevel
> of the empty mirror,
> flying wherever
> it feels like, gay!

Four figures constitute the poem's broken sentence: the bubble in the spirit level, the compass needle, the runaway mercury, and the rainbow-bird flying from the empty mirror. They are all eerily non-human, and the space in which they meet is deafeningly empty of human presence. The poem reverts to the world of Bishop's early fantasies, in which objects play out her human concerns. The objects of the poem belong to a haunted interior very much like the mirror world of 1951's "Insomnia" in emotional intensity, and the syntax pushes us near the breathlessness of the mysterious and truncated "O Breath" from 1949's *Four Poems*, in which the speaker looks at the breast of a lover, saying: "Beneath that loved and celebrated breast," there is "something moving but invisibly," exclaiming further:

> (See the thin flying   of nine black hairs
> four around one   five the other nipple,
> flying almost intolerably   on your own breath.)
> Equivocal, but what we have in common's   bound to be there,
> whatever we must own   equivalents for,
> something that maybe I   could bargain with
> and make a separate peace   beneath
> within   if never with.

In this last poem there is no white ditch severing the movements of each line's thought—yet those gerunds of "Sonnet" take up the same divisions, the same ruptures, and this time argue a release and a healing. "O Breath" named its separations as unbridgeable; "separate peace" was possible between what may have been lovers of different genders, if we think that nine black hairs argue a male body into the poem, but those staggered prepositions spoke against any true recognitions or accommodation of difference: the poet ends, "never with."

"The Gentleman of Shalott" is an early allegory of gender identity published in *North & South;* it is perhaps another notable attempt, besides "Crusoe in England" or "Insomnia," the bitter love song looked at in a previous chapter, to deal publicly with lesbianism. If we read "The Gentleman of Shalott" as a parable about the choice of a same sex world, the poem seems only faintly tinged with melancholy about this choice. "Half is enough," the poem concludes. Displaying Bishop's general fascination with problems of binary form, this poem traces the fortune of Tennyson's "The Lady of Shalott," now a gentleman whose mirror is not the surface of a lake, but a strip of reflecting glass placed at the edge of a half self. The problem seems to be self-consideration:

> He felt in modesty
> his person was
> half looking-glass,

for why should he
be doubled?
The glass must stretch
down his middle,
or rather down the edge.
But he's in doubt
as to which side's in or out
of the mirror.
There's little margin for error,
but there's no proof, either.
And if half his head's reflected,
thought, he thinks, might be affected.

But he's resigned
to such economical design.
If the glass slips
he's in a fix—
only one leg, etc. But
he can walk and run
and his hands can clasp one
another. The uncertainty
he says he
finds exhilarating. He loves
that sense of constant re-adjustment.
He wishes to be quoted as saying at present:
"Half is enough."

Like Bishop's glum Crusoe, the Gentleman lives in an apparently solipsistic world of one-of-a-kind particles, where union takes place between fractured sameness: but "why should he be doubled?" Why should the essential pared-down self take on an other, or be part of an inherently connected world of beings? In an abstract comic form, the question seems to simmer here, long before the far more anguished essays on the same issue are allowed to burst free from the almost seven-year-old of "In The Waiting Room." In this parable it is the mirror of like gender, perhaps, that enables twinned legs to walk or run, or hands to clasp, or women to achieve fulfilling love with each other. When the mirror slips, and the aegis of the identical is withdrawn, the "economical design" must result in a toppling, lurching instability both isolating and immobilizing: a "fix," indeed. But these dangers are underplayed; the need for "constant re-adjustment" is arousing, the uncertainty of these dilemmas "exhilarating."

The poem is immensely playful; there is an ebullience to the challenges that the situation poses that irony only partly disperses. And then, too, contained within the mystery of Bishop's favored binary forms is the logical puzzle, resonant with further implications, as to whether the Gentleman is truly doubled or split, plenary or lacking— either point of view is possible. Perhaps there is a lulling regularity in the inevitable oscillation from state to state. For us as readers there is a further pairing within the temporality of Bishop's poetry: we can choose to view the late statements on identity as a straight line of development, culminating in a climax of increasing bleakness at the end of Bishop's life, or we can view either terminus, "late" or "early," as decisive and say, with the fortitude that memory prompts, "Half is enough." Half on occasion may in fact be double, and this little parable may be the later sonnet's prevailing counterweight. We do not often know if the separate moments of our lives, whether blistering or radiant, should be thought cumulative in impact or merely equal and incommensurate.

"Exchanging Hats," a poem of 1956 published posthumously, offers a certain somber hope for altering points of view on gender roles. Ostensibly joking, and probably even referring, veil over brim, to a folklore mine of jokes about changing hats, the poem eyes its hat-switching aunts and uncles, and says

> —oh, even if the joke falls flat,
> we share your slight transvestite twist
>
> in spite of our embarrassment.
> Costume and custom are complex.
> The headgear of the other sex
> inspires us to experiment.

Perhaps in a future world gender can be determined at will, a flip of the newly-accustomed wrist giving the unembarrassed wearer maleness through a fedora, femaleness by bonnet. And even in the existing world Bishop's "headgear" could be understood to mean the gears of the head which drive us to adopt one gender or the other: the wording is suggestive. Still, as it contemplates change, the poem grows to darkness: "Unfunny uncle," says Bishop, and then, addressing both sexes equally,

> Aunt exemplary and slim,
> with avernal eyes, we wonder

what slow changes they see under
their vast, shady, turned-down brim.

We may get to what those avernal eyes peer at in the fume-laden, out-size, and hellish opening to the future that "avernal" implies, but it doesn't look good; finally, vision seems bought and brought at a high price.

Bishop had doubts about the meanings loaded into "avernal," how-ever. In a letter to Ilse Barker about the poem she says, "I was afraid that it was a good idea that I had spoiled. However — I think the original 'anxious' would be better in the last stanza, rather than 'aver-nal' — that's a bit too much." Moving to "anxious" and normalizing the poem's changes of perspective would have removed a great burden of guilt and self-accusation from the poem; it seems too bad that the move was never made.

"Sonnet," like the speaker of "Santarém," names its caught crea-ture as "divided"; its inner compass needle wobbles and wavers, "un-decided." Although the fluctuating mercury measure of sickness and health in the thermometer has to break its glass skin and run away to gain a freedom that looks highly like expiration, the iridescence flash-ing out from the narrow bevel of the empty mirror knows no limits of choice for its flight: its feelings without the ghost of a human image in the mirror to affect them, are inherently gay. In "O Breath," in the mirror of the other, choice is contested and always equivocal. In "Insomnia" the world of the woman-loving woman is radically other for both, and in "The Gentleman of Shalott" the mirror of same-sex choosing is a world in which, within the present of the poem, "half" remained "enough." Even for the posthumously published "Exchang-ing Hats," while "Costume and custom are complex," and in the 1956 poem's world the assumption of gender at least partly arbitrary, the eyes that note "slow changes" are still "avernal." Yet within "Son-net's" measuring instruments, acceptance and gaiety merge in the closing pun.

If we read all of these poems as a chronological and sequential record of a developing thought, the final poem is more than striking. Like the Indian bird women of "Brazil, January 1, 1502" retreating before their colonial rapists, the rainbow bird in "Sonnet" seems in its flight close to retreat: if not a site of violation, love is still a place out of sight and beyond the range of hearing. But never having published her poems both erotic and tender, and after having tabled the veiled and angry inquiries about love and gender of the late forties and fifties, more than half a life later Bishop opens these subjects again. If the language and symbols are no less veiled, if the poem's deep need is still to remain at a distance from the sex and gendering that are its obliquely disclosed subject, this time the conclusion is significantly different, even if the affirmation comes at the cost of a shattering or an effacement of self that can hardly be described as easy.

·III·

Bishop's refusal to assume school or class membership either as woman, lesbian, or confessional poet, may point to renunciations of group membership that constitute the strength of her work. Unlike Berryman and Lowell, both of whom saw themselves, often frantically name-dropping in print as they did so, as new boys within the old boys' school of poets, she brushes this parish aside and drops back within a broader circuit—ultimately, like Robert Frost, a poet both maverick and mainstream. Perhaps her greatest importance to us is the positioning that kept her a sharp step back from confessional style (that is, boxed in within a too-specific personality), and several revealing technical steps outside of the formal disjunctions of high modernism. It is her odd centrality that is most compelling: her marvelous language perfectly balanced between golden and colloquial, her ear fresh and wholly American, her subject an original reading of the traditional, and her Poetical Character, a firm believer in dream, mystery, and surprise, but set in egalitarian resistance to the poet as prophetic divine.

A woman virtually orphaned before the age of six, raised by successive grandparents and aunts, who at six horrified one grandmother by her staunch allegiance to the flag of the other grandmother, who spent a substantial part of her life on another continent, Bishop's strength in poetry, both early and late, defines itself as a revision of certain critical identities. She denies certain antitheses, confounds certain pairings. A woman, she refused to be confined within limited gender boundaries. A modernist, in her own shrewdly selective way, she reached back to a grandparent generation of Victorians for both form and substance. A poet, she used all the resources of prose to broaden lyric form. A master of the verbal art, she used description with the skill of a consummate painter and draftsman. Lastly, she refused to set the goals of art and science at odds, finding that her road to Hopkins' "least degree of virtue" lay by another great Victorian, Charles Darwin.

To the figure of the moralist lurking in her mind and work, Bishop also added the figure of the scientist, and did this quite naturally and with fairly little fuss. In Bishop's love of patient description we have a persuasive example of a Wordsworthian wise passivity, of a Keatsian negative capability; in her fidelity to the ideal of the scholar-dreamer-artist content to bring to bear all of one's human resources of eye, hand, and mind to the chosen task, she resembles the best of her predecessors, her aesthetic generously syncretic. Like the sun that shines in her "Large Bad Picture," no matter what the worked intention of the artist may turn out to be, Bishop's governing principle of light is "comprehensive and consoling."

Her fondness for Darwin's minute attentions testify to the enlarging effect of the dedicated mind. In Bishop's preoccupation with small, successive acts, we seem to be given a license to join a series of words like *small, understated, determined, modest,* and so on: the words weave a moral figure that goes on the one hand, back to the religious energies of the wealth of the harvest that springs from the mustard seed, and on the other back to Blake's romanticism. She may have mocked Blake with her scatterbrained sandpiper, and feared the disintegrative forces that a myopic obsession with the grains or atoms of life can summon. Yet this fear seems countered by the awesome release of powers that Blake describes in his "Auguries of Innocence" as "a World in a Grain of sand [. . .] Infinity in the palm of your hand/ and Eternity in an hour." Bishop's cool pragmatism, skeptical self-possession, and determined secularism, however, prevent any lifting abstractions from drift or dilution. Yet it is finally a transfigurative energy that Bishop recognizes. In her crucial description of that slide into the unknown, that "self-forgetful, perfectly useless concentration" that is, after all, the moment of epiphany, it seems important to recognize the large and generous view of human effort that her words, all of her words, imply.

ENDNOTES

1. In the Footsteps of Elizabeth Bishop

1. *Brazil*, by Elizabeth Bishop and the Editors of *LIFE* (New York: Time Inc., 1962).

2. All subsequent citations of unpublished prose refer to manuscripts held by the Vassar College Library. Any exceptions to this rule will be specifically noted.

3. Throughout this and succeeding chapters, all quotations from Bishop's published poetry are taken from the text of *Elizabeth Bishop: The Complete Poems, 1927–1979* (New York: Farrar, Straus & Giroux, 1983).

4. Claude Lévi-Strauss, *Tristes Tropiques*, translated by John Russell as *A World on the Wane* (New York: Criterion Books, 1961). p. 91.

5. All subsequent quotations from Bishop's published prose, in this and other chapters, except as noted otherwise, will be taken from the text of Elizabeth Bishop, *The Collected Prose* (New York: Farrar, Straus & Giroux, 1984).

6. Charles Wagley, *Amazon Town: A Study of Man in the Tropics* (New York: Macmillan, 1953).

2. "It is marvellous to wake up together"

7. I take my text for "The Extasie" from *The Poems of John Donne*, vol. 1, edited by Herbert Grierson (London: Oxford University Press, 1958), p. 53.

3. The Body's Roses

8. Mary McCarthy, "Symposium: I Would Like to Have Written ..." in Lloyd Schwartz and Sybil P. Estess, eds., *Elizabeth Bishop and Her Art* (Ann Arbor: University of Michigan Press, 1983), p. 267. Hereafter referred to as *EBHA*.

9. Lee Edelman traces the details of these references thoroughly in his article, "The Geography of Gender: 'The Waiting Room,'" *Contemporary Literature* (Summer 1985), 26:179–196.

10. Octavio Paz, "Elizabeth Bishop, or the Power of Reticence," *World Literature Today* (Winter 1977) 51 (1):15. Hereafter cited as *WLT*.

11. Marianne Moore, "A Modest Expert," from *The Complete Prose of Marianne Moore*, edited by Patricia C. Willis (New York: Penguin, 1987), pp. 406–408.

12. George Starbuck, " 'The Work!': A Conversation with Elizabeth Bishop," *Ploughshares* (1977), 3(3/4):29.

13. Robert Lowell, from "Thomas, Bishop, and Williams," *Sewanee Review* (Summer 1947), 55:497–99.

14. Howard Moss, "A Long Voyage Home," review of *The Collected Prose*, in *The New Yorker*, April 1, 1985, p. 104.

15. Elizabeth Spires, "The Art of Poetry, xxvii: Elizabeth Bishop," *Paris Review* (Summer 1981), no. 80, pp. 56–83.

16. David Kalstone, "Prodigal Years, 1947–49, Elizabeth Bishop & Robert Lowell," *Grand Street* (Summer 1985), 4(4):181.

17. Letter to Phyllis Sutherland, January 5, 1961, Vassar College Library.

18. Adrienne Rich, "The Eye of the Outsider: The Poetry of Elizabeth Bishop," *Boston Review*, April 1983, pp. 15–17.

4. *"Time's Andromedas"*

19. Bonnie Costello, "Fluctuating Charms: Images of Luminosity, Iridescence, and Metamorphosis," *Marianne Moore: Imaginary Possessions* (Cambridge: Harvard University Press, 1981), pp. 133–158.

20. I am here taking my quotation directly from an interview of Moore by Howard Nemerov, republished as "Poetry and Criticism," in *The Complete Prose of Marianne Moore*, edited by Patricia C. Willis (New York: Penguin, 1987), p. 590.

21. *Poems of Gerard Manley Hopkins*, edited by W. H. Gardner (New York: Oxford University Press, 1956), p. 89.

22. Marcel Proust, *Remembrance of Things Past*, translated by C. K. Scott Moncrieff (New York: Random House, 1934), 1:138–140.

23. Herbert Leibowitz, "The Elegant Maps of Elizabeth Bishop," *The New York Times Book Review*, February 6, 1977.

24. Ezra Pound, *Gaudier-Brzeska: A Memoir* (Norfolk, Conn.: New Directions, 1960), p. 89.

25. M. W. Croll, "The Baroque Style in Prose," appearing in Kemp Malone and Martin B. Ruud, eds., *Studies in English Philology* (Minneapolis: University of Minnesota Press, 1929), pp. 427–456.

26. James Merrill, "Elizabeth Bishop, 1911–1979," from *EBHA*, p. 259.

27. "It All Depends" [In Response to a Questionnaire], *EBHA*, p.281.

28. Alexandra Johnson, "Geography of the Imagination," *Christian Science Monitor*, March 23, 1978, p. 24.

5. *The Mappings of* North & South

29. Thomas J. Travisano, *Elizabeth Bishop: Her Artistic Development* (Charlottesville: University of Virginia Press, 1988), p. 82.

30. This is Bishop's description of the poem's genesis in an interview with Alexandra Johnson, "Geography of the Imagination," *Christian Science Monitor*, March 23, 1978, pp. 24–25.

31. Helen Vendler, "Domestication, Domesticity, and the Otherworldly," *WLT*, pp. 23–28.

32. Robert Harbison, *Eccentric Spaces* (New York: Knopf, 1977), pp. 126–128.

33. Franz Kafka, *Letters to Friends, Family, and Editors*, translated by Richard and Clara Winston (New York: Schocken Books, 1977), p. 16.

34. David Kalstone, *Becoming a Poet*, Robert Hemenway, ed. (New York: Farrar, Straus & Giroux, 1989), pp. 64–67.

35. Barbara Page, "The Key West Notebooks of Elizabeth Bishop," a presentation on Elizabeth Bishop for the Modern Language Association Convention, Washington, D.C., 1989.

36. Kalstone, *Becoming a Poet*, p. 65.

6. For a World *"Minute and vast and clear"*

37. Richard Mullen, "Elizabeth Bishop's Surrealist Inheritance," *American Literature* (March 1982), 54:63–80.

38. The correspondence with Houghton Mifflin can be found in the Elizabeth Bishop papers, Houghton Library, Harvard.

39. A particularly tormenting entry in the notebook, and I acknowledge that until the day that some sharper pair of eyes than mine makes out the scrawled word, nothing definitive can be said about it.

40. J. Hector St. John Crevecoeur, *Letters from an American Farmer* (New York: Albert & Charles Boni, 1925), pp. 43–45.

41. These details are taken from Elizabeth Spires' interview with Elizabeth Bishop, "The Art of Poetry, xxvii: Elizabeth Bishop," pp. 56–83.

42. Max Ernst, *Beyond Painting: And Other Writings by the Artist and His Friends* (New York: Wittenborn, Schultz, 1948), p. 8.

43. Ernst, *Beyond Painting*, p. 11.

44. Hugh Kenner, "The Experience of the Eye," from Harold Bloom, ed., *Marianne Moore*, Modern Critical Views Series (New York: Chelsea House, 1987), p. 15.

45. Anne Stevenson, "Letters from Elizabeth Bishop," *Times Literary Supplement*, March 7 1980, pp. 261–262. Also discussed in her study of Bishop, *Elizabeth Bishop* (New York: Twayne, 1966), pp. 66–75.

46. Helen McNeil, "Elizabeth Bishop," from Helen Vendler, ed., *Voices and Visions: The Poet in America* (New York: Random House, 1987), p. 424.

47. Helen Vendler, "Domestication, Domesticity, and the Otherworldly," *WLT*, p. 26.

48. Svetlana Alpers' discussion of Dutch art in the seventeenth century, *The Art of Describing*, would be particularly relevant in giving us another context within which to read this deceptively plain-spoken poetry and its often oblique relation to the tactics of modernism. Besides the obvious parallel in subject matter, the Dutch focus on genre scenes, on objects, textures and domesticity, Alpers' account of the Dutch manipulation of size and scale distortion, and her discussion of

perspective and its relation to narrative, offer a great deal that applies interestingly to Bishop's habits in poetry. Svetlana Alpers, *The Art of Describing: Dutch Art in the Seventeenth Century* (Chicago: University of Chicago Press, 1983).

49. Elizabeth Bishop, "Gregorio Valdes." *The Collected Prose*, Robert Giroux, ed. (New York: Farrar, Straus & Giroux, 1984), pp. 51–59.

50. Bishop, "The U.S.A. School of Writing," *Collected Prose*, p. 46.

7. Miss Moore and Miss Bishop

51. I take the text for this poem from the bilingual edition, *Selected Poems of Pablo Neruda*, edited and translated by Ben Belitt (New York: Grove Press, 1961), pp. 88–95. In consultation with Sylvia Benitez-Stewart, I've altered the English somewhat.

52. Letter to Roberta Lynn Keller, 1976, Vassar College Library.

53. Lynn Keller, "Words Worth a Thousand Postcards: The Bishop/Moore Correspondence," *American Literature* (October 1983), 55:405–429.

54. Letter to R. L. Keller cited earlier.

55. Bonnie Costello, "Marianne Moore and Elizabeth Bishop: Friendship and Influence," *Twentieth Century Literature* (Summer/Fall 1984), 28:130–149.

56. Bishop, *The Collected Prose*, p. 130.

57. David Kalstone, *Becoming a Poet*, p. 5.

58. Bonnie Costello, "Marianne Moore and Elizabeth Bishop: Friendship and Influence," in Harold Bloom, ed. *Marianne Moore* (New York: Chelsea House, 1987), p. 120.

59. Lynn Keller, "Words Worth a Thousand Postcards: The Bishop/Moore Correspondence," p. 420.

60. Costello, "Moore and Bishop," in Bloom, ed. *Marianne Moore*, pp. 121–122.

61. George Starbuck, " 'The Work!': A Conversation with Elizabeth Bishop," *EBHA*, p. 320.

62. Costello, "Moore and Bishop," in Bloom, ed., p. 122.

8. Skunk and Armadillo

63. Robert Lowell, "Thomas, Bishop, and Williams," *Sewanee Review* (Summer 1947), 55:497–99.

64. Robert Lowell, "William Carlos Williams," *Collected Prose* (New York: Farrar, Straus & Giroux, 1987), pp. 40–41.

65. Lowell, *Collected Prose*, p. 77.

66. The letters at issue appear in *Paterson*, signed "Cress," or "C." William Carlos Williams, *Paterson* (New York: New Directions, 1963), pp. 15–16, 59–60, 63, 80–81, 93–94, 101, 105–113.

67. This occurs notably in "The Shako," "Falling Asleep Over the Aeneid," "Thanksgiving's Over," and in Lowell's imitation of Franz Werfel's "The Fat Man in the Mirror."

68. Lowell, *Collected Prose*, pp. 292–295.

69. Although the title of the draft appears to refer to the Ark of the Covenant in which the Mosaic tables of the law are carried, Bishop's large, dark, and sheltering barn and barnyard space seem more to belong to Noah's ark, the physical embodiment of the covenant, or promise that the Lord makes to Noah in Genesis 6:18 to save him from the flood.

70. My discussion in these pages depends on unfinished drafts of Lowell's poems for Bishop to be found in the Lowell papers, Harvard University Library.

71. Kalstone, *Becoming a Poet*, pp. 237–239.

72. Kalstone, *Becoming a Poet*, pp. 210–212.

73. Robert Lowell, "On 'Skunk Hour,' " *Collected Prose*, pp. 225–228.

74. John Berryman, "Despondency and Madness: On Lowell's 'Skunk Hour,' " *The Freedom of the Poet* (New York: Farrar, Straus, Giroux, 1976). pp. 321–322.

75. Penelope Laurans, " 'Old Correspondences': Prosodic Transformations in Elizabeth Bishop," *EBHA*, pp. 75–95.

9. Brazilian Choices

76. David Bromwich, "Elizabeth Bishop's Dream-Houses," *Raritan* (Summer 1984), 4:77–94.

77. Barbara Page, "Nature, History, and Art in Elizabeth Bishop's 'Brazil, January 1, 1502,' " *Perspectives on Contemporary Literature* (1988), vol. 14.

78. Kenneth Clark, *Landscape into Art* (Boston: Beacon Press, 1962), pp. 9–15.

79. Elizabeth Bishop, and the Editors of LIFE, *Brazil* (New York: Time Inc., 1962), p. 114.

80. Personal correspondence with the author, May 1, 1990.

81. Ashley Brown, "An Interview with Elizabeth Bishop," *Shenandoah* (1966), 17(2):3–19.

82. Charles Tomlinson, "Elizabeth Bishop's New Book," *Shenandoah*, 17 (Winter 1966), pp. 88–91.

83. Bromwich, p. 87.

84. Alan Sinfield, *Dramatic Monologue* (New York: Methuen & Co., 1977), p. 25.

85. Charles Wagley, *Amazon Town: A Study of Man in the Tropics* (New York: MacMillan, 1953).

86. The useful texts here were Mircéa Éliade, *Shamanism: Archaic Techniques of Ecstasy* (Chicago: University of Chicago Press, 1951); Paul Radin, *Primitive Religion: Its Nature and Origin* (New York: Dover Publications, 1957); Jon Christopher Crocker, *Vital Souls: Bororo Cosmology, Natural Symbolism, and Shamanism* (Tucson: University of Arizona Press, 1985).

87. For this observation I am indebted to the novelist, translator, and anthropologist, Howard Norman.

10. The Gallery of Her Glance

88. Kalstone, *Becoming a Poet*, pp. 203–208.

89. An Anthology of *Twentieth-Century Brazilian Poetry*, Elizabeth Bishop and

Emanuel Brasil, eds. (Middletown, Conn.: Wesleyan University Press, 1972), pp. 102–103.

11. Geography III

90. John Hollander, "Questions of Geography," *Parnassus* (Spring/Summer 1977), 5:359–366.

91. David Kalstone, "Elizabeth Bishop: Questions of Memory, Questions of Travel," *Five Temperaments: Elizabeth Bishop, Robert Lowell, James Merrill, Adrienne Rich, John Ashbery* (New York: Oxford University Press, 1977), pp. 21–22.

92. Elizabeth Spires, "The Art of Poetry, xxvii: Elizabeth Bishop." *Paris Review* (Summer 1981), pp. 56–83.

93. Octavio Paz, "Elizabeth Bishop or the Power of Reticence," *WLT*, p. 15.

12. Last Poems

94. Adrienne Rich, "The Eye of the Outsider: The Poetry of Elizabeth Bishop," *Boston Review* (April 1983), p. 16.

95. This dating is given in a footnote by Phyllis Stowell, "The Question of Santarem," *Studia Mystica* (Spring 1988), 11(1):50. Early drafts turn up in a notebook dating from 1959, with alternate titles "Naked Dog," "Rio Blues," and "Goodbye to Rio."

96. Thomas J. Travisano, *Elizabeth Bishop: Her Artistic Development* (Charlottesville: University of Virginia Press, 1989), p.85.

INDEX

Hardwick, Elizabeth, 165, 169, 223, 225-30
Hardy, Thomas, 85, 227, 228
Harvard Advocate, The, 215
Harvard University, 264
Hawthorne, Nathaniel, 47, 181
Herbert, George, 44, 61
High modernism, 185, 285
High Modernists, 69
High Romanticism, 127
Histoire Naturelle (Ernst), 121
Historic context (EB works), 101, 239, 271; Brazilian poems, 193-94
History (Lowell), 176
His Toy, His Dream, His Rest (Berryman), 242
Hollander, John, 243
Homosexuality, 31; of EB, 45, 63, 168 (*see also* Lesbianism); Moore on, 143-44; in works of EB, 64-65, 66-69
Hopkins, Gerard Manley, 54, 60, 83, 84, 85, 149-50, 151, 228, 286, EB on, 90-94, 95
"House Guest" (poem, EB), 46, 235
House poems (EB), 99-100
Hudson, W. H., 203-4
Hulme, T. E., 69
Hutchinson, George, 54, 261
Huxley, Aldous, 85, 210
Hypostasis, 86

Identity (EB works), 246
Identity as poet (EB), 45-46, 58, 62-63, 96-97, 243, 264, 285
Identity as woman (EB), 45-46, 62-63, 285
Identity as writer (EB), 202
Illusionism, 119, 120
Imagery (EB works), xii, 29, 32, 111, 239-40; consistency of, 80; oneiric, 123
"Imaginary Iceberg, The" (poem, EB), 108-9, 117

"Imber Nocturnus" (Night Storm), (poem, EB), 35
Imitations (Lowell), 223, 224-25
Impersonality (EB works), ix, 36, 60, 95
Imprisonment (motif), 37; *see also* Prison figure
"In a Room in 1936" (draft of poem, EB), 153
"In Prison" (prose piece, EB), 26, 47-48, 158-59
"Insomnia" (poem, EB), 29-31, 78, 136, 167, 193, 215, 281, 284
Intelligence-Officer, The (Hawthorne), 47
"In the Village" (story, EB), 49, 50, 171, 179, 180-81, 191, 193, 230, 245
"In the Waiting Room" (poem, EB), 29, 46, 54, 65, 119, 211, 230-32, 244, 245, 248, 269, 280, 282-83
Intimacy, 12; issue of, in EB works, 75, 79
Intimate relations, between women, 233
Intimate relations, poems of (EB), 135, 136, 142, 193
"Into the Mountain" (juvenile story, EB), 246
Inversion, 30, 31
"Invitation to Miss Marianne Moore" (poem, EB), 136-40, 141, 142, 224, 274
Iridescence, 81-82, 83, 284
Irony (EB works), 47, 115, 152, 278, 280, 282
"Island, The" (Jarrell), 249
"It is marvellous to wake up together" (unpublished poem, EB), x-xi, xii, 23-24, 27-52, 70, 263; cage in, 44-45, 47-49; dating of, 37-38; eroticism in, 36, 39-40, 43, 45, 49, 193; water/storm imagery of, 35, 43